I0103861

The Ethics of Happiness

An Existential Analysis

Stephen J. Costello, Ph.D.

The Ethics of Happiness:

An Existential Analysis

Copyright ©2010 by Stephen J. Costello

ALL RIGHTS RESERVED. No part of this book may be reproduced, stored in a retrieval system, or transmitted by any form or by any means, electronic, mechanical, photocopying, recording, or otherwise, except as may be expressly permitted by the applicable copyright statutes or in writing by the publisher

ISBN: 1-55605-424-6   978-1-55605-424-2

Library of Congress Control Number: 2010941165

WYNDHAM HALL PRESS
5050 Kerr Rd
Lima, Ohio 45806
www.wyndhamhallpress.com

Printed in The United States of America

Dedication
I dedicate this book to Darren Cleary, whom I hold in admiration and awe, and who changed me from a cheerful pessimist to a tragic optimist.

'We hold these truths to be self-evident: that all men are created equal; that they are endowed by their Creator with certain inalienable rights; that among these are life, liberty, and the pursuit of happpiness'.

> Thomas Jefferson (1743-1826)
> President of the United States

'One feels inclined to say that the intention that man should be "happy" is not included in the plan of "Creation"'.

> Sigmund Freud (1856-1939)
> Austrian Psychoanalyst

'The last end of human life is bliss or happiness'.

> St. Thomas Aquinas (1225-1274)
> Italian Philosopher and Theologian

'Some people cause happiness wherever they go, others whenever they go'.

> Oscar Wilde (1855-1900)
> Irish Playwright

'To explore the whole sphere of the modern soul, to have sat in its every nook – my ambition, my torture, and my happiness'.

> Friedrich Nietzsche (1844-1900)
> German Philosopher

Table of Contents

Acknowledgements

First and foremost, I would like to thank my family, especially my parents, Val and Johnny, for all their encouragement, support and interest.

My profound gratitude goes to Darren Cleary, a remarkable person and to whom this book is dedicated. I admire, respect and love you deeply and your friendship has transformed my world. Knowing you has provided my life with so much meaning, fascination, exuberance, purpose, enjoyment and hope.

Thank you to my close friends – John Rice, who has been there for me through thick and thin, Oisín Breathnach, Helen Sheehan, Thomas O'Connor, Fionnuala MacAodha, Hugh Cummins, Emil Alhén, Liam Kearney, István Mészáros, Terence Hartley, and Fr. John Harris, O.P. – for your advice, friendship, and help.

To all my logotherapy colleagues especially Dr. Robert Barnes, Manfred Hillman, Doren Francis, Dr. Ann Graber, Alex Vesely, Dr. Cynthia Rice, and Dr. Robert Hutzell, for our common dedication to Franklian psychology and philosophy, as well as to Richard Kearney, mentor and friend.

I thank you all from the depths of my heart.

Prelude

It is a kind of happiness to know to what extent we may be unhappy.

La Rochefoucauld

Why is it so hard to be happy?, so difficult to sing a hymn to happiness? Is happiness included in the 'plan of Creation', in this 'Vale of tears'? What can we do to be happy? And what exactly *is* happiness? Is it a passing condition or a permanent state? What is the difference between pleasure, happiness and joy? Are we humans supposed to be happy here? Is happiness really possible to attain and subsequently retain? Should we deliberately pursue it or just let it happen? Isn't there a saying: 'Those who search for happiness never find it'? What have the philosophers to say on the subject of happiness? (When one psychoanalyst heard that I was writing a book on happiness, he said to me 'happiness is a symptom that has to be cured'!). These are some of the questions that this book seeks to answer and address.

For Jacques Lacan, 'happiness happens' (Lacan, 1992, p. 13). That is the etymology of the word. Happiness means 'to happen'. It is an encounter so, an episode, a happen-ing. Happiness comes and goes – it's like a ghost: the *spirit* of happiness. There seems to be a gap separating imagination and reality, expectation and attainment. Thomas Carlyle observed that happiness is inversely proportionate to the quantity of our expectations, i.e., how much we think we are entitled to. Happiness equals what we have, divided by what we expect. According to psychoanalytic theorists such as Freud and Lacan, it is desire that renders happiness problematic, if not impossible. Desire is always deferred. It is irrepressible. This means that when we get what we desire we are still not happy. Regret is built in to the very substance of desire. We shall examine this psychoanalytic, more specifically, Lacanian position, on the subject later in the book.

In the film 'Annie Hall', Woody Allen approaches an apparently happy couple and asks them whether they are happy, to which they respond in the affirmative. Allen asks: 'How do you account for it?' She replies: 'I'm very shallow and empty and have no ideas and nothing interesting to say' and he says: 'And I'm exactly the same way'! They managed to work out something so, observes Allen.

Woody Allen's character, who believes that life can be divided into the horrible (which includes cripples, etc.) and the miserable (the rest of us, who should be thankful we are only miserable) also says: 'That's the most fun I've ever had without laughing'. Allen is Freudian through and through. So with Woody Allen, we can ask: 'how do we account for human happiness?'

Lacan once said that all he had been doing since the age of twenty was exploring the philosophers on the subject of love. My aim in this book is to explore what the philosophers have to say on the subject of happiness. Hence, this work, which draws on philosophy, existential analysis (Viktor Frankl's logotherapy) as well as on psychoanalysis (Freud and Lacan), poetry and religion, too. However, the main thrust throughout is logo-philosophical, in that I am concerned with the meaning of happiness, with what happiness means.

Happiness is one side of the coin; depression (radical unhappiness) is *ostensibly* on the other side. In between there is, what I like to call, 'divine discontent'. The philosopher Kant asked: 'what can I hope for?', which is the religious or eschatological question. Perhaps the divine discontent of the *metaxy* (the 'in-between' state of humanity) is the most we can hope for. T. S. Eliot once said that we humans can't bear too much reality. Well, we can't tolerate too much pleasure either. Too much pleasure *is* painful. Lacan labels this *jouissance*. Think of being tickled. Isn't there a moment when all that pleasure becomes painful, too difficult to endure, to sustain? Shylock asks: 'If you tickle us, do we not laugh?' But laughing can lead to crying. Tickling testifies to the impossibility of satisfaction. Likewise, too much sexual ejaculation is painful. Goethe felt that nothing was 'harder to bear than a succession of fair days' (cited by Freud, 1982, p. 13). We are saying here that *jouissance* suffuses pleasure. It encircles it. But pleasure is not happiness. We need to explore this more thoroughly in the pages that follow.

We are accustomed to saying there is a thin line between genius and insanity, between mania and depression, between love and hate, between liability and reliability, between happiness and too much happiness, which always borders on its supposed opposite. Happiness and unhappiness, then, are two sides of a Moebius strip, like love and hate.

So, this is the structure I have set up in this book: after discussing the nature of philosophy and encircling possible definitions of happiness (the introduction), I will then proceed to deal with the philosophy of happiness from a historical and hermeneutical perspective. This is important as the meaning of the signifier /happiness/ changes down the centuries. The book proceeds as follows: Science and happiness (chapter one), Aristotle on happiness as virtue (chapter two), Epicurus on happiness as pleasure (chapter three), Boethius on happiness as goodness (chapter four), Aquinas on happiness as contemplation (chapter five), Pascal on happiness as diversion (chapter six), Schopenhauer on happiness as the absence of suffering (chapter seven), and Nietzsche on happiness as power (chapter eight). I then discuss Freud's famous eleven paths to happiness, together with a philosophical free-association of, and commentary upon, each path: in the Freudian formulation we may regard happiness as neurosis (chapter nine). Chapter ten concentrates on happiness as *jouissance*, drawing on the insights of Jacques Lacan and Miguel de Unamuno. Chapter eleven details Wittgenstein's view of happiness as meaning while chapter twelve confronts Ricoeur's conception of hermeneutics with Lacan's idea of the Real, as applied to the question of happiness and its relationship to hope and desire. Chapter thirteen returns to Thomas Aquinas in relation to the question of happiness in 'Heaven'. Chapter fourteen charts the work of Charles Taylor and Bernard Lonergan on the 'fullness' that is beyond happiness or 'flourishing', understood as *eudaimonia*, while the final chapter (chapter fifteen) draws on Viktor Frankl's logotherapy and existential analysis and adumbrates a tri-dimensional model of happiness which distinguishes between pleasure, happiness and joy. This chapter is the culmination of the work. The subject of happiness is one that traditionally pertains to the philosophical study of *ethics*. And so my philosophical, existential analysis concerns itself with the ethics of happiness, one that will, and must not shy away from, confronting the question directly: is happiness ethical at all? We shall see.

Introduction
Philosophy and Happiness

A man who likes nobody is much more unhappy than the one whom nobody likes.

La Rochefoucauld

Ludwig Wittgenstein once opined that philosophy is a sickness and the cure is philosophy. Let us proceed with the cure to our sickness, to our guiding question: 'what is happiness?'

Philosophy is a permanent necessity of the human being, a vocation, an invocation, an exhortation to question. Amid the jungle of existence there arises, perpetually, the question: 'Why?' Philosophy is one activity we do in order to engage with the world, in order to satisfy our thirst for knowledge. There are other ways. Philosophy is simply one stripe on a tiger's back – it is not the tiger itself. Philosophy is the love of wisdom – a wisdom, as Proverbs says that 'is better than rubies' (*Proverbs*, VIII: 11) but it is a love that can never be consummated. So at the heart of philosophy is failure. Philosophers are lovers – lovers of wisdom but are not necessarily wise. Philosophers are not saints or sages. We philosophise because we live. And at the heart of this philosophical work is failure, too, because, and let us admit it at the outset, happiness cannot really be defined.

Everyone has his or her own definition of the word. Happiness means a long-lasting, steadfast and deep, enduring, consistent contentment to one person, while another may view it as a momentary experience of euphoric, almost ecstatic but inevitably short-lived joy and elation. Is happiness a subjective state, something personal or objective? This is the problem with other concepts such as Goodness or God or Love. How are we to define these? Such a task appears quite impossible. Is happiness impossible too?

In his *Philosophical Investigations*, Wittgenstein draws our attention to the way we use a whole range of ordinary words and points out that we can't give a reasonably satisfactory definition even of the word 'game'. We all are embarked on different 'language games' that makes defining words extremely problematic. The later Wittgenstein challenged his readers to produce a set of conditions that games have in common.

> Consider ... the proceedings that we call "games". I mean board-games, card-games, ball-games, Olympic games, and so on. What is common to them all? – Don't say: "There *must* be something common or they would not be called "games"" – but *look and see* whether there is anything common to all ... Look for example at board-games, with their multifarious relationships. Now pass to card-games; here you find many correspondences with the first

group, but many common features drop out, and others appear. When we pass next to ball-games, much that is common is retained, but much is lost. – Are they all "amusing"? Compare chess with noughts and crosses. Or is there always winning and losing, or competition between players? Think of patience. In ball games there is winning or losing; but when a child throws his ball at the wall and catches it again, this feature has disappeared. Look at the parts played by skill and luck; and at the difference between skill in chess and skill in tennis. Think now of games like ring-a-ring-a-roses ... (Wittgenstein, 1953, pp. 66-7).

What we find, Wittgenstein concludes, is not a set of features that is common to them all but a complicated network of similarities criss-crossing and overlapping, which he characterised as 'family resemblances'. If you view members of a family, we find that some are similar in build, or in the way they talk or walk while others have certain similar facial features etc. On the basis of such similarities we may recognise them as belonging to the same family, but there is no need or reason to suppose that there must be some set of features that all the members have in common. Aristotle's understanding of happiness as *eudaimonia* or 'flourishing' is vastly different from Lacan's notion of happiness in its guise as *jouissance*, to take just one example.

The word 'happiness', then, acts as a signifier and is open to multiple meanings and shifting definitions, divergent interpretations. Is 'happiness' a concept to which nothing corresponds? Even attempting to define happiness is probably misconceived but just because we can't define it doesn't mean that we can't use or understand the term in our own way – or write a book about it.

The subject of happiness has attracted a lot of philosophical attention. We may mention a few thinkers who have pondered on the subject.

For Plato, health and happiness involved the harmony of the parts but Aristotle, and later, Shakespeare, both prioritised *virtue* (excellence of character) over happiness. For Aquinas, happiness was ultimately consumated in the beatific vision (*beatitudo*), where we would see God, no longer in a glass darkly, but come face to face with the 'uncaused cause' (*ens causa sui*) - Augustine's 'self-loving love'. Aquinas held that happiness or *hilaritas mentis* ('cheerfulness of heart') was one of the virtues. The realisation of happiness, in the Aristotelian and Thomistic sense, is man's true end (*telos*) and destiny. For both Aristotle and Aquinas, happiness means union with God. Christianity urges us to be of 'good cheer', while we, paradoxically, live in this 'vale of tears'. According to the teachings of Christianity, we can never be fully happy here in our exiled state since the Fall and due to Original Sin. Though, it appears that many people who believe in a loving God and in the redemptive power of Christ are happy. For theists, life has ultimate meaning because each one of us has been made in the image and likeness of God Himself ('every hair on your head has been counted' and 'I will not leave you orphans'). There is the promise of Paradise 'where every tear will be wiped away'. As Christ said to the thief crucified beside him: 'This day you will be with me in Paradise'.

The oldest answer in the world to the problem posed by happiness is to be found in religion, because the kind of happiness we yearn for belongs to the deepest realms of the human heart. For Christians, the belief in the Resurrection of the body, as articulated in the Apostles' Creed, sustains them. What is required of Christians is 'joyful acceptance' of life and 'love of Creation' rather than the weary resignation and resigned insouciance of the Stoic. It involves an unconditional 'yea saying' to life, while keeping our gaze firmly fixed on the great Beyond – *in* the world, but not *of* it.

Albert Camus wrote about the utter absurdity of life and opened his *magnum opus*, *The Myth of Sisyphus*, saying that the only philosophical question is whether we should commit suicide, an option he rejects. Drawing on the myth of Sisyphus, who was condemned by the gods to labour all his life by pushing a boulder up a hill knowing he hadn't the strength to topple it over, Camus proclaimed: 'One must *imagine* Sisyphus happy', though in reality such a happiness is impossible.

For Arthur Schopenhauer, the nineteenth-century 'dark' philosopher, happiness is realised in death or worldly detachment, as it is for the Buddha too, though Schopenhauer thought there was some consolation and saving grace to be found in art.

Alain, penned a book on happiness in 1928 entitled *Propos sur le bonheur*, stating that happiness is a *duty*. Not to be outdone by the French, the Spanish philosopher, Julián Marías wrote a book on happiness in 1987 entitled *La felicidad humana* (*Human Happiness*). For this Spanish follower of Ortega y Gasset, happiness involves a thrust into the future and is linked to *hope*, as it is for Paul Ricoeur too, the twentieth-century French philosopher. For G. K. Chesterton, the British writer, happiness is inextricably connected with *gratitude*. The contemporary French philosopher, André Comte-Sponville, opined: 'Happiness is not a matter of luck. It has to be created'. And the British philosopher, Bertrand Russell, wrote in his *The Conquest of Happiness*, which Wittgenstein called 'vomative' (Monk, 1991, p. 294), that the 'key to happiness is accepting one unpleasant reality every day'. He also said that nothing amuses him so much as unhappiness. For Russell, the secret of happiness is to face the fact that the world is 'horrible, horrible, horrible'.

Another philosopher (also a psychoanalyst), Jonathan Lear, attempts to reconcile Aristotle with Freud in his book, *Happiness, Death and the Remainder of Life* and discusses the Aristotelian conception of happiness alongside the Freudian death drive.

The psychologist Abraham Maslow adumbrated a *psychology* of happiness. And Alan Watts penned a book entitled: *The Meaning of Happiness* in 1940, which sought to conjoin the findings of psychology with the 'wisdom of the East'. Watts writes: 'A life without meaning is unhappiness' (Watts, 1940, p. 179). However, there is much truth in his view that: 'Those who search for happiness do not find it because they do not understand that the object of their search is the seeker' (Watts, ibid., p. 174). Edward de Bono, the famous guru of 'lateral thinking', wrote a book that was published in 1977 with the title: *The Happiness Purpose*, the subtitle of which was '*If I had to design a new religion this would be it*'. He proposed a new religion based on the belief that the purpose of life is happiness and the best foundation for such a happiness is self-importance. 'The happiness purpose' is to be achieved through thinking, humour and dignity, with love being replaced by the 'more reliable practice of respect'.

And in 1991, Dorothy Rowe, the well-known British psychologist, wrote *Wanting Everything*: *The Art of Happiness*. Her basic thesis was that we don't get everything we want from life. This leads to frustration, anger, resentment and unhappiness. We then evolve strategies to overcome these feelings such as power, possessions, envy or selfishness etc, none of which leads to happiness. If only we understood the nature of human longing and the conditions that prevent its fulfilment we could ultimately arrive at a position of wanting, which does lead to happiness. She is a humanistic hopeful.

One of Freud's expressed aims for psychoanalysis was to replace neurotic (or hysterical) suffering with 'common human unhappiness', (or 'general human misery', depending on the translation) as he expressed it in his *Studies on Hysteria*. For Freud, we are psychically constituted so as not to be completely happy. The psychoanalytic and religious registers of human experience have much in common here.

Augustinian Christianity insists that 'our hearts are restless until they rest in thee O Lord' – desire and its apogee. The psalm chosen by the Church for Compline every Saturday runs:

"What can bring us happiness?" many say.
Lift up the light of your face on us, O Lord.
You have put into my heart a greater joy
than they have from abundance of corn and new wine (Psalm 4).

The question is answered in psalm 15:

Preserve me, God, I take refuge in you.
I say to the Lord: "You are my God.
My happiness lies in you alone".

The psalm concludes:

You will show me the path of life,
the fullness of joy in your presence,
at your right hand happiness for ever.

Christianity talks a lot about *joy*– Easter joy. The Psalmist says: 'The fullness of joy is found in the presence of the Lord' (Psalm 16: 11). It recognises that ultimate and utter happiness eludes us in this life because of the gulf between my desire and the only entity capable of fulfilling that desire in its entirety – Divinity Itself. We do ask and I, for one, want to know, together with the Psalmist: what will bring us happiness? My quest is as personal (all quests are) as it is logo-philosophical.

So is Solon, the Athenian lawgiver, right when he says that no one is happy until they die –'he is at best fortunate' – or Bertrand Russell who said that the secret of happiness is to face the fact of life's sheer horribleness or Pascal who cried out: 'Oh, how happy is a life we throw off like the plague' or Freud when he supposed that happpiness was simply not included in the 'plan of Creation', or Aquinas who thinks we are made for nothing less, or Viktor Frankl who advises us to let happiness happen?

Are we made for happiness or are we constitutionally incapable of being happy? And perhaps happiness consists in not *wanting* to be happy or in wanting *not* to be happy. Schopenhauer suggested that the surest way for us not to become very unhappy was not to expect to be very happy (Schopenhauer, 1974, p. 408). Like Freud, Schopenhauer believes it is much easier to be unhappy. He notes that 'it is quite easy to be very unhappy, whereas to be very happy is not exactly difficult but absolutely impossible' (Schopenhauer, ibid.). Voltaire agrees: 'Happiness is only a dream and pain is real'. And for Swift, happiness is the gift of being well deceived. In *On the Genealogy of Morals* (essay 3, aphorism 28), Nietzsche talks of the 'fear of happiness', just as Erich Fromm would talk about the 'fear of freedom'. Don't they all have a certain point?

I have chosen the following outstanding thinkers in the Western intellectual tradition with whom to dialogue on this topic of happiness: Aristotle, Epicurus, Boethius, Aquinas, Pascal, Schopenhauer, Nietzsche, Freud, Simone Weil, Unamuno, Ortega y Gasset, Wittgenstein, Sartre, Iris Murdoch, Paul Ricoeur, Lacan, Slavoj Zizek, Charles Taylor, Bernard Lonergan, Owen Flanagan, and Viktor Frankl. The work of poets such as Yeats, Tennyson, Keats and Auden amongst others, are cited also. The philosophers represented here are drawn, in the main, from the Continental tradition of philosophy.

I realise only too well that the task I have set for myself is a nicely impossible one. What Augustine said of time in Book XI of his *Confessions*, holds for happiness as well: he said that so long as no one asked him to explain time he knew what it was; but if someone asked him to explain it and he tried to do so, he no longer knew.

This book is, as we have said, on the philosophy of happiness but it would be churlish indded to omit any discussion of the subject that stems from science even if it is a philosophy of science so the first chapter will offer such an analysis before we return to the beginnings and proceed historically by looking to Aristotle and attempting to unravel his hermeneutic of human happiness.

Chapter One
Science and Happiness

It's funny, this thing about happiness. It's a commodity that was imported from America in the fifties.

Franesca Annis (actress).

There are a number of contemporary philosophers, mainly exemplars of the Anglo-American analytic tradition, who draw on neuroscience and the philosophy of mind for illuminations and insights in order to further their own reflections and researches on the subject of happiness and, indeed, on other philosophical subjects. I intend, in this chapter, to discuss in some detail the broad contours of one important recent philosopher who is representative of this 'school'. It is merely intended to be indicative of a particular tradition within philosophy, an alien tradition from the rest of the philosophers in this book. So though this particular chapter may jar, to a certain extent, with the style and substance of the rest of the book I felt it was worth considering as it does represent one important strand within philosophical thought.

My 'subject' is Owen Flanagan and his book, *The Really Hard Problem*: *Meaning in a Material World*. For Flanagan, the 'really hard problem' is consciousness and how it emerges from neuronal activity. He attempts to make sense of meaning and mystery and magic *naturalistically*, that is to say, without any reference to transcendent reality. Flanagan construes man as muscle and tissue rather than embodied spirit but he is in accord with traditional philosophy in holding to the assertion that we all want happiness and to live meaningful lives, to achieve *eudaimonia*, to be a 'happy spirit' (though he fails to bring this intuition to final fruition philosophically). He draws mainly on neuroscience and evolutionary biology to support his supposition that we are finite material beings living in a material universe. Interestingly and perhaps contradictorily, he also draws on Buddhism and mindfulness meditation for empirical evidence to help us to understand the causes and constituents of happiness/human flourishing, understood in its broadly Aristotelian sense. What he unfortunately calls 'eudaimonics' can aid us to live lives of increasing meaningfulness, he contends. In the Introduction he explicitly states that he no longer believes in God (Flanagan, 2009, p. xiii) but wants to make sense of meaning naturalistically; to this end, he recommends adopting an attitude of 'optimistic realism' in what will be an empirical-normative enquiry into human flourishing, a *eudaimonistic scientia* or 'eudaimonics' for short. Flanagan asserts that we are not embodied souls (he actually means embodied spirits) but animals and so he conceives of happiness along the lines of a philosophical (and not so philosophical, in that he is heavily indebted to neuroscience and Buddhist thought) naturalism. Darwin's theory is his cornerstone and so it is no wonder that he borrows insights from genetics and biochemistry. One can't help suspecting that his indebtedness to Buddhism and other Eastern mindfulness practices is due to the fact that, as he says himself, they are 'non-theistic' (Flanagan, ibid., p. 4). My own position may be characterised as a philosophical Christian one. I am a philosopher who, when philosophising, is a Christian in drag!; Flanagan is a philosopher who is a scientist in drag. Both of us are hypocrites in the Levinasian sense, in that we have dual mandates (this is a good thing!), double allegiances. In *Totality and Infinity*, the French philosopher Emmanuel Levinas explains: 'It is perhaps time to see in hypocrisy not only a base contingent defect of man, but the underlying rending of a world attached to both the philosophers and the prophets' (Levinas, 1969, p. 24). Levinas, so, draws on the twin traditions of Judaism and philosophy. Is he a philosophical Jew or a Jewish philosopher? Or both Jew and philosopher simultaneously? However, and perhaps it is being a bit mean, Flanagan is not a philosopher in the Platonic sense though to be fair to him he does reinterpret Plato in interesting ways (Parmenides and Plato founded philosophy or, if you prefer, philosophy is Parmenides' and Plato's invention). Analytic philosophy, it seems to me, departs significantly from the traditional conception of philosophy. To return to Flanagan's text.

Drawing on the work of Nelson Goodman, Flanagan labels a sextet as 'spaces of meaning'. This sextet is art, science, technology, ethics, politics and spirituality. The list is not exhaustive. By moving in these spaces I live meaningfully. I, and about 80% of the population do; 20% don't and can't as they live, by contrast, in a state of abject and absolute poverty. We weave a tapestry of 'sense and meaning' (Flanagan, ibid., p. 14) in these particular spaces. He agrees with Aristotle that we seek *eudaimonia* though his understanding of what this means is not Aristotelian. For Flanagan, *eudaimonia* is flourishing but there is no connotation, as there is in Aristotle, of it being a state of spiritual blessedness. Because art, science, ethics, religion and politics etc are human practices and the human is an animal, albeit, a very smart social animal (note, he is no longer Aristotle's 'rational animal') then natural science can explain the nature and function of art, and ethics and religion too (see Flanagan, ibid., p. 21). However, despite his later disclaimer, isn't this scientism, that is to say, the view that the methods employed in the natural sciences should be employed in the human sciences as well, viz., reductionism?

So, for Flanagan, the above practices or features of life contribute to meaning and happiness. Flanagan translates Plato's transcendentals of the True, the Good and the Beautiful into Darwinian terms; they become universal ways by which we orient ourselves to the world in order to live meaningfully and achieve *eudaimonia*, which is what we all seek. 'Ethics and politics track what is good, art and music track what is beautiful, and science tracks what is true' (Flanagan, ibid., p. 40). But one could easily take issue with this and claim, for instance, that religion tracks what is true. But though 'hedonic well-being is firmly on our radar' (Flanagan, ibid., p. 43), Flanagan realises that selfish motives abound. Flanagan, like Darwin is Humean rather than Hobbesian here: humans are egoists with fellow-feeling. We are selfish animals with some capacity for sympathy, so. We are a mixed bag of motivations.

'Positive Psychology', in a comparative consensus, lists the virtues that are mandatory for flourishing/happiness. They are Seligman's (see Seligman, 2002): justice, humaneness, temperance, wisdom, transcendence and courage. The reader will note that four out of these six are the cardinal virtues of Plato as set out by him in the *Republic*! Flanagan disputes that transcendence is a virtue even though he recognises it as a religious or, should I say, 'spiritual' impulse. So our natures (yes, he uses the word) are mixed and *eudaimonia* occurs when we grow the better seeds in our nature: fitness first, followed by flourishing. Our basic needs must first be met (he could have drawn here, but didn't, on Maslow's famous hierarchy of needs) before we can aim at living well (Ricoeur will add to 'living well', 'with and for others in just institutions'). 'Alienation' is precisely not being able to discover what one wants which, for Flanagan, is liberty, fitness, and flourishing. And, as we said, many humans are precluded through poverty from flourishing so that ethics must turn to politics, as Aristotle insisted. 'Education and meaningful work are not universally available. Beauty is hard to find amidst squalor. The lack of basic political freedoms, massively unequal distributions of wealth, and ethnic hatred provide dramatically sub-optimal environments even for basic decency and true friendship' (Flanagan, ibid., p. 59). Flanagan is at pains to point out that his claims are based on 'empirical observation' (Flanagan, ibid., p. 60) and on a philosophical anthropology but a page later he opines that our 'karma, good or bad, carries on' (Flanagan, ibid., p. 61). But is karma empirical? Can karmic causation be proved scientifically? Flanagan does this a lot – he slips in viewpoints or perspectives from different Eastern spiritual traditions into his so-called strict philosophical naturalism which leaves this reader a little perplexed.

I have to say that his discussion of Buddhist epistemology which follows is outside the scope of this philosopher's ability to assess but suffice to state that, with the Dalai Lama, he is seeking the convergence and conciliation of science with (non-Christian) spirituality. He concludes his chapter 'Science for Monks: Buddhism and Science' by categorically stating that most religions are incompatible with Darwinism and that Catholicism is inherently incompatible with Darwinism in teaching that man possesses a spiritual soul created directly by God, that all men have descended from Adam who has transmitted to them original sin, that each of us is made in the image and likeness of God, that life is not random mutation but the product of intelligent design. Unlike Catholicism, 'eudaimonics is empirical' (Flanagan, ibid., p. 112).

Flanagan conflates happiness and meaning (see Flanagan, ibid., p. 119); my point, which I will outline in chapter fifteen, argues contrariwise, that happiness is a by-product of meaning. Interestingly, what does accord with my own assertion of there being three types of 'happiness' (and 'happiness' is a polysemic term) – is Flanagan's distinction between 'hedonic' happiness, happiness as 'subjective well-being' (experiences of 'flow') and happiness as 'eudaimonistic', which parallels my tripartite division exactly and respectively (see Flanagan, ibid., p. 150 and chapter fifteen of this book).

In terms of statistics and the GSS (General Social Survey), 32% of Americans describe themselves as very happy, 56% as pretty happy and 12% as not too happy. So the vast majority (88%) are happy. However, one must bear in mind, as we said above, that there are different meanings attached to the signifier/happiness. There is, for example, Aristotelian happiness, Buddhist happiness, hedonistic happiness, the Marquis de Sade's view on happiness and, as Flanagan humorously puts it, the 'joy-joy-click-your-heels' (Flanagan, ibid., p. 162) type of happiness. He poses intriguing questions: Was Jesus happy? Can we say that the Buddha was happy? The answers are not obvious. But Flanagan informs us that he knows enough about Buddhism to know that there is such a thing as happiness, which in this perspective involves or is manifested as a stable sense of serenity and contentment as well as being caused or constituted by enlightenment or wisdom, virtue and goodness. And if mindfulness practices can increase this sense of optimal well-being then they are to be recommended. Just as there is no one view or version of happiness, so too is there no one single meaning of life (see Flanagan, ibid., p. 201). This would be like, to draw on Frankl's analogy, asking a chess-player which is the best move in chess. Much depends on the circumstances and the context. However, it is very unFranklian to state, as Flanagan does, that 'you have a right to have happiness' (Flanagan, ibid., pp. 210, 214), which I would dispute.

So is there an ethics of happiness? For Flanagan, ethics is ecology and 'eudaimonics' is broader than ethics even though it does commend itself to us ethically. In a footnote Flanagan puts it thus: 'Living in the space of ethics conceived in minimalist conventional terms is not enough for flourishing' (Flanagan, ibid., note 8, p. 232). Perhaps happiness really is a skill and not a state as Aristotle originally thought and taught, a skill that we can learn to cultivate and practice? Understood thus, 'eudaimonics' can help us contribute to the accumulation of good effects and aid us in living a meaningful life.

There are many more thinkers we could cite in the area of mind science, such as the Churchlands, Daniel Dennett, Sam Harris, Sissela Bok, but I have taken Owen Flanagan as one important and illustrious illustration of this particular philosophical tradition who has served our purposes to provide an account from a different perspective to my own which has contributed to and furthered our understanding of the topic of happiness. While I am unable to analyse his outline and discussion of Buddhist thought on this subject, I would like to say something critical about brain sciences in general which he draws on and which is germaine to my own non-neuroscientific analysis of the subject. To this end, I have found Paul Ricoeur's dialogue with the neuroscientist Jean-Pierre Changeux instructive in this regard. Ricoeur's critical comments will serve as a hermeneutic response, albeit indirectly, to Flanagan and others in the field of contemporary analytic philosophy of mind.

In *What Makes Us Think?: A Neuroscientist and a Philosopher Argue About Ethics, Human Nature, and the Brain* (2000), the hermeneutic philosopher Paul

Ricoeur and the neurobiologist Paul Changeux engage in critical dialogue and creative dispute on some subjects that are apposite for our own enquiry.

Ricoeur hints at the very beginning that the reductionism present in much that passes for 'mind science' that has informed much of analytic philosophy is understandable given the fact that reductionism is a reaction against ontological dualism. Ricoeur thus welcomes naturalism in its attempt 'to shore up ethics by appeal to the biological facts uncovered by the science of the brain and observation of the behaviour of living beings' (Ricoeur, 2000, p. 21). Much of human experience has a biological basis, and ethics (as distinct from Kantian morality), has deep roots in life but at some point Ricoeur will want, he says, to pass over into the normative sphere. The brain, however, does not think even though when I am thinking there is something always going on in my brain, even when I am thinking of God! (see Ricoeur, ibid., p. 40). Ricoeur rejects the eliminative arguments made by the Churchlands (Paul and Patricia) and their related claims for a materialist ontological monism which Ricoeur finds 'naive' (Ricoeur, ibid., p. 41). The mental includes the neuronal but not the other way round. Aristotle distinguished four causes. Neuroscience confines itself to understanding the material and formal causes but ignores or has nothing to say about the efficient or final causes. Its methodology is limited and partial. It sees aspects of the whole but not the whole itself. Ricoeur: 'To do psychology I am obliged to restrict this field [the total experience of life], whereas the task of phenomenology is to restore its full scope' (Ricoeur, ibid., p. 129). A naturalist approach only recognises as legitimate the objectifying methods of the natural sciences. It advances and seeks to defend a materialist conception of mind; it has this in common with some strands of Buddhism; Buddhist doctrine is essentially agnostic, 'rejecting from the outset any notion of revealed truth' (Ricoeur, ibid., p. 289), in Ricoeur's words and perhaps this is why it endears itself to certain philosophers of mind.

Mind or brain scientists tells us that there is a certain relationship between the structure of the brain and the psyche but we are never told what the relationship is. This is a crucial point. Ricoeur has this to say: 'I do not know what it means to say "consciousness occurs in the brain". Consciousness may know itself – or not: this is the whole question of the unconscious – but the brain will forever remain an object of knowledge; it will never belong to an experience of one's own body. The brain does not "think" in the sense that thought conceives of itself' (Ricoeur, ibid., p. 52).

For Ricoeur, phenomenology has an advantage over the neurosciences, which rely on metaphysical anthropomorphisms (see Ricoeur, ibid., p. 89). The question he poses is this: How does knowing more about what goes on in the brain actually enrich my intersubjective knowledge? Consciousness is always outside of itself for the phenomenologist – hence the employment of the word 'intentionality'. Consciousness aims at something other than consciousness; all consciousness is consciousness of something other than consciousness. Ricoeur cites Sartre's studies of emotions which show that emotion is at once intentional and meaningful. And Ricoeur would wish, he says, to talk about 'spirit' and 'transcendence' and he can do this operating as he is from within a phenomenological rather than materialist framework because he wants to have access to all of human experience. As he states: 'human experience isn't only scientific' (Ricoeur, ibid., p. 175). When Changeux tells him not to underestimate the potential resources of the neurosciences, Ricoeur replies thus: 'But what will it prove? That cerebral activity underlies all mental phenomena? This is the working hypothesis of the neurosciences! The reproach that I would bring once more against your program is that it groups together under the banner of neurobiology all related disciplines without taking into account either the variety of the respective referents of these sciences or of the variety of their styles of research – instead of leaving it up to interdisciplinary collaboration to create a synergistic relation among fields, with each member of the constellation being free to compete with the others for hegemony' (Ricoeur, ibid., pp. 176-7). In relation to choice and ethics and our experience of life, Ricoeur opines that we know much more through the reflection of moralists and novelists than through the neurosciences (see Ricoeur, ibid., p. 197). Neuroscience would be well advised to draw upon a wider field of observation concerning human beings. In order to understand morals or desire, to take but two examples, 'I have no need to know anything about the brain' (Ricoeur, ibid., p. 200), according to Ricoeur. Ricoeur wishes to affirm the autonomy of phenomenology in relation to the neurosciences.

For Ricoeur, the ultimate aim of moral life is bound up with religion (he is Kantian in this respect) and it is to liberate in each of us our basic goodness. There is the propensity for evil but the good is an original inclination. Evil is a propensity, good is a predisposition. Ricoeur dismisses the concept of original sin, which is a late rationalising interpretation in the history of Christianity, an 'anti-gnostic gloss' (Ricoeur, ibid., p. 285). For Changeux, his interlocutor, happiness is something that links the cognitive with the affective, the prefrontal with the limbic (see Ricoeur, ibid., p. 221). The difference in perspective here is obvious and Ricoeur worries and wants to challenge Changeux's ambition 'to take over neighboring sciences, little by little, and ultimately common experience as well' (Ricoeur, ibid., p. 241). Darwinism, with its emphasis on survival is, for Ricoeur, 'very selfish' (Ricoeur, ibid., p. 281), as it ignores the Other who is the locus of any ethical and religious considerations. The concern of religion, by contrast to ethics, is to save the fundamental goodness of mankind. For Changeux, this has nothing to do with religion but is the concern of everybody.

The above short excursus, which aims only to give a taste and flavour of the debate, is revealing on many levels not least as it demonstrates the divergences in perspective between the neurosciences and current Continental phenomenology. What I hope the dialogue does succeed in showing and questioning is the inbuilt assumptions and presumptions of the neuroscientists, showing, at the very least, that there are questions they must answer in their intellectual interactions with other scholars on our shared quest for meaning and understanding.

Chapter Two
Aristotle: Happiness as Virtue

Happiness lies in the taste, and not in the things, and it is from having what we desire that we are happy – not from having what others think desirable.

La Rochefoucauld

Traditionally, philosophy has seen the happiness of human beings as consisting in knowing the immaterial substances, such as the soul and God. According to Aristotle (384-322 BC), each one of us wants to be happy in the fullest sense of the word. *Eudaimonia* (translated as 'happiness') may also be translated as 'well-being' or 'flourishing'. Aristotle defines happiness as 'an activity of the soul in accordance with virtue'. Aristotle's theory of happiness *requires* a theory of virtue. This is the case with Spinoza too. In proposition XLII of Part V of his *Ethics* Spinoza had said: 'happiness is not the reward of virtue but virtue itself'. However, according to the Spanish philosopher, Miguel de Unamuno, nothing is more dreary and desolating than 'this happiness, this *beatitudo* of Spinoza, that consists in the intellectual love of the mind towards God' (Unamuno, 1954, p. 98). It is anti-vital. The voice of Spinoza is the voice of reason and reason, according to Unamuno, fails to satisfy the needs of the heart. Unamuno asks about him: 'Was he happy, Benedict Spinoza, while, to allay his inner unhappiness, he was discoursing of happiness?' (Unamuno, ibid.). Unamuno continues: 'Was he happy, the poor Jewish intellectualist definer of intellectual love and of happiness? For that and no other is the problem …. And what profits it to discuss or to define happiness if you cannot thereby achieve happiness?' (Unamuno, ibid., p. 99). For Unamuno, happiness is 'a thing that is lived and felt, not a thing that is reasoned about or defined' (Unamuno, ibid., p. 100). But more of Unamuno in chapter ten. Returning to Aristotle.

What will give us happiness, according to Aristotle, is the most complete development and exercise of our capacities that is compatible with living in society. For the Aristotelian, 'to exist is to act'. In other words, life is about *action* and actualising our potentialities.

Self-indulgence and self-assertion will bring us into conflict. So Aristotle develops his doctrine of the 'Golden Mean' – the mean between two extremes, according to which a virtue is the midway point between two extremes of vice. For example, generosity is the mean between the two extremes of meanness (a deficiency) and profligacy (an excess). Modesty, to take another example, is the mean between shamelessness and shyness. According to Aristotle, happiness and mental health is dependent on the harmony of the parts. In other words, we need to achieve a balance and attain the golden mean. This involves juggling between action (*praxis*) and theory (*teoria*), between knowing and doing. The aim, as for Plato, is harmony and balance, achieving a still and centred personality that is in concordance rather than conflict. This is the way to achieve happiness. Moderation in all things is the message of Aristotles's 'practical wisdom' (*phronesis*). He sets out this ethical vision in *The Nicomachean Ethics*, the central thesis of which is that virtue leads to happiness, and happiness is our aim, our end (*telos*). We will see that it is this key Aristotelian notion that Frankl will critique later.

What is virtue? Virtue, for Aristotle, is an acquired disposition to do what is good. Virtue needs *three* things: knowledge, will and habit (steadfast operation). It is not its own reward. Virtue is the path to happiness. Augustine calls virtue an 'ordered love'. For Augustine, all virtue is love. And for Aquinas, virtue is ordered to goodness and goodness is an object of desire. Virtue is the perfection of potential. Virtue orders our love. Cicero says that virtue is to a soul what health and beauty are to a body. Virtue is not the only prerequisite for happiness any more than happiness is the only prerequisite for virtue. Both Plato and Aristotle claim that happiness can derive only from a life based on the Good. Central to the good life, that is to say, the happy life, is the virtue of friendship.

For Aristotle happiness is that activity that most fulfils us; therefore, Aristotle suggests it ought also to be concerned with the most perfect objects of intellect. So for Aristotle, happiness is an activity deriving from wisdom, since wisdom (*sophia*) is the crowning virtue of our most perfect ability, intellect (*nous*), and that activity is happiness. For both Aristotle and Aquinas, the happiness of human beings is twofold:

1) There is an imperfect happiness in this life that consists in the contemplation of immaterial substances, though our intellect does not know what such substances are.
2) The other happiness is the perfect happiness of the 'next life', when we will see the substance of God himself and other immaterial substances, such as angels.

Aquinas argues that human beings compulsively *will* total happiness, which, according to Boethius, is the perfect state, in which every good is collected together. So we yearn to be happy. But as Aristotle holds: *what you want depends on what you are*. There is in man a natural compulsion to want to be happy. We *will* to be happy and no good will be powerful enough to compel will to will unless it be good in every respect. Total happiness is the only perfect good. So it would seem that we all want to be blissfully happy. In his discussion of free will, of will as rational desire – will is the desire of our reason – Aquinas said that happiness 'can be reached by many paths'. (Freud named *eleven* such paths). But for Aquinas, total happiness is to be found in God alone. This is the bliss of the beatitude held out as a hope to the believer. For Aquinas, everybody *intends* happiness or bliss. In his

Treatise on Law, Thomas notes that the last end of human life is bliss or happiness. It is the ultimate human goal of life, according to Thomas. For Aristotle, happiness consists in *activity*. This is happiness as, and through, *virtue*.

Aristotle relates virtue (excellence of character) to happiness. Virtue perfects the soul. For Aristotle, happiness is achieved through civic action and involvement in the *polis* (city state). Aristotle had said that man is, by nature and definition, a political animal. Centuries later, the existentialists would emphasise this type of political engagement and social commitment. The ethics of the Greeks is, as Schopenhauer pointed out, to make it possible to lead a happy life, a *vita beata*. Aristotle distinguishes between the happiness man can find in political (active) life, through practising virtue in the city (politics is founded on ethics for Aristotle), and philosophical happiness, which is a life devoted to the activity of the mind. The summit of philosophical happiness is the contemplation of the divine Intellect – accessible only in rare moments. So, for the most part, the philosopher must content himself with the inferior way of happiness, which consists in the search or the quest for the divine Ground of being, in Aristotle's existential analysis.

Aristotle began his *Nicomachean Ethics* by asserting that the Good is 'that at which all things aim' (Aristotle, ibid., p. 63). The teleological thrust is towards happiness. The end is happiness but views of what happiness is differ hugely. So what does happiness consist in? Happiness is something about living well. For some it is money or pleasure or fame or popularity but such a person can as quickly change his mind. For example, when a person falls ill he says happiness is health, when he is hard up he says that it is money. Plato held the view that above and beyond these particular goods there is another that is Good in itself and the cause of whatever goodness there is in all these others.

Aristotle observes that everyone is impressed by someone who pontificates on the subject and says something that is over their heads! For vulgar people, the Sovereign or Supreme Good or happiness is pleasure and the life of enjoyment (this, as we shall soon see is Epicurus's view). Aristotle dismisses this way of life as being mere 'bovine' existence. It is only one possible life. According to Aristotle, there are three main types of life:

1) the life of pleasure
2) the political life
3) the contemplative life

Aristotle privileges the contemplative life over all the others. Of course pleasure is essential to life; Aristotle made this clear in Book X of his *Ethics* but it is not the whole of life. Do we toil and suffer all day long just to amuse ourselves? Wealth, too, can never be the good that we are seeking because it serves as a means for obtaining something else – it is not an end in itself, whereas the life of intellect has its end in itself. The Good for man must be the *ultimate* end and object of human life; it must be something that is in itself completely satisfying and happiness fits such a description. Happiness is something we always choose for itself 'and never for any other reason' (Aristotle, ibid., p. 73). Aristotle notes: 'Happiness, then, is found to be something perfect and self-sufficient, being the end to which our actions are directed' (Aristotle, ibid., p. 74). The function (*ergon*) of a man is an activity (*arete*) of the soul and happiness is that activity. Happiness is not a state since if it were we could call a person happy even if they slept all through their life, passing it by in a vegetable state. Activities are either necessary and to be chosen for the sake of something else or to be chosen for themselves. Happiness is to be chosen for itself. It is self-sufficient.

However one day can't make you happy. It involves a lifetime: 'One swallow does not make a summer; neither does one day. Similarly neither can one day, or brief space of time, make a man blessed and happy' (Aristotle, ibid., p. 76).

Aristotle asserts that 'happiness is virtue' (Aristotle, ibid., p. 78) because an activity in accordance with virtue implies virtue. Though, other things help, such as friends, good ancestry, children and personal beauty 'for a man is scarcely happy if he is very ugly to look at, or of low birth, or solitary and childless' (Aristotle, ibid., p. 80).

The next question Aristotle asks is: can happiness be learnt or acquired or cultivated, or does it come to us by chance or through divine dispensation? If anything is a gift from the gods we would expect it to be happiness seeing as happiness is the best of all human possessions, Aristotle answers. But even if it is acquired by moral goodness it is still one of our most divine possessions. As to happiness just happening, Aristotle feels that if 'the most important and finest thing of all should be left to chance [that] would be a gross disharmony' (Aristotle, ibid., p. 81). Happiness, that 'virtuous activity of the soul' (Aristotle, ibid.) is, in essence, 'not only complete goodness but a complete life' (Aristotle, ibid.) too.

Another question that Aristotle poses is: is it only when one's life is at an end that a person can be called happy? Ought we call no man happy as long as he lives and adopt Solon's phrase 'look to the end'? Can we only be happy once we are dead? This is a paradox, for Aristotle, once we define happiness as a kind of activity. 'It is virtuous activities that determine our happiness' (Aristotle, ibid., p. 83). In this life the happy man will spend his time 'in virtuous conduct and contemplation' (Aristotle, ibid.). Aristotle concludes book one of the *Ethics* with these words:

> We are now in a position to define the happy man as "one who is active in accordance with complete virtue, and who is adequately furnished with external goods, and that not for some unspecified period but throughout a complete life". And probably we should add "destined both to live in this way and to die accordingly"; because the future is obscure to us, and happiness we maintain to be an *end* in every way utterly final and complete. If this is so, then we shall describe those of the living who possess and will continue to possess the stated qualifications as supremely happy – but with a human happiness (Aristotle, ibid., pp. 84-85).

In book ten, Aristotle returns to discussing the life of happiness. He maintains that 'pleasure and pain permeate the whole of life' (Aristotle, ibid., p.

312) but rejects Eudoxus's view that pleasure is the Good and desirable in itself. But the opposite view, that pleasure is not a good, is likewise open to criticism he feels. Here he stands between the Scylla of hedonism and the Charybdis of puritanism. Happiness is not the same as pleasure so. This is a central point, one with which Frankl will concur and which will occupy our own analysis in the final chapter.

It is happiness, not pleasure, that is the end of human conduct. Happiness must be distinguished from amusement. Some people assume that happiness is amusement since many people who are regarded as happy have recourse to such amusements and these are seen to be conducive to happiness. However, for the good man 'virtuous acitivity is most desirable. It follows that happiness does not consist in amusement' (Aristotle, ibid., p. 327). He goes on to say: 'Indeed it would be paradoxical if the end were amusement; if we toiled and suffered all our lives long to amuse ourselves' (Aristotle, ibid.). This is childish – it is also Pascal's view. The happy life is one lived in accordance with goodness 'and such a life implies seriousness and does not consist in amusing oneself' (Aristotle, ibid.). So if happiness is an activity in accordance with virtue, which Aristotle says it is, then it is reasonable to assume that this is in accordance with the highest virtue, which for Aristotle is *contemplative activity*. Aristotle asserts that 'contemplation is ... the highest form of activity' (Aristotle, ibid., p. 328). We are more capable of continuous contemplation than we are of any practical activity. But he also assumes that 'happiness must contain an admixture of pleasure' (Aristotle, ibid.) because such an activity in accordance with philosophical wisdom is 'the most pleasant of the virtuous activities' (Aristotle, ibid.). And since happiness implies leisure, it must be an intellectual rather than practical activity. Such a happy human life is complete, 'for nothing that pertains to happiness is incomplete' (Aristotle, ibid., p. 330). Aristotle asserts that for man 'the best and most pleasant life is the life of the intellect, since the intellect is in the fullest sense the man. So this life will also be the happiest' (Aristotle, ibid., p. 331). The gods spend their time in contemplation and they are supremely happy, so that the 'perfect happiness is a kind of contemplative activity' (Aristotle, ibid., p. 333). Among human activities contemplation is the one most akin to the gods so it follows that man is happy by contemplating since it resembles divine activity itself.

Happiness, then, is co-extensive with contemplation, and the more people contemplate, the happier they are; not incidentally, but in virtue of their contemplation, because it is in itself precious. Thus happiness is a form of contemplation. But its possessor, being only human, will also need external felicity, because human nature is not self-sufficient for the purpose of contemplation; the body too must be healthy, and food and other amenities must be available (Aristotle, ibid., pp. 333-4).

Nothing is gained from contemplation except the act of contemplation itself. However, we shouldn't feel that this is pie in the sky philosophising. Aristotle's theorising is characterised by what has been termed his 'robust common sense' and realism. And in the *Politics*, Aristotle explores the practical implications of all this. The purpose of government is, says Aristotle, to enable its citizens to live the full and happy life as discussed and outlined in his ethico-political philosophy. But it's only by being a member of society that one can do this. Happiness and personal fulfilment are not to be found in isolation. There is a strong connection between self (soul) and society (the state). *There are inescapable social and political dimensions to any happy life.* The function of the state is to make possible the optimal development and happiness of the individual. Only by achieving an ethical stance in oneself can one seek to change the political situation in society. For the Greek philosophers, politics (justice in the state) is founded on ethics (justice in the individual), as we said earlier. This is the great Greek insight and insistence. As Aristotle says in the *Ethics*: the '*student of ethics must therefore apply himself to politics*' (Aristotle, ibid., p. 342). As political animals it is incumbent upon us to retain a lively interest in both soul and society – in ethics and politics, in other words. (Plato proffered the view that nothing would change in the *polis* unless and until philosophers became kings or kings, philosophers).

In *The Art of Rhetoric* Aristotle notes: 'There is pretty much an objective at which everybody aims, both each in private and all together, both in pursuit and in avoidance. And this, to put it in a nutshell, is *happiness* and its elements' (Aristotle, 1991, p. 87). In this work he defines happiness thus: '*Let happiness, then, be virtuous welfare, or self-sufficiency in life or the pleasantest secure life or material and physical well-being accompanied by the capacity to safeguard or procure the same*' (Aristotle, ibid.). According to Aristotle, the elements of happiness are the following: gentle birth, a wide circle of friends, wealth, creditable offspring, comfortable old age, physical virtues such as health and beauty, status, good luck and virtue (also prudence, courage, justice and moderation). A man would enjoy the greatest self-sufficiency if he possessed *internal* advantages (those connected with the body and the soul) and *external* advantages (those connected with good birth, friends, cash and status). This is how life is secure. Good birth, status and eminence excite envy. Creditable offspring are straightforward elements. Wealth is seen as abundance in money and land and possessions in terms of furniture, cattle and slaves but being rich, according to Aristotle, lies more in using than in having. Good repute is taken to be a serious figure or to possess something that everybody wants. It is to do with honour as a mark of reputation. Health is the excellence of the body, which is free from disease. Beauty will differ for each stage of life. The beauty of a young man, Aristotle opines, is to have his body useful for competition and force, being pleasant to look at for enjoyment too. That is why the pentathletes are the most beautiful. Prowess is composed of size, strength and speed, such as runners, wrestlers and boxers possess. A good old age is a slowness to age and freedom from pain. The enjoyment of a wide circle of friends is self-evident as a good. Good fortune is the presence or acquisition of the good things of life for which chance is responsible. However, ultimately Aristotle makes happiness synonymous with contemplation. And this implies leisure time. Happiness implies leisure.

Happiness depends on leisure because we occupy ourselves so that we may have leisure. The exercise of the practical virtues takes place in politics whereas the virtue of contemplation and the activity of the intellect has no other end beyond itself. So, can it be attained? Aristotle's answer is this: anyone who does achieve it does so because of the divine element in him. If the intellect is divine compared with a person so the life of the intellect is divine compared with the life of a human being. We ought to live according to the highest that is in us and put on immortality and think not mortal but divine thoughts. The life of the intellect will be the happiest life for man. Life in conformity with the other virtues will be secondary happiness. The exercise of the moral virtues will bring secondary happiness. Perfect happiness consists in contemplative activity. God is happy but in what does His happiness consist? What is God's activity? Surely not just actions or brave actions? We can't say of God that He risks His person in the cause of honour. Surely God's life is spent in some activity for we can't imagine God to be asleep all the time? God's life is a form of contemplation and as He is supremely happy (in the sense that He is perfect and needs nothing outside himself) so human activities that are most akin to God's will be the happiest. Animals can't be happy whereas only God is supremely happy and man is happy in so far as he contains something that resembles divine activity. Animals cannot be happy because they have no way of participating in contemplation. Happiness is co-extensive with contemplation and the more that people contemplate the happier they are. Aristotle concludes his entire philosophical programme thus: happiness is a form of contemplation. It is Aquinas's view too, as we shall shortly see.

However, being only human and not divine, man will also need external happiness because he is not self-sufficient. The body must be healthy and food must be available etc. One cannot be happy without external goods, as we have said. This does not mean, though, that it will be necessary to have such goods on a grand scale; Aristotle speaks of a modest means. A man's life will be happy if he lives in accordance with virtue. This is the opinion of the wise. The person who exercises his intellect and cultivates it is in the best state of mind. God Himself will take pleasure in that part of us which is the best and related to Himself. The wise person is the happiest so.

So onto the next question: how can this be put into practice? This theoretical knowledge *must* be put into practice. Many people perform good actions out of fear or from a desire to avoid punishment, opines Aristotle. They live under the sway of their feelings and pursue their own pleasures. Surely to encourage people toward perfection (didn't Christ say as much: 'be ye therefore perfect just so as your heavenly father is') and to dislodge from their characters habits that have long been embedded there is impossible? Aristotle wonders as much. His answer: goodness can only be induced in a suitably receptive character. How do we become good? Is it through effort and habit or nature or instruction? According to Aristotle, it is bestowed by some divine dispensation. Discussion and instruction are not effective in all cases. The example Aristotle gives is of a piece of land. In order for it to prosper the land must be nourished – only then will the seed grow. Likewise, the mind of the pupil must be prepared in its habits if it is to enjoy the 'right' things. Feelings do not yield to argument. We must have a character to work on that has some affinity to virtue – 'one that appreciates what is noble and objects to what is base'. Training in goodness must begin at an early age. The right upbringing, supervision and habit are all important.

To sum up: happiness is the end sought in human life since it is chosen only for itself and never for any other reason. We may also choose pleasure or intelligence partly for themselves but we also choose them for the sake of happiness in the sense that we believe that they will be instrumental in promoting it. Man is a social animal so he will also need friends, a partner etc. to have a happy life. So if we all agree that happiness is the end and aim of life, can we also agree on the following: that each thing has its own function, Aristotle asks. For example, a painter achieves proficiency in the performance of his particular function. Shoemakers have a function. The eye has a function. What is the function of a human being? What is his *proper* function (precisely as man)? It can't be nutrition or growth as these are also shared by plants. It can't be sentience as the animals share in this. It is rationality. The function of man is an activity of the soul in accordance with virtue. This entails and implies the use of reason. Happiness isn't a state in that a state can be present in a person without him exercising the virue entailed. It is not a possession but an exercise in virtue. So how is happiness acquired? Can happiness be learnt? Is it acquired through habit and practice? Does it occur by chance? It is a gift from God? If anything is a gift from God to man, surely happiness is such a gift? Even if it is not a gift but is acquired by moral goodness it is one of our most divine possessions. A dog cannot be happy nor can a child be happy – its age debars it from contemplative activity. Happiness requires a complete adult human life, for Aristotle.

The virtues are dispositions not feelings or faculties. And the soul, for Aristotle, is the essential form of the body. It is who we fundamentally or substantially are. It is the whole person. Happiness, so, is not a mental state or an emotional condition. Happiness is about *flourising*; it is not a subjective feel-good factor or psychological state – it is ontological, metaphysical. The Greek word, as we have already noted, is *eudaimonia*, which is very hard to translate into English. The *eudaimon* lives and acts well. It is not living well as we understand it but well-living, well-acting. The 'happy' man is the one who fulfils his function, is he who flourishes, who actualises his potentialities. My happiness ends with the end of my life but in a certain sense also my plans and projects survive me. My successes or failures are not terminated by my termination – they may be fulfiled or frustrated by others after me. Interferences may occur after my death. So in a sense I cannot succeed until I am dead. So the happy person is one who is engaged in something. It is not about having some power but it is about exercising one's powers (dispositions). That's what Aristotle means by 'activity'.

The term 'soul' may be confusing too. It does not mean having a 'real self' that is housed in an alien body. To have a soul or *psuche* is simply to be alive for Aristotle, to be animated (*anima*=soul). 'Activities of the soul' are just the activities that living creatures can do by their nature. Sticks and stones cannot be happy since they are not endowed with life.

Finally, virtue or *arete* can be translated as goodness or virtue or excellence. But it is ultimately about doing something well. This takes time. Happiness is not pleasure or ecstasy. It cannot be brief or momentary. Happiness cannot be short-lived. A happy person performs with some success that most perfect of tasks. He thinks. He reflects. He practices the moral virtues of courage, temperance, patience, truthfullness, friendliness, modesty, righteous indignation etc. and the intellectual virtues of practical wisdom or prudence (*phronesis*), intelligence or understanding (*nous*) and wisdom (*sophia*). Happiness culminates in contemplation. The 'contemplator' is not a monk (necessarily) or an ascetic. Remember Aristotle said that a moderate supply of external goods is a precondition of happiness. The contemplative person *is* enjoying himself. Contemplation is not an exercise in reasoning. It is not an intellectual quest. It is not logic. For Aristotle, 'those who know have a more pleasant life than those who search'. Contemplation is not (Eastern) meditation, which involves a letting go and relaxation, a surrender to nothing. For Aristotle, contemplation is a consciously directed activity and is about something. The contemplative person will be somebody who has already acquired knowledge. To contemplate is to survey one's existing knowledge. It involves an appreciation of knowledge and truth. It is something divine. No one can live this life for more than a portion of his time. Many people cannot aspire to it at all.

The happy man, so, will spend his time in virtuous conduct and philosophical contemplation. Furthermore, the happy person cannot become miserable. He will not be dislodged from his happiness easily by the strokes of bad fortune but will bear them nobly. Happiness is always the final and complete end. Happiness is something precious and perfect, the cause of which is divine. And it is achieved through the virtuous mean between two extremes. This metaxological position is reminiscent of St. Benedict's motto: '*Ne Quid Nimis*': 'All things in moderation'. 'Nothing to excess' (see 41 and 42 especially, of the *Rule of St. Benedict*. This was pointed out to me by Abbot Emeritus Christopher Dillon, OSB, of Glenstal Abbey in a private conversation with the author, for which I thank him).

What of the criticisms of Aristotle's recipe for happiness (see books I, II and X and Jonathan Barnes's criticisms in his introduction to the *Ethics*)? Can we not achieve happiness without doing anything particularly well? After all, the vast majority of people have nothing outstanding about them. Aren't there such things as 'happy failures'? We can answer these objections by saying that if happiness involves some success, then it is true in that I cannot succeed or fulfil myself as a human being without doing something well, without exercising some virtue. Another criticism: surely happiness doesn't consist in a *single* activity that is right for everybody to do? Can there not be several felicitous activities? After all there are different wines and different jokes that make different people laugh or please the palette etc. Of course, different things make different people happy in the usual sense of that term. But there must be something, some one thing, which constitutes human happiness. This will amount to doing well as a human being, according to

Aristotle. Another criticism: Is Aristotle's view of human reason adequate and well-rounded? Surely the joy of the chase is more enjoyable and even exceeds the capture – the life of contemplative and tranquil repose and review? What about affection, sympathy, aesthetic appreciation? Is the contemplator of truth really happier and better than the lover of men and the admirer of beauty? Perhaps one can be friend, aesthete, lover and thinker. Perhaps human excellence is a deeper, broader river than Aristotle imagined or thought. Perhaps. But Aristotle would have located sympathy and sensibility on a lower level than contemplation. He would have said that intellect is the perfect faculty of the soul. Finally, would we really want to be happy in Aristotle's use of the term? Some may say: 'if happiness consists in bouts of intellectual activity within a life of moral rectitude, then I no longer want to be "happy"'. Aristotle would no doubt answer that if people prefer sensual delights over the austere pleasures of a life of virtue then they abjure their very humanity and lead a bestial life, eek out a mere bovine existence in the world. Such a person wouldn't be a man at all but an earthworm. A 'real' man would think, from time to time, on God and the mind, on the *summum bonum*. This Aristotelian answer will, of course, never convince the world if it chooses to be stubborn or willful or both. Nor should it, perhaps. Let us now examine Epicurus's philosophy of happiness; it stands in marked contrast to Aristotle's, as we shall see.

Chapter Three
Epicurus: Happiness as Pleasure

The happiness or unhappiness of man depends as much on their humours as on fortune.

La Rochefoucauld

The Epicureans came after the Cynics and Sceptics and before the Stoics. The Epicureans were non-religious, politically inactive and pleasure seeking philosophers. For this crowd of philosophers, non-existence is our inescapable destiny. The good in this life, happiness in this world, should be our aim. The way to achieve this, they thought, is to withdraw into private communities. This is the farthest remove from the publicly engaged philosophy of Aristotle. Epicurus (341-270 BC) emphasised the importance of sensual pleasure, much like Eudoxus whom Aristotle criticises. 'Pleasure is the beginning and goal of a happy life', he asserted in his *Letter to Menoeceus* (Epicurus, 1991, p. 128). Epicurus understood philosophy to be a guide to pleasure: 'The man who alleges he is not yet ready for philosophy or the time for it has passed him by, is like the man who says that he is either too young or too old for happiness' (Epicurus, ibid., p. 122).

He and his followers set up a philosophical school to promote happiness, which remained influential for the next five hundred years. The question the Epicureans asked was: 'what will make me happy?' They felt that just as medicine cured physical suffering, philosophy should alleviate mental suffering. Epicurus proclaimed that philosophy is an activity, which, through discourse and reasoning, procures for us a happy life. The task of philosophy was to interpret our desire and distress and save us from erroneous schemes and strategies for happiness. They insisted that we should not act on first impulses but instead discern the rationality of our desires by employing the Socratic method of dialectical reasoning. By so doing, philosophy would guarantee our true happiness. But apart from his love of the pleasures of the table, Epicurus, like Aristotle before him, highlighted the necessity of friendship for anyone pursuing the happy life. 'Of all the things that wisdom provides to help one live one's entire life in happiness, the greatest by far is the possession of friendship' (Epicurus, 1993, p. 27). Emerson defined friendship thus:

> Friendship requires that rare mean betwixt likeness and unlikeness .... Better be a nettle in the side of your friend than his echo. Let it be an alliance of two large formidable natures, mutually beheld, mutually feared, before they recognise the deep identity which beneath these disparities unites them. Let him be to thee forever a sort of beautiful enemy, untameable and devoutly revered (cited in Hederman, 2001, p. 204).

Epicurus himself lived in a large house a few miles from Athens with a group of friends, all of whom had their individual quarters but there were common rooms for conversations and meals. Moreover, the set up seems to have worked out well. It is thought that it might have been the first commune. Though money and wealth is unlikely to make you feel miserable, Epicurus felt that if we have money without friends, freedom and a reflective (or analysed) life (Socrates had said that the unexamined life was not worth living), we would never be fully happy. In order to discern what is essential for happiness, Epicurus divides our desires into *three* groups:

1) natural and necessary desires
2) natural but unnecessary desires
3) neither natural nor necessary desires

Natural and necessary desires would include: friends, freedom, reflection (on disease, death, poverty etc.) and food, shelter and clothes. Natural but unnecessary desires included grand houses, private baths, banquets, servants, fish and meat. Fame and power constituted desires that were neither natural nor necessary. Ultimately for Epicurus, happiness is not being in active pain but pursuing, instead, a life of pleasure. Happiness as pleasure, then – nothing more but nothing less either. But surely we can't equate happiness with mere pleasure? This would be utterly reductionistic and in fact erroneous too. As we said in the previous chapter on Aristotle, though pleasure may be a *part* of happiness, the two terms are not coextensive. This crucial distinction between pleasure and happiness will be further delineated in our chapter on Frankl.

The Stoics succeeded the Epicureans and for Marcus Aurelius, happiness is to be found in the present moment. Goethe summed up this Stoic position well when he opined: 'Only the present is our happiness' (cited in Hadot, 1995, p. 217). Happiness entails profitting from the present. Wouldn't this insight involve having to be without memory (the past) or desire (the future)? What Epicureanism and Stoicism have in common is that both these philosophies were therapies of the soul, spiritual exercises, their goal being freedom, self-mastery and happiness. The pleasure of the present was emphasised. In his *Meditations*, Marcus Aurelius observes: 'All the happiness you are trying to achieve by long, roundabout ways, you can have it right now ….that is, if you leave everything past behind you, entrust the future to providence, and if you arrange the present in accordance with piety and justice' (Marcus, 1968, 12, 1, 1-2). Happiness is now or never. Both these ancient philosophical schools, as opposed as they are, share a concern with concentrating cosnciousness upon the present moment as a way to ensuring the achievement of happiness. The difference, perhaps, is that the Epicurean *enjoys* the present moment of happiness, whereas the Stoic *wills* it; what is a pleasure for the former is a duty for the latter.

We will now explicate Boethius's view of happiness which, as we shall see, stands much closer to Aristotle's view than it does to Epicurus's.

Chapter Four
Boethius: Happiness as Goodness

The happiest person in the world is the one who is content with little.

La Rochefoucauld

Boethius (ca. 475-525 A.D.) was an eminent philosopher, public figure and exceptional Greek scholar under the Gothic emperor Theodoric. He was a member of an ancient and aristocratic family who fell from favour and was imprisoned in Pavia. His father had attained to the consulship as would Boethius' two sons. His family exerted huge influence. He married Rusticiana, daughter of Symmachus, Prefect of Rome and Head of the Senate. While waiting for his brutal execution – he was to be bludgeoned to death at the place of his exile in Pavia – he wrote *The Consolation of Philosophy* (Boethius, 1969), which is a dialogue of alternating prose and poetry (39 poems to be exact) between the ailing prisoner and his 'nurse' Philosophy, whose instruction in the nature of fortune and happiness bring him to health and enlightenment. He regarded the hour of his greatest happiness as being when he was in prison and he heard that his two sons were appointed consuls together. But though actively engaged in politics, Boethius considered philosophy to be his *summum vitae solamen* – his chief solace in life. He was also a Christian who wrote a number of treatises and tracts in theology and may be seen as a forerunner of the scholastics.

The Consolation of Philosophy is, as the title says, a type of consolation – a moral meditation and medication. The book talks a lot about illness, remedy and cure. It was a hugely popular work in mediaeval Europe and Boethius' ideas suffuse the thought of both Chaucer and Dante, with Dante setting Boethius among the twelve lights in the heaven of the Sun. Dante tells us that the words of Boethius provided him with his greatest consolation after the death of Beatrice. *The Consolation of Philosophy* combines poetic intensity with brilliant philosphical insight in a light and lyrical manner.

Boethius stands at the crossroads of the Classical and Mediaeval worlds. The title of his work says it all – it is less about argument than it is about a philosophical meditation and the consolation that philosophy can bring generally and in the face of death particularly. Boethius' book restores and celebrates a Platonic tradition of dialoguing – it is somewhat akin to Plato's *The Last Days of Socrates*, which similarly discusses Socrates' final hours before his own execution by hemlock. Boethius' book tells of Philosophy, personified throughout, as descending to Boethius from on high and leading him by various paths to God Himself. The schema is Platonic and mirrors Plato's description in Book VII of the *Republic* of the soul's ascent in the famous allegory of the Cave – from seeing shadows to seeing the sun as a metaphor for the Form of the Good. We may also compare the book to Sir Thomas More's *Dialogue of Comfort Against Tribulation*, which was also written in prison and under the threat of execution. Boethius' bitter experiences led him, in the work we are here considering, into a rediscription and re-examination of the nature of happiness. In its conversational commentary and tone it is akin to the writings of Pseudo-Dionysius and Augustine. It is a philosophical rather than theological consolation, so there is no talk of the Trinity or Paradise or the Incarnation etc. He draws a distinction between faith and reason. The Boethian doctrine of salvation is the ascent of the individual by means of philosophical introspection and meditation to the knowledge of God; it is close to Neoplatonic philosophy and post-Augustinian Christianity. Turning now to the text itself.

We see Boethius in a state of much distress and deep despair – from happy youth to hapless age. As the first poem opens: 'Foolish the friends who called me happy then/Whose fall shows how my foothold was unsure' (Boethius, 1969, p. 35). As Boethius is giving vent to his sorrow and anger, he becomes aware of a woman standing over him, with an awe-inspiring appearance and burning eyes. On the bottom of her gown there is embroidered two Greek letters: *Pi* and *Theta*, which correspond to the two kinds of philosophy, practical (*Pi*) and contemplative (*Theta*). The former includes moral philosophy and ethics, the latter metaphysics, theology and physics. She tells him that it is a time for healing not lamenting. When he turns to look at his physician (the piece is replete with medical metaphors) he discovers it was his nurse in whose house he has been cared for since childhood – Philosophy. He gains some consolation from knowing that many illustrious philosophers suffered similar fates: Anaxagoras was banished from Athens, Zeno was tortured, while Socrates was put to death. While Boethius displays his grief, Philosophy remains unperturbed, stoic like in silence, and says that he is full of grief and alternating between fits of rage, wrath, anguish and disturbing passions and so in need of a cure. The cause of his illness is that he has forgotten his true nature and Philosophy attempts to restore his health so that treacherous passions become dispelled in the resplendent light of truth. He is told to banish grief as his mind is clouded and bound in chains.

In Book II (there are five in all), Philosophy says that she has discovered and diagnosed the nature of his condition – that he has been pining for his former good fortune and this has catapulted him into the slough of despondency. Philosophy reveals that change and inconstancy is Fortune's normal behaviour and that Fortune has lured and enticed him with a false happiness that is destined to pass away. Just as a farmer entrusts his seed to the fields, he balances the bad years against the good and so should he have done. Things change quickly on the wheel of chance and in one short hour one can see 'happiness from utter desolation grows' (Boethius, ibid., p. 56). Wealth, honours, fame and power are all under Fortune's jurisdiction. In life there are both fruit and flowers, cloud and cold – inconstancy is Fortune's very essence and sometimes 'the overthrow of happy realms' is carried out 'by the random strokes of Fortune' (Boethius, ibid., p. 58) and the mind of man is plummeted in a 'deep seated melancholy' (Boethius, ibid., p. 59). Philosophy says that this is not a cure for Boethius' condition but an application to help soothe his grief and console his heart. Philosophy reminds him of how fortunate he has been in so many ways, having enjoyed the blessings of a wife and two consular sons etc. Philosophy admonishes him thus:

> You are a happy man, then, if you know where your true happiness lies, since when the chief concern of mortal men is to keep their hold on life, you even now possess blessings which no one can doubt are more precious than life itself. So dry your tears. Fortune has not yet turned her hatred against all your blessings (Boethius, ibid., p. 62).

Philosophy continues:

> But I can't put up with your dilly-dallying and the dramatization of your care-worn grief-stricken complaints that something is lacking from your happiness. No man is so completely happy that something somewhere does not clash with his condition. It is the nature of human affairs to be fraught with anxiety.... Some men are blessed with both wealth and noble birth, but are unhappy because they have no wife. Some are happily married but without children ... Some again have been blessed with children only to weep over their misdeeds. No one finds it easy to accept the lot Fortune has sent them.... Remember, too, that all the most happy men are over-sensitive. They have never experienced adversity and so unless everything obeys their slightest whim they are prostrated by every minor upset, so trifling are the things that can detract from the complete happiness of a man at the summit of fortune.... No one is so happy that he would not want to change his lot if he gives in to impatience. Such is the bitter-sweetness of human happiness.... It is evident, therefore, how miserable the happiness of human life is; it does not remain long with those who are patient, and doesn't satisfy those who are troubled (Boethius, ibid., pp. 62-63).

Philosophy reveals the secret of happiness: that it lies within. She observes:

> Why then do you mortal men seek after happiness outside yourselves, when it lies within you? .... I will briefly show you what complete happiness hinges upon. If I ask you whether there is anything more precious to you than your own self, you will say no. So if you are not in possession of yourself you will possess something you would never wish to lose and something Fortune could never take away. In order to see that happiness can't consist in things goverend by chance, look at it this way. If happiness is the highest good of rational nature and everything that can be taken away is not the highest good – since it is surpassed by what can't be taken away – Fortune by her very mutability can't hope to lead to happiness (Boethius, ibid., p. 63).

Such a happiness, based on chance and which comes to an end at death, is unreliable as Fortune changes all the time. This is a false happiness but Philosophy says to Boethius she knows he is convinced that the human mind cannot die and so others have sought happiness actually through death and even suffering and torment. She proclaims: 'It seems that the happiness which cannot make men unhappy by its cessation, cannot either make them happy by its presence' (Boethius, ibid., p. 64).

Philosophy then proceeds to show up how barren and poor riches really are: from precious stones to the beauty of the countryside, the sea, the sun, the stars and sky and moon, flowers and fine clothes etc., none of which belong to man. Life is full of plenty as well as poverty, pearls as well as perils. And he who has much, wants much. Philosophy poetically exclaims: 'O happy was that long lost age/ Content with nature's faithful fruits' (Boethius, ibid., p. 68).

Like riches, power, fame and high office, Fortune is not worth pursuing either and is of no intrinsic good or value. However long a life of fame and fortune is, 'when compared with unending eternity it is shown to be not just little, but nothing at all' (Boethius, ibid., p. 74). A philosopher (someone who deserves the title) practises virtue and seeks out heaven in freedom and despises earthly affairs. Fortune may seem to bring happiness but deceives man with her smiles. As Fortune is capricious, wayward and inconstant so also is human happiness – 'how fragile a thing happiness is' (Boethius, ibid., p. 76). Book II ends with Philosophy crying:

Love promulgates the laws
For friendship's faithful bond.
O happy race of men
If Love who rules the sky
Could rule your hearts as well! (Boethius, ibid., p. 77).

Book III begins by Philosophy telling Boethius that she is trying to bring him to his true destination, which is true happiness. She criticises him thus: 'Your mind dreams of it ... but your sight is clouded by shadows of happiness and [you] cannot see reality' (Boethius, ibid., p. 78). Boethius begs her to show him the nature of true happiness, which Philosophy promises to do. She tells him that 'all are striving to reach one and the same goal, namely, happiness, which is a good which once obtained leaves nothing more to be desired. It is the perfection of all good things and contains in itself all that is good' (Boethius, ibid., p. 79). And perfect good does not, as some suppose, reside in wealth or respect, in fame, enjoyment, in power, position, popularity (whose 'acquisition is fortuitous and its retention continuously uncertain') (Boethius, ibid., p. 89) or pleasure. All men desire happiness and are looking for it in all these pursuits but they will not find it in these, though some people through the possession of these, snatch at a false appearance of happiness. But nothing satisfies greed – it is insatiable and once dead 'his fickle fortunes him forsake' (Boethius, ibid., p. 84). Philosophy says of the pursuit of bodily pleasures that it is 'full of anxiety and its fulfilment full of remorse' (Boethius, ibid., p. 90) and if bodily pleasure can produce happiness, why then the animals are very happy because their whole life is directed to the fulfilment of their bodily needs and requirements. All these paths to happiness are side-tracks.

If you want to hoard money you have to take it by force; if you want high office you will have to grovel to those who bestow it; if you want to outdo others in honour you will have to humiliate yourself by begging; if you want power you will have to expose yourself to risks and plots; if you want fame you will find yourself on a hard road and worn with care; if you decide to lead a life of pleasure some others will pour scorn on you and see you as a slave of the body. All these things are puny as is man himself when compared to an elephant in size, a bull in strength, a tiger in speed. 'Look up at the vault of heaven ... and stop admiring things that are worthless' (Boethius, ibid.). Beauty is ephemeral too.

The sleek looks of beauty are fleeting and transitory, more ephemeral than the blossom in spring. If, as Aristotle said, we had the piercing eyesight of the mythical Lynceus [one of the Argonauts who could see in the dark and discover hidden treasure] and could see right through things, even the body of an Alcibiades [an Athenian military leader of the fifth century, whom we will encounter later on; he was famous for his wealth and beauty and notorious of the use he made of them, as the footnote tells us], so fair on the surface, would look thoroughly ugly once we had seen the bowels inside (Boethius, ibid., p. 92).

The supreme good is happiness but it is not, as Eudoxus or Epicurus believed, to be found in pleasure. Man is a drunkard who cannot find his way home. Happiness is, rather, a state of self-sufficiency with no wants. True 'and perfect happiness is that which makes a man self-sufficient, strong, worthy of respect, glorious and joyful' (Boethius, ibid., p. 96). Nothing in the mortal state of things can furnish such a state of complete happiness – they are only shadows of the truly good. Only an imperfect happiness exists in perishable goods, which means 'that there can be no doubt that a true and perfect happiness exists' (Boethius, ibid., p. 99). God is filled with supreme and perfect goodness. And the perfect good is true happiness, so it follows that true happiness is to be found in God. This is Philosophy's conclusion. 'God is the essence of happiness' (Boethius, ibid., p. 101). And 'supreme happiness is identical with supreme divinity' (Boethius, ibid., p. 102), a position Aquinas will adopt. Through the possession of happiness people become happy and since happiness is divinity it is through the possession of divinity that a person becomes happy. 'Each happy individual is therefore divine' (ibid.). Heaven is man's true homeland and 'God is happiness itself' (Boethius, ibid., p. 110). Boethius' tragic melody and tearful melancholy is over and he addresses Philosophy thus: 'The conclusion of this highest of arguments has made me very happy, and I am even more happy because of the words you used. I am now ashamed of the stupidity of all my railing' (Boethius, ibid., pp. 111-12).

But in Book IV, Boethius admits that the greatest cause of his sadness is the realisation that evil exists and the wicked go unpunished and virtue unrewarded.

Philosophy answers thus: all men desire the good, and happiness is the good itself and both good and bad men strive to reach the good and men become good by acquiring goodness so they obtain what they are looking for. But if the wicked obtained what they want – that is goodness – they could not be wicked. Both groups want it but only one attains it so it demonstrates the power of the good and the weakness of the bad. They desire good through the things that give them pleasure but they don't obtain it, 'because evil things cannot reach happiness' (Boethius, ibid., p. 123). Philosophy says simply: 'Goodness is happiness' (Boethius, ibid., p. 124) and the punishment of the wicked is their very wickedness. Someone who 'robs with violence and burns with greed' (Boethius, ibid., p. 125) is like a wolf; someone who is wild and restless and is forever engaged with lawsuits is like a dog yapping; the person who lies in ambush in order to steal is like a fox; the person of quick temper is like a lion; the timid coward is like a hind; the lazy person is like an ass; the fickle person is like a bird with ever-changing interests; the person wallowing in impure lusts and filth is like a sow. 'So what happens is that when a man abandons goodness and ceases to be human, being unable to rise to a divine condition, he sinks to the level of being an animal' (Boethius, ibid.).

So the good are happy while the bad are unhappy and they are more unhappy, according to Philosophy, if they go unpunished. When the wicked receive their punishment they receive something good since the punishment itself is good because of its justice. 'So the wicked are much more unhappy when they are unjustly allowed to go scot free, than when a just punishment is imposed on them' (Boethius, ibid., p. 129). Punishment must alternate between a penal severity and a purifying mercy. The wicked are used to the dark and haven't yet come into the light. Further, Philosophy opines that those who commit an injustice are more unahppy than those who suffer it. Plato had said that it was better to suffer injustice than to do it. The guilt of the wicked could be cut back by punishment 'like a malignant growth' (Boethius, ibid., p. 131) and wickedness is compared to 'a disease of the mind' (Boethius, ibid., p. 132). Health means goodness and wickedness sickness (a Platonic motif).

Philosophy, (and Boethius too), brings this dialogue to an end by saying that evil is necessary for some good. We think of the sufferings of Job. Philosophy addresses Boethius thus: 'Providence stings some people to avoid giving them happiness for too long, and others she allows to be vexed by hard fortune to strengthen their virtues of mind by the use and exercise of patience' (Boethius, ibid., p. 139).

The Consolation of Philosophy concludes with these words of Philosophy's: 'Avoid vice, therefore, and cultivate virtue; lift up your mind to the right kind of hope, and put forth humble prayers on high' (Boethius, ibid., p. 169). For we live in the sight of a God who *sees* all things.

Descartes concludes his Third Meditation on a similar note when he notes: 'For, just as faith teaches us that the sovereign felicity of the other life consists in the contemplation of the divine Majesty alone, so even now we can learn from experience that a similar meditation, although incomparably less perfect, allows us to enjoy the greatest happiness we are capable of feeling in this life' (Descartes, 1968, p. 131). And Wittgenstein, for his part, opines: 'Christianity is indeed the only *sure* way to happiness' (cited in Monk, 1991, p. 122). These three very different philosophers are alike in this respect – their conviction of Christianity as guaranteeing happiness to us mortal creatures. However, it is a happiness that is not attainable in this life. Arguably it is Aquinas, whom we shall consider next, who makes the proposition that partial happiness is attainable here but perfect happiness awaits us elsewhere, central to his thought.

Chapter Five
Aquinas: Happiness as Contemplation

I nearly wept. I had not wept for years and years and years, and did not then. But such a sadness flooded me, such a sense of wasted life and happiness which might have been and could not be.

Iris Murdoch

St. Thomas Aquinas, that great hermeneutic synthesiser of Greek philosophy, especially Aristotelianism, with Christian theology held, together with Aristotle, though in a different way, that the ultimate of human happiness is to be found in contemplation. The locus of this desire for happiness is the realm of the mind. For Aquinas, all gratifications point to the ultimate one – all happiness has some connection with eternal beatitude. All satisfactions this side of Heaven fail to satiate completely – they are not what we seek. As André Gide remarked in his *Journals*: 'The terrible thing is that we can never make ourselves drunk enough'. Nothing is enough, sufficient, adequate. The happiness that is contemplation is not just the happiness of the philosopher. All satisfactions remain directed toward one ultimate and final end: partial happiness in this life, perfect happiness in the 'next life'. Virgil says in Dante's poem: 'Amid a thousand twigs, one sweet fruit is sought'. The question is: can our most intense desires be entirely satisfied by an act of the intellect? We posed this as a criticism in the section on Aristotle; we shall now attempt to answer the objection that the question implies more fully.

We desire happiness, for Thomas, just as the falling stone in some sense 'seeks' the depths. According to Aquinas, we seek happiness *by our nature*, in other words, by virtue of our creation. All beings endowed with reason want happiness by nature. Aquinas: 'Man desires happiness naturally and by necessity' (Aquinas, *S.T.*, I, 94, I). 'By nature the creature endowed with reason wishes to be happy' (Aquinas, *C.G.*, 4, 92). 'To desire to be happy is not a matter of free choice' (Aquinas, *S.T.*, I, 19, 10). 'The desire for the ultimate goal is not among the things under our control' (Aquinas, *S.T.*, I, 82, I ad 3). So we want to be happy and we can't not want it. The will is incapable of not willing happiness. It is as natural as the falling stone that 'seeks' the depths, as the flower that turns to the light, as the beast that hunts its prey. The very desire for happiness is inherent in man's composition. Man is here understood as a created spiritual being. His will is free but the desire for happiness springs from his innermost core. The will is unrestricted by external coercions. This desire pierces the heart and points back to an ultimate non-human origin. Aquinas: 'The will strives in freedom for felicity, although it strives for it by necessity' (Aquinas, *Pot.*, 10, 2 ad 5). That said, we can't answer the question: why do you want to be happy? But as Diotima says in Plato's *Symposium*: 'Nor is there any need to ask why a man desires happiness; the answer is already final'. Our spirit thirsts for 'that drink called happiness'. The phrase is the Thomist, Josef Pieper's one (see Pieper, 1958, pp. 80, 81, 84).

So we have a nature dictated desire for happiness though what this state consists in is hidden. The soul of man craves something else besides mere pleasure. Happiness comes to us as something unforseen, not subject to intention or planning. Happiness comes unbidden, as a gift of being. We are not, in Pieper's words, 'forgers of our own felicity' (Pieper, ibid., p. 26). Food, drink, houses, money, a beautiful partner – none of these can quench our thirst for happiness. With happiness comes gratitude. So, we desire happiness by nature but *we cannot make ourselves happy*. We are not happy by virtue of our being. Aquinas: 'In the present life perfect happiness cannot be' (Aquinas, *In Eth.*, I, 10, no. 129). We do not possess in this life ultimate gratification. We are restless wanderers, living the viatoric life. We are nonhappy and cannot conceive of the truly happy person or of Heaven where the thirst is finally quenched, we hope. Only God is perfectly happy by His very existence. Aquinas: 'To God alone may perfect beatitude be attributed, by virtue of His nature' (Aquinas, *S.T.*, I, 62, 4). God *is* His happiness. Aquinas: 'God and happiness are the same' (Aquinas, *C.G.*, I, 101). If we are happy we share in a happiness that is not of ourselves. God's happiness does not depend on happenings in this world. It cannot be intensified or diminished by any events in the realm of creation. Put another way: God's happiness is not affected by evil in this historical world. According to Thomas, the divine Joy is the only reality capable of quenching our ultimate desire.

Aquinas: 'To seek happiness is nothing but to seek the satiation of the will' (Aquinas, *S.T.*, I, II, 5, 8). We are hungry for happiness, thirsting for it. Hunger and thirst are the energy of human nature, just as happiness is a drink, is drinking. But this satiation comes from 'somewhere else'. But how do we drink this drink? We shall see.

If happiness is the quenching of a thirst, the person who thirsts looks away from himself to the source. Aquinas: 'That which produces happiness is something outside of the soul' (Aquinas, *S.T.*, I, II, 2, 7 and *C.G.*, 2d.15, 3, 3, ad I). If the person who thirsted were himself the drink, how could he continue to thirst? So the quenching of the thirst must come from outside himself. No one can be happy (can satisfy his own thirst) by his own being or doing.

In his *City of God*, Saint Augustine observed that ancient philosophy offered no less than two hundred and eighty-eight different opinions on what the ultimate happiness of man consists in! Aquinas is content with offering just the one.

We humans crave but so many seem content with possessing an illusory spectre of the desire for happiness, Thomas says. In reality we want too little. If we are oriented toward something else then we cannot have the preservation of our own existence as our ultimate goal. The allaying of the thirst can't consist in the continued existence of the person who thirsts. Aquinas: 'The good of man depends upon God's cognition, and therefore man's happiness depends upon his glory before God' (Aquinas, *S.T.*, I, II, 2, 3). Nietzsche thought happiness consisted in the will to power but power, according to Aquinas, 'has the quality of beginning, but happiness that of the ultimate end'. Power is located in history, just as happiness transcends time.

Cicero had said in his *De Oratore*, that they are usually called happy who, after they have won honour and glory in action, are able to spend their lives in a completely ordered community where they may pursue their work, unimperilled and enjoy their leisure with dignity. This is not enough. These goods are not insignificant but they are not *the* gratification towards which our deepest thirst is directed. Man is endowed with a thirst for happiness but this thirst cannot be realised in the finite realm. Even if the whole world were to be given to him, it would not be enough – in fact, it would be far too little, to satiate his ultimate desire, to make him completely happy. Question: what, so, is the drink called happiness that alone can satisfy man's most ardent desire? Answer: God. *God is the drink known as happiness*. Or if you prefer: goodness but a goodness so good that there is nothing in it that is not good. Our unlimited, boundless desire for happiness, despite despair, is terrifying and can be satisfied only by the boundless, infinite reality. We do not want merely to survive but to thrive; we do not simply want to muddle through but to live. Only the whole good can quench our thirst. Thus Aquinas: 'The whole good cannot be found anywhere in the realm of created things; it is encountered in God alone' (Aquinas, *S.T.*, I, II, 2, 8). We stretch out to grasp this, to receive it into the shelter of ourselves. The infinite good alone bears the name of (final) happiness.

We must distinguish joy from happiness – they are two different things, according to Pieper (see Pieper, 1958, pp. 47-8). Joy is always secondary – it is the response to happiness, according to Pieper. Happiness causes joy and we seek the good even at the cost of joy. Happiness is not gladness or joy but happiness without joy is unthinkable. Beatitude is possible and can be conceived only with pleasure and enjoyment and rapture on the part of spiritual-sensual man, and happiness is a good proper to man alone. The term *delectatio* does denote delight and delectation but does not correspond exactly with either of these terms. Rather, it connotes spiritual joy. There is desirability in happiness – one that confers the profoundest pleasure. Joy is joy *for*; there is no joy for joy's sake as there is with happiness. Possessing the good, says, Aquinas, is the cause of rejoicing. Partaking of the good is primary; joy is secondary. The drink known as happiness, which is something outside the soul, cannot be equated with joy. We can desire things even though possessing them does not bring joy. Such things may be sight, memory, knowledge, being good – Aquinas's tentative list (see Pieper, ibid., p. 49). Three of these involve awareness of reality through seeing, knowing and remembering. The good is every drink that quenches thirst. Joy appeases desire. We desire joy for the sake of the good, says Aquinas and every joy is consequent to a good so that there exists a joy consequent to the supreme good. The supreme good is happiness, so joy is the response to happiness.

Let us ask again: what is happiness? Happiness means attaining the whole good. We don't become happy by the fact that happiness as a drink exists. We must partake of it, receive it into us. How? This depends both on the drink and the drinker. It is like being overcome by a huge wave. It is like liquid being poured into some vessel. It cannot be seized or assimilated. We enter into it.

Aquinas distinguishes between created and uncreated happiness (Aquinas, *S.T.*, I, II, 3, I). God, as uncreated cause makes us happy but this happiness is not something that solely descends upon us from outside – we are participants in, though not creators of, our own happiness. Happiness is not a mere feeling or feel good factor – it takes place in the mind, in the innermost, alert silence of the mind of man. For Aristotle, happiness, as we have seen, takes place by action not by passivity. It is an activity of the soul – an act. But happiness is a gift too, for Aquinas. So both then: it comes as a gift and we create the conditions for its attainment. To explain this with an example, we can cite Christ who gave sight to the blind but they saw with their own sense of sight.

Three propositions may be adduced, according to Pieper (see Pieper, ibid., p. 52):
1) Happiness means perfection,
2) Perfection means realisation,
3) Realisation means action.

Firstly, happiness is perfection in that once attained there is nothing left to wish for. Aquinas: 'In perfect felicity the whole man is perfected' (Aquinas, *S.T.*, I, II, 3, 2). Secondly, a person attains to this perfection in that he realises its promise; he actualises its possibility. Aquinas: 'Felicity must consist in man's attainment of uttermost degree of being real' (Aquinas, ibid.). Thirdly, only by acting does a person attain happiness. Aquinas: 'Action is the ultimate realisation of the person who acts' (Aquinas, ibid.). *Happiness is drinking the drink*!

So, what type of action, then? Let us start by saying what type of action it is not. It is not action that is geared to getting success in the external world. It is an activity that is *within* the acting person himself. The effects of this drink called happiness are *within* – they work inward. Outward acts perfect the inner work. This work does not absorb or conern or consume the Creator.

Aquinas: 'The essence of happiness consists in an act of the intellect' (Aquinas, *S.T.*, I, II, 3, 4). So the fulfilment of existence occurs when we become aware of, get to know, reality. The whole of our being is directed towards the attainment of *insight*. The happy person is one who *sees* therefore. Happiness consists in seeing reality as it is. It is the ultimate satisfaction. We crave to see. We live to see, in contemplation. And a life must change. A person's perfection is not in love or the will. Hugh of St. Victor did say: 'To know truth and love the good – in this happiness consists'. However, for Aquinas, happiness does not consist in an act of the will but in cognitive activity. Happiness always takes the form of cognition. Now Augustine had said in his *De Trinitate* that happy is he who has everything he wants. Now Aquinas points out that it is impossible, *à la* Augustine, to speak about happiness without speaking of the will. Aquinas rewords it thus: 'He who has everything he wants is happy in that he has what he wants' (Aquinas, *S.T.*, I, II, 3, 4 ad 5). But....! 'He is happy in that he has what he wants – which having, however, takes place by something other than an act of will' (Aquinas, ibid.). This is the crucial point. *Happiness cannot be willed.* Happiness does consist in having everything that the will can will but this having is different from willing. This having is cognition. Happiness consists in cognition, in contemplation, in other words. It does not mean loving what we have but having what we love. Having the beloved occurs through cognition, in seeing, in contemplating. Augustine stands in agreement with Aquinas. 'Having' is cognition. 'Being happy means possessing something eternal. We labour to this end: that we may see. For Thomas, our whole reward is seeing. We want the universal reality. For this we hunger, thirst and long. It is the conquest of actuality, of repletion, of spiritual insight. Cognition seeks to seize reality. To know something or someone is to 'have' them, to grasp and understand them. Knowing is having. And the soul is all that is – it is reality itself. John 17:3: 'Eternal life is knowing Thee'.

'I know him'. 'I love him'. Knowledge then bespeaks of the most intimate, closest presence. To love is to affirm and affirmation is expressed in yearning and joy. These are the two modes of the act of love. Yearning is desire. It is craving, striving, seeking for. Joy is bliss, rapture, delight. This is the expression of the love that has obtained the beloved object of desire. We do not desire desire. What is sought by the will can't itself be an act of the will. All motion seeks rest. Rest resides not in willing but in knowing. What is loved becomes present to the will through cognition (something other than an act of the will or love). And cognition is seeing, intuiting, contemplating. (Seeing is an act of the intellect). Happy is the person who sees what he loves. And without love there can be no happiness – love's premise is happiness. Unhappiness, so, is the failure to possess what one loves. Love may be necessary for happiness but it is not enough. (It is a necessary but not sufficient condition, as we philosophers say). The eye does not love – it sees. Loving involves an act of the intellect. Contemplation is a knowing inspired by and suffused with love. Contemplation can't exist where love is absent. Pieper puts it thus: 'Contemplation is a loving attainment of awareness. It is intuition of the beloved object' (Pieper, 1958, p. 75).

Now for the next question: what constitutes contemplation? *Three* things (see Pieper, ibid, pp. 76-79):
1)   Silent perception of reality;
2)   Intuition;
3)   Knowing accompanied by wonder.

Contemplation involves attention and receptiveness to reality. It is a form of knowing that is not arrived at by thinking (contemplating is not thinking) but by intuiting, by seeing. Intuition is knowledge of what is present. Thinking attests to the failure of intuition. Finally, contemplation can be characterised by this form of knowing accompanied by marvel or amazement. This is possible for the person who can't see the whole of reality but only a part of it. God cannot be amazed at anything because He knows everything. He doesn't wonder. He loves. And love is the source of this contemplation, as 'deep calls unto deep', as the perfect calls to the imperfect. As such, there is no such thing as nonreligious contemplation, according to Pieper (Pieper, ibid., p. 80). All contemplation is religious. That said, it is equally true that almost anything encountered in the world can trigger awareness of the divine reality.

The ultimate satiation with the drink known as happiness occurs on the other side of death when we will see God no longer in a glass darkly but face to face. This is the *hope*. Aquinas maintains that this is the opinion of the philosophers as well as the saints (Aquinas, *C.G.*, 3, 39). Contemplation is the eternal beatitude of men and angels and of God Himself. This is an eschatological assertion but there is also the anthropological one – that man in his historical existence here on earth yearns to see. Earthly contemplation concerns a focusing of the inner gaze even though it senses a more complete satisfaction from someone else. Human happiness does not consist in the knowledge of God, which is to be had by logical demonstration. Faith, as nonseeing, kindles the longing that gratifies it. The knowledge of faith is a knowledge of what is absent. Earthly contemplation can quench man's thirst more than anything else as it affords a perception of the (absent) presence of God. Thus Aquinas: 'Imperfect beatitude, such as can be had here, consists primarily and principally in contemplation' (Aquinas, *S.T.*, I, II, 3, 5). And: 'As far as contemplation extends, so far does happiness extend' (Aquinas, *In Eth.*, 10, 12). Contemplation is insightful, intuited knowledge and spiritual vision.

If we are to partake in the object of this intellectual act, of that drink called happiness, it means that God is present in the world and we can, in some sense, see Him when our gaze is directed towards the depths of things. God isn't outside the world but the sustainer and source of all that is in the world. Seeing becomes true contemplation only when love is directed towards the divine, infinite, ultimate ground of reality and when this beloved object shows itself to the inner gaze in tranquil consolation and peaceful revelation. The yearning for happiness is united with the senses, with reason, with the play of imagination and with faith and the supernatural life. Such divine satiation arrests and transfigures us. The happy life is the one, so, that passes in a contemplative way of seeing (as well as hearing, smelling, tasting, but primarily seeing) the things of creation. Through contemplation, we see the beloved, divine object of desire. Contemplation consists in this loving gazing. The poet Gerald Manley Hopkins talks of 'inscapes', of passionately attending to the world of created things. Contemplation sees and seeks out the depths in things, as another poet – Rilke – put it. However, whatever is experienced in contemplation is not communicable. The fruits of contemplation and contemplation itself cannot be communicated. It takes place 'in the soul', that is to say, in the depths and innermost core of the whole person. Here, silence is the only true form of speech. When Saint Thomas himself enjoyed such an experience he said that everything he had previously written appeared to him like so much straw. Silence, so, in the face of absolute mystery but it is not the silence of resignation, as Pieper makes clear, rather, it is the silence of reverence (see Pieper, 1964, p. 110).

Like morality, love points beyond itself. The essence of love lies in affirming the other as other. Love must aim at something other than itself. Loving means wanting the other to be happy. In charity (*caritas* or love) we love others 'as companions in the sharing of beatitude', as Aquinas puts it (Aquinas, *Car.*, 7). Loving means desiring the beloved to be happy. Love is desiring and joy in possession.

The meaning of the active life is to make possible the happiness of the contemplative life. Understood like this, politics must aim at something that is not political. Aquinas puts it thus: 'The whole of political life seems to be ordered with a view to attaining the happiness of contemplation. For peace, which is established and preserved by virtue of political activity, places man in a position to devote himself to contemplation of the truth'. Contemplation keeps the end *in sight*.

A characteristic of the happy person is *simplicity (simplicitas)*. The person who really sees gathers the whole of reality into a single look. And everything seems utterly simple. Thus Nietzsche: 'Man's happiness is based upon there being for him an indisputable truth'. Happiness yearns for truth, just as it demands eternity. Nietzsche said as much when he observed that it is 'always one thing which makes for happiness: ... the capacity to feel unhistorically'. The happy person steps out of, transcends, time and resides in the reposeful *hit et nunc* of being. He sees things as they are. 'We prefer seeing to all else', Aristotle says in the first chapter of his *Metaphysics*. There is such joy in seeing. Contrariwise, too much stimulation and empty stimuli can kill the soul's receptivity, with an informational overload.

Is all this idealistic, too other worldly? What about evil and all the horrors of humankind? It is not in our mere power that the possibility of happiness exists. It exists due to an Other and it exists *in spite of* evil. There is the 'dark night' on the way of contemplation; there is the sight of the historical Gethsemane. However, happiness consents to the world *as a whole*. Such a consent takes place amid the tears and horrors, the grief and the terror. We may put it like this then: *happiness is founded on sorrow*. But the happy person presumes that all will come right with the world, that everything created is loved by God, that happiness is ultimately 'something utterly divine' as Aquinas calls it (Aquinas, *In Eth.*, I, 14; no. 169). *Happiness does not exist because of us. It exists despite us.* And our earthly contemplation, our earthly form of happiness, is imperfect, a foretaste of Eternal Life and Happiness. The happiness of contemplation is not easy or comfortable. It does entail the 'dark night of the soul'. Contemplation doesn't ignore evil or guilt or sin or sorrow. The happiness that derives from contemplation is the only true happiness though *it is founded on sorrow*, on the realisation of one's limitations due to our creaturely status and contingency. There is unrest in all this gentle repose. Earthly contemplation glimpses a light. Created things are in darkness. But the unknowable reality never denotes something in itself dark but only something that has so much light that we cannot absorb it all. Aquinas, one last time: 'though the eyes of the bat do not avail to behold the sun, it is seen by the eye of the eagle'

(Aquinas, *In Met.*, II, I, no. 286). Everything is seen then in an all-seeing embrace of love.

At the risk of repetition, we can summarise the Thomistic teaching on happiness, as adumbrated by Aquinas in his *Summa Theologica* and *Summa contra Gentes*, in ten main points thus:

1) Human happiness does not consist in bodily pleasures (in the goods of the body). It is not located in these.

2) Happiness is a good proper to man alone.

3) Man's ultimate happiness consists in contemplation of truth and is sought for its own sake.

4) Man's ultimate end fulfils his natural apetite in such a way that once he achieves it he desires nothing more. This cannot happen in this life because the more knowledge we gain the more our desire for such knowledge increases. Therefore, man's ultimate happiness is not in this life. In fact, no one is happy in this life. True happiness in this life is, in fact, impossible.

5) In that final happiness every human desire will be fulfilled as we will enjoy the vision of the Truth through which everything that the intellect naturally desires to know becomes known to it.

6) In that ultimate happiness there will be perfect pleasure, one not mixed with sadness or worry, anxiety or grief.

7) Through the vision of the divine, intellectual substances attain the true happiness in which all desire is at rest.

8) Since perfect happiness (*beatiudo*) for man consists only in the enjoyment of God from the vision of the divine essence as first cause, it follows that whoever devotes himself to things that are less than God as his end is prevented from participating in true happiness.

9) *Partial* happiness can be achieved in this life but only *perfect* happiness can be achieved in the life to come.

10) God is He alone in Whom all the perfect happiness of man consists and the supernatural virtues direct man to supernatural happiness. This supernatural happiness is salvation.

Next we explore Pascal's view of happiness, which directs us away from Thomas's metaphysical concerns, towards the enjoying distractions afforded by the material world.

Chapter Six
Pascal: Happiness as Diversion

It does not take much to make a wise man happy; nothing can make a fool contented; this is why nearly all men are wretched.

La Rochefoucauld.

Blaise Pascal (1623-1662) was a brilliant mathematician and scientist who was also a religious philosopher and committed to Catholicism. He is usually labelled a 'Jansenist' but doctrinally Pascal was never wholly at one with his Jansenist friends. On November 23rd, 1654 he experienced a personal revelation that resulted in his total conversion, one that led him to see intellectual achievement as a distraction from the search for reality. His famous *Pensées* ('Thoughts') were published posthumously in 1670.

The two poles of Pascal's argument are evident from the beginning of the book and may be defined thus: 'Wretchedness of man without God / Happiness of man with God'. He says that Ecclesiastes shows that 'man without God is totally ignorant and inescapably unhappy' (Pascal, 1995, no. 75). Pascal had a theory of the three orders, which stemmed originally from mathematics. Just as lines, squares and cubes can't be added together as being of different orders, so in the realm of human knowledge that which is proper to the *body* (the senses), to the *mind* (reason) and to the *heart* are of different orders and must be distinguished. For Pascal, the heart is the channel for intuitive knowledge, for apprehending pre-rational first principles and assenting to supra-rational propositions. Once the facts come through our senses, we codify, classify and categorise the manifold impressions of the senses. Reason analyses them and formulates hypotheses that can be tested experimentally but in neither case does the heart play a part. In supernatural matters, it is the heart that performs a decisive role. Reason is here inadequate. Paradoxically, Pascal appeals to reason in order to communicate truths that are outside its province. Only reason can persuade reason of its own inadequacy. 'The heart', he says, 'has its reasons, of which reason knows nothing'. La Rochefoucauld expressed similar sentiments when he said: 'The head is always the dupe of the heart' (La Rochefoucauld, 1997, maxim 102); 'It is not all who know their heads who know their hearts' (La Rochefoucauld, ibid., maxim 103) and 'The head cannot long play the part of the heart' (La Rochefoucauld, ibid., maxim 108).

He distinguishes between the God of the philosophers (the God of reason) and the God of Abraham, Isaac, and Jacob (the God of Revelation). Against Deism, the religion of the philosophers, which states that man can know God without Christ, Pascal maintains that without the Fall man would still be happy. Without Redemption man remains wretched and without the Incarnation man cannot know God through Christ. By partaking of humanity Christ sanctified a state that is neither that of the apes nor of the angels. Man's only goal, according to Pascal, is happiness and happiness is attainable through God. The wretchedness of man without God is the result of making himself his own centre (i.e., humanism); the happiness of man with God is the result of making Christ his centre (i.e., supernaturalism).

Defining the human condition as one of 'inconstancy, boredom, anxiety', Pascal devotes the whole section on 'Diversion' in his *Pensées* to showing how man tries to keep boredom at bay. Realising the wretchedness of human existence, man has taken to *diversions*. For Pascal, 'nothing could be more wretched than to be intolerably depressed as soon as one is reduced to introspection with no means of diversion' (Pascal, 1995, no. 36). *Diversion is the key to happiness*, which Pascal says is the 'world's supreme good' (Pascal, ibid., no. 44) – diversions such as gambling and hunting (we prefer the hunt to the capture, says Pascal). According to Pascal, we recall the past and anticipate the future but seldom, if ever, live in the present. Heidegger made a similar point some centuries later; for Heidegger man is fundamentally finite, a creature of contingency and facticity, thus the title of his great work, *Sein und Zeit* (*Being and Time*). We live on a line of time. For Heidegger, man is constituted by temporality. Because we exist in time we are what we are not in the sense we are 'no longer' (the past) and 'not yet' (the future). We are what we can be (the possible). There is the missed encounter with the present; there is the past of history (or memory) and there is the future of possibility (or desire). That's why Wilfred Bion, the British psychoanalyst, recommennds that analysts be without memory or desire so that they can be fully in the present moment with their suffering patients. There is something Buddhist-like in this exhortation but desire, as Spinoza, Hegel and Lacan never tire of telling us, is the essence of man. Desire sustains us in existence. (Buddhism extinguishes desire but Buddhists still desire – they desire to not to want to desire). Desire keeps us going, giving us 'the courage to go on', as Beckett put it. We find it so difficult to live in the present and practise 'mindfullness of being', as both the Buddhists and the Jesuits recommend (on that note, the *Spiritual Exercises* of Ignatius Loyola, founder of the Jesuits, are all about desire). Our minds either harp back to the past or fantasise about the future. This leads Pascal to exclaim: 'Thus we never actually live, but hope to live, and since we are always planning how to be happy, it is inevitable that we should never be so' (Pascal, ibid., no. 47). To be happy we must give up trying to be happy. Frankl, as we shall see, tells us that happiness must not be aimed at directly.

Pascal also holds that it is not good for us to be too free or to have all one needs (see Pascal, ibid., no. 57). There must be some lack. Desire springs from lack. We desire what we don't have and if we never lacked we would not desire. So lack is important in the life of man.

Pascal again: 'If our condition were truly happy we should not need to divert ourselves from thinking about it' (Pascal, ibid., no. 70). But we do. We devise all sorts of means to distract ourselves from thinking about life and death, love and sex, age and disease, depression and abandoned affairs that leave a hole in the heart of being. Heidegger said that anxiety (*angst*) is the fundamental mood of our being-towards-death though we contrive to forget or cover up this fact and facet of our mortality, this inevitability of our species. Thus we live 'inauthentic' lives. Our experience of being-in-the-world (*In-der-Welt-Sein*) is also an experience of non-being or not being. We are aware that we exist and that we can *not* exist – death is our destiny. Unlike fear, anguish lacks an object, occurring when nothing (nothingness) is the matter. (In his seminar on *Anxiety* (*L'Angoisse*) Lacan said that anxiety is the only affect that doesn't deceive and that the cause of anxiety is not lack but the lack of a lack, i.e., too much presence). There is an end in view – death. Our nonexistence cannot be gainsaid. All our existence is haunted by the fact of our ultimate and utter nothingness. This awareness, which we normally keep concealed, is accompanied by *angst*, that most fundamental and basic of all our ontological/existential (not just psychological) moods. Nothingness is within us, constituting the very basis of our being. Lacan went so far as to say that life is meaningful only in so far as it culminates in death. Death gives life meaning. We die every day we live. According to Plato/Socrates, philosophers make dying their profession. Similarly, the French philosopher, Montaigne, said 'to philosophise is to learn how to die'. But due to our anguish we seek Pascalian diversions to distract ourselves a while even though for Heidegger such a refusal to acknowledge our being-towards-death is an act of inauthenticity. Heidegger lambasts those who flee from this awful realisation and who seek refuge in distractions. (Sartre termed it *mauvaise foi* – 'bad faith'). However, Pascal's point is likewise to acknowledge this but then to distract us from it because we can't alter it or change the status of our utter contingency. Know that this is so but seek to distract yourself from the realisation that this is so, seems to be Pascal's point.

    Pascal puts little trust in reason or in the dreams of philosophy to make us happy. He proclaims that philosophy isn't worth even an hour's effort (Pascal, ibid., no. 84). Yet, we have within us the capacity to be happy (Pascal, ibid., no. 119). Unhappy as we are, 'we have an idea of happiness but we cannot attain it' (Pascal, ibid., no.131). Our fallen nature does not permit full happiness but great is the man who knows that he is wretched.

    Section VIII of the *Pensées*, entitled 'Diversion', is the key section of the book on the subject of happiness. Pascal begins by saying:

> If man were happy, the less he were diverted the happier he would be, like the saints and God. Yes: but is a man not happy who can find delight in diversion? No: because it comes from somewhere else, from outside; so he is dependent, and always liable to be disturbed by a thousand and one accidents, which inevitably cause distress (Pascal, ibid., no. 132).

    Try as we may, we seem unable to be happy. La Rochefoucauld says that 'we are bad company for ourselves' (La Rochefoucauld, 1997, maxim 141). But diversion can alleviate the unbearable lightness of being and distract us awhile from our distractions.

'Being unable to cure death, wretchedness and ignorance, men have decided, in order to be happy, not to think about such things' (Pascal, 1995, no. 133). We block them from our minds; we ignore their existence; we turn our backs on them. *Denial* is the name Freud gives to this defense mechanism but some defense mechanisms are necessary, indeed, essential. Pascal continues: 'Despite these afflictions man wants to be happy, only wants to be happy, and cannot help wanting to be happy. But how shall he go about it? The best thing would be to make himself immortal, but as he cannot do that, he has decided to stop himself thinking about it' (Pascal, ibid., no. 134). We take refuge in fantasy or we flee our concerns by escaping into activities of various sorts, anything that takes us out of ourselves. 'I have often said that the sole cause of man's unhappiness is that he does not know how to stay quietly in his room' (Pascal, ibid., no. 136). And perhaps also, this might entail the capacity to be alone in the presence of another person, as Winnicott, the British psychoanalyst, held. Flight, though, is of no avail because, as Freud reminds us, the ego cannot escape from itself. We look around, at the bloody, drunken chaos of life and see the dung-heap on which we will end our lives. Pascal talks about the natural unhappiness of our feeble mortal condition. We are so wretched that 'nothing can console us when we really think about it' (Pascal, ibid.). So what to do? Again and again Pascal advises that we redirect our attention and look elsewhere (Iris Murdoch advised this too). The solution to discomfort, discontent, disenchantment, dissatisfaction, despair? Three words: distraction, distraction, distraction or, in Pascal's language, *diversion*, which in the French – *divertisement* – connotes diversion as well as enjoyment. Freud might call this *suppression*. We deliberately decide to distract ourselves, to divert ourselves, to direct our attention away from self towards otherness, to anything that is not the self.

> The only good thing for men therefore is to be diverted from thinking of what they are, either by some occupation which takes their mind off it, or by some novel and agreeable passion which keeps them busy, like gambling, hunting, some absorbing show, in short by what is called diversion. That is why gaming and feminine society, war and high office are so popular. It is not that they really bring happiness, nor that anyone imagines that true bliss comes from possessing the money to be won at gaming or the hare that is hunted: …. What people want is not the easy peaceful life that allows us to think of our unhappy condition, nor the dangers of war, nor the burdens of office, but the agitation that takes our mind off it and diverts us. That is why we prefer the hunt to the capture. That is why men are so fond of hustle and bustle; that is why prison is such a fearful punishment; that is why the pleasures of solitude are so incomprehensible…. he [man] becomes unhappy as soon as he thinks about himself (Pascal, ibid.).

Roger Scruton, the British philosopher, penned a passionate and beautiful *apologia* for hunting entitled: *On Hunting* (1998). On a Pascalian note he admitted that he was wretched until he discovered the diversion of hunting, which changed his life: 'My life divides into three parts. In the first I was wretched; in the second ill at ease; in the third hunting' (Scruton, 1998, p. 7). Like dancing, hunting is done for no other purpose than itself. It is for nothing. Kant's words on the aesthetic seem relevant here; one could say that hunting or any diversion exhibits 'a purposiveness without purpose'. It is auto-telic, having its end in itself. Scruton feels that 'since discovering hunting, my priorities have changed' (Scruton, ibid., p. 63). He is now no longer an academic but lives by his wits through freelance writing. Hunting obviously gives him freedom and a meaning to life or, at least, distracts him a while from life, making sense even of German philosophy! He writes: 'Hunting gives sense to everything – even to Heidegger' (Scruton, ibid., p. 161).

Some fellow philosophers find such 'trivial' diversions incomprehensible. Pascal admonishes them:

> That is all that men have been able to devise for attaining happiness; those who philosophize about it, holding that people are quite unreasonable to spend all day chasing a hare that they would not have wanted to buy, have little knowledge of our nature. The hare itself would not save us from thinking about death and the miseries distracting us, but hunting it does so (Pascal, 1995, no. 136).

Pascal maintains that telling somebody to rest is the same as telling someone to be happy; it is not to understand human nature at all. It's the same as saying: 'whatever you do don't look behind you' and what do we do? Yes, we do the exact thing we were instructed not to do. It's not just children that can't do what they're told. According to Pascal, we would do anything to be disturbed. St. Teresa of Avila once said: 'be not disturbed' but we want to be disturbed, desperately. And who can blame us? 'It is wrong then to blame them; they are not wrong to want excitement – if they only wanted it for the sake of diversion. The trouble is that they want it as though, once they had the things they seek, they could not fail to be truly happy' (Pascal, ibid.). So we want a violent or vigorous occupation to take our minds off ourselves 'and that is why they choose some attractive object to entice them in ardent pursuit' (Pascal, ibid.) such as hunting or dancing – in dancing 'you must think where to put your feet', old-fashioned dancing, that is. All we want, though we don't know it, is the hunt not the capture, as Pascal repeats over and over. 'They think they genuinely want rest when all they really want is activity' (Pascal, ibid.). We remember that for Aristotle, happiness is doing something. It is some *activity*. Doing nothing requires much more effort. We have an instinct that seeks out external diversion though somewhere inside us we feel:

> ...that the only true happiness lies in rest and not in excitement .... All our life passes in this way: we seek rest by struggling against certain obstacles, and once they are overcome, rest proves intolerable because of the boredom it produces. We must get away from it and crave excitement.... Man is so unhappy that he would be bored even if he had no cause for boredom, by the very nature of his temperament, and he is so vain that, though he has a thousand and one basic reasons for being bored, the slightest thing, like pushing a ball with a billiard cue, will be enough to divert him (Pascal, ibid.).

So be not bored. Pascal gives the example of a man to whom money is given but on condition that he does not gamble. Pascal says that you will make him unhappy. If you make him play for nothing, he will likewise become bored. He must create a target for his passions that arouses desire, anger, and fear. 'However sad a man may be, if you can persuade him to take up some diversion he will be happy while it lasts, and however happy a man may be, if he lacks diversion and has no absorbing passion or entertainment to keep boredom away, he will soon be depressed and unhappy. Without diversion there is no joy; with diversion there is no sadness' (Pascal, ibid.).

To give an example: Terry Dobson, who was a well-known Aikidoka (a practitioner and teacher of the Japanese martial art of Aikido), wrote a moving account of his personal journey in a book entitled *It's a Lot Like Dancing*. He had gone to Japan and decided to commit suicide. Before he was about to do the deed he happened on a *dojo* (a place where the Way of Harmony [Aikido] is practised) and after a few minutes looking at the amazing spectacle in front of his eyes and seeing the strength and grace and seeming effortlessness of the old Japanese man hurtling his strong attackers through the air with style and speed, he decided all at once that this is what he must do. He would devote the rest of his life to learning this martial art of Aikido and so he did. At the end of the book he wonders why he didn't become a serial killer. Aikido was his distraction and it had literally saved his life.

According to Pascal, busy people don't have time to be depressed. They don't have a single hour of the day to think about themselves. So busy yourself to keep depression at bay. Learn to dance well. Take up a martial art. Pascal puts it to the test: leave a king, he says, entirely to himself with nothing to satisfy his senses, no cares to occupy his mind, no company and complete leisure to think about himself and 'you will see that a king without diversion is a very wretched man' (Pascal, ibid.). So we cannot be too occupied or busy enough. As T. E Lawrence noted, in a Franklian vein: 'Happiness is a by-product of absorption'. And when we have time off Pascal advises that we spend it on diversion and sport to keep ourselves fully occupied. 'How hollow and foul is the heart of man!' (Pascal, ibid.). It is even 'easier to bear death when one is not thinking about it' (Pascal, ibid.). Perhaps. But if Pascal's answer to happiness is distraction, then, I would submit, we need to be distracted occasionally from our distractions, while bearing in mind that sometimes distraction is psychologically healthy, a 'dereflection' in Frankl's language.

We cannot concur with Pascal that happiness consists solely in diversions though it is understandable and indeed essential that we engage in such diversionary pursuits from time to time, as I have said. In *De L'évasion* (*On Escape*), Levinas observes that what he calls 'escape' (Pascal's 'diversion') 'is the need to get out of oneself, that is, *to break with the most radical and unalterabley binding of chains, the fact that the I [moi] is oneself [soi-même]* (Levinas, 2003, p. 55). When we are ill at ease or suffering some malaise or disquiet we attempt to get out of the situation, to escape from something unbearable. Levinas defines malaise as a dead weight in the depths of our being. However, ultimately pleasure is a deceptive escape (contra Epicurus and Pascal). Pleasure fails; it develops with an increase in promises, promises that are never kept. 'Pleasure is disappointment and deceit' (Levinas, ibid., p. 63). It distracts from ethical considerations. So despite all this *ennui*, this abounding boredom, there is, for Levinas, the face of the Other, this Other one can never abandon.

Can't we say that all these endless diversions bring boredom in their wake? Safranski notes: 'Boredom lurks in the measures of diversion. Whatever is mobilised against it is already invariably infected by it'. We may note in passing that Baudelaire's poem, *Spleen II* is a monument to the failure of diversion. Aquinas's word for it is *acedia*; it is a sickness of the soul.

In *The Fundamental Concepts of Metaphysics: World, Finitude, Solitude*, Heidegger spends much of the time analysing boredom. According to the Heideggerian hermeneutic, we can detect and distinguish three points or movements in this regard. 1) Immersion in everydayness and habit, absorption in wordliness; 2) Anxiety or boredom throws this world into question, revealing the Nothing that lurks beneath it – the nothing to do or even care about; 3) Movement of return, whereby something is freshly revealed. We are recalled to a primordial astonishment that there is something not nothing and we see the world anew. How does this Heideggerian tir-partite schema relate to Pascal's theorising on diversion? We can say that Pascalian diversion leaves us in Heidegger Act I. In Act III, when we return to the world of diversion, the latter no longer operates as a shield against the Nothing. The Nothing (*Das Nicht*) shows through. Paul Valéry opined: 'God made the world out of nothing, but the nothing shows through'. Just so. This return is the meaning of *dwelling*, for Heidegger (not as the abolition of homelessness but as its acceptance). To dwell is to pitch one's tent *à la* Buber on shifting ground. Homelessness is to home what the Nothing is to Being. In each case the former reveals the latter; they are equiprimordial. Being, as Heidegger remarks, is the uncanny other of the Nothing. To be or not to be? Being is to be preferred to non-being, but knowing that existence is haunted by nothingness. For ultimately anxiety, as Voegelin notes, 'is the response to the mystery of existence out of nothing' (Voegelin, 1990, p. 71). The hope is that the God beyond being can soothe a man's soul and assuage his mortal anxiety. 'The search for order is the response to anxiety' (Voegelin, ibid.). Perhaps then will we be more inclined to face reality and less inclined to fight or flee it.

Now it is time to explore Schopenhauer's 'negative' account of happiness, in that, so conceived, happiness is seen as not being something, namely, as not suffering. (For Frankl, suffering is a key component of the 'tragic triad' of human existence). The hope is that suffering does not have the final word.

Chapter Seven:
Schopenhauer: Happiness as the Absence of Suffering

Happiness and unhappiness normally go to those who already have most of one or the other.

La Rochefoucauld

Arthur Schopenhauer (1788-1860) was, together with Nietzsche, one of the greatest of the nineteenth-century 'dark' philosophers. His most famous work was *The World as Will and Representation* (1818), which influenced Freud, Freud translating the concept of the 'will' into the unconscious. Both Schopenhauer and Freud were cheerful pessimists but Schopenhauer is merry too, much like Hume, whom he admired. If Schopenhauer inspired Nietzsche (who called him 'the only serious moralist of our century'), both these philosophers were to influence Freud. Freud took the term the 'id' from Nietzsche and from Schopenhauer he took the notion of the death drive – Schopenhauer has a chapter in the aforementioned book with the title 'Denial of the Will to Live'. Schopenhauer's fame came in 1851 with the publication of his *Parerga and Paralipomena*, a collection of essays and aphorisms.

For Schopenhauer, every individual is embodied Will and the nature of Will is to strive to live. Will is will to live (Freud's self-preservative instincts; Darwin's survival of the fittest, which also means the destruction of the weakest). This means that every individual is an ego whose primary interest is in staying alive and which overrides every other, including every other individual. The outcome is conflict. The suffering so engendered is the stuff of life itself. According to Schopenhauer, *happiness is merely the dimunition of suffering*. Happiness is, so, seen in negative terms by Schopenhauer. Similarly, Buddhists (and Schopenhauer was influenced by Buddhism) believe that happiness is the *absence* of suffering. The way out of this is denial of the Will – the refusal to enter the contest. The power to do this resides in the conscious intellect, which is capable of understanding the nature of the Will. The only real good, ultimately, is extinction – the realisation that life is as nothing. 'So long as we are given to the throng of desires with its constant hopes and fears …. We never obtain lasting happiness and peace'. Nature is red in tooth and claw. As Schopenhauer says: 'Man is a wolf to man' (Freud would later render it into Latin: *homo homini lupus*). Violence and injustice are rife, rampant and the human world is like the animal world. (See the marvellous painting by George Stubb, which depicts this, entitled 'Horse Attacked by a Lion' from 1769). Each life is a meaningless tragedy and ends in death. For Schopenhauer, 'Will' rather than 'reason' directs us. Reason is, as David Hume, the Scottish philosopher, put it, 'the slave of the passions and can pretend to no other office other than to serve and obey them'. People are perpetually unsatisfied and unhappy. Death, then, is the cure for the sickness of life. Or, as Lacan would likewise assert, life is a disease and the cure is death.

One way in which we can find momentary relief from the dark dungeon and dung-heap of the world, according to Schopenhauer, is through the arts (painting, poetry, sculpture and, above all, music), which relaxes and releases us from the relentless rack of willing. Art can temporarily silence the ego. Schopenhauerian happiness, thus, resides in *detachment* rather than Pascalian *divertisement*. We are here reminded of one of the Buddha's sayings: 'Happy is he who has overcome his ego … who has attained peace … who has found the truth'. Though egoism is prevalent, ubiquitously so, Schopenhauer also contends that aside from egoism there are *two* other fundamental motives of human activity – malice and compassion (the latter being a cardinal virtue in Buddhist ethics). Schopenhauer showed compassion to animals and plants – he loved and venerated nature. And it is precisely through this veneration of all things that we may perhaps be saved.

> Consider the insect on your path: a slight unconscious turning of your step is decisive as to its life or death. Look at the wood-snail, without any means of flight, of defense, of deception, of concealment, already prey for all. Look at the fish carelessly playing in the still open net: the frog restrained by its laziness from the flight which might save it; the bird that does not know of the falcon which soars above it; the sheep which the wolf eyes and examines from the thicket (cited in Murdoch, 1992, p. 71).

For Schopenhauer: 'Work, worry, toil and trouble are indeed the lot of almost all men their whole life long. And yet if every desire were satisfied as soon as it arose how would men occupy their lives, how would they pass the time?' (Schopenhauer, 1974, p. 43). Happiness is the abolition of desire and the extinction of pain. He writes that 'the happiness of a given life is not to be measured according to the joys and pleasures it contains but according to the absence of the positive element, the absence of suffering' (Schopenhauer, ibid.). Human happiness consists of 'health, food, protection from wet and cold, and sexual gratification' (Schopenhauer, ibid.). Schopenhauer congratulates himself (as does Freud congratulate him in his preface to the fourth edition of *The Three Essays on the Theory of Sexuality*) on being the first philosopher to make a serious study of sexual love, though Plato had discussed the Greek love of youths in his *Phaedrus* and *Symposium*. The material basis is physical pleasure. For everything becomes and is, ultimately, nothingness.

> That which *has been* no longer *is*; it as little exists as does that which has *never* been. But everything that *is* in the next moment *has been*. Thus the most insignificant present has over the most significant past the advantage of *actuality*, which means that the former bears to the latter the relation of something to nothing (Schopenhauer, ibid., p. 51).

Every evening, we are poorer by a day. The greatest wisdom and happiness 'consists in enjoying the present and making this enjoyment the goal of life' (Schopenhauer, ibid., p. 52). Because of the nature of the world, which is in a state of permanent Heraclitean change and unceasing motion, there is no possibility of repose but only unrest.

> In such a world, where no stability of any kind, no enduring state is possible, where everything is involved in restless change and confusion and keeps itself on its tightrope only by continually striding forward – in such a world, happiness is not so much as to be thought of .... In the first place, no man is happy but strives his whole life long after a supposed happiness which he seldom attains, and even if he does it is only to be disappointed with it; as a rule, however, he finally enters harbour shipwrecked and dismasted. In the second place, however, it is all one whether he has been happy or not in a life which has consisted merely of a succession of transient present moments and is now at an end (Schopenhauer, ibid., pp. 52-3).

Life is a task, the task of maintaining itself in being and man is a creature who is a compound of desires that can never be fully satisfied. As Schopenhauer puts it:

> We begin in the madness of carnal desire and the transport of voluptuousness, we end in the dissolution of all our parts and the musty stench of corpses. And the road from the one to the other too goes, in regard to our well-being and enjoyment of life, steadily downhill: happily dreaming childhood, exultant youth, toil-filled years of mankind, infirm and often wretched old age, the torment of the last illness and finally the throes of death (Schopenhauer, ibid., p. 54).

Is it any wonder we can't be happy? Life is a *desengaño*, a process of disillusionment.

Schopenhauer regarded reading as a surrogate for thinking. And he divided thinkers into *two* classes: the sophists, who want to appear as thinkers and the true philosophers, who really think for themselves. 'The pleasure and happiness of their existence consists in thinking' (Schopenhauer, ibid., p. 93) and 'there is no happiness on earth', Schopenhauer says, 'to compare with that which a beautiful and fruitful mind finds in a propitious hour in itself' (Schopenhauer, ibid.), though he recognises, with Hume, the Scottish sceptic, that philosophy is not for everyone. Religion is the metaphysics of the masses. He endorses a wise saying: *Primum vivere, deinde philosophari* ('First live, then philosophise').

If hope is the confusion of the desire for a thing with its probability, happiness and unhappiness 'is no more than the ratio between what we demand and what we receive' (Schopenhauer, ibid., p. 168). This is because enjoyment, for Schopenhauer, is only negative – it is the removal of a pain. He compares states of human happiness and apparent good fortune to certain groups of trees: seen from a distance they look beautiful but up close their beauty disappears. In relation to money and the happiness it is suppoeds to bring, Schopenhauer has this to say: '*Money* is human happiness *in abstracto*; consequently he who is no longer capable of happiness *in concreto* sets his whole heart on money' (Schopenhauer, ibid., p. 170).

Though Schopenhauer loved a nineteen-year-old singer, a relationship that lasted intermittently for ten years, he redirected his attention to a succession of poodles, which provided him with huge happiness. Some philosophically minded Frankfurters bought poodles in homage to the great philosopher. He had a rigorous daily routine: he wrote for three hours every morning, played the flute for an hour, dressed in white tie for lunch (he had an enormous appetite), visited his club where he read *The Times*, took a two-hour walk with his dog, attended the opera or the theatre in the evening, where he usually became enraged by late-comers and those who coughed and generally made noise. But increasingly he isolated himself from human company, for which his mother rebuked him in a letter. Above all, he longed for recognition, the recognition the nearby Hegel was achieving, whose philosophy he describes as 'repulsive and nonsensical gibberish, recalling the rantings of a bedlamite'. Fame would come posthumously, though, to this good-natured gruff. He longed to be admired. In the preface to the *World as Will and Representation* he wrote:

> Our greatest pleasure consists in being admired [Hegel called this the desire for "recognition"]; but the admirers, even if there is every cause, are not very keen to express their admiration. And so the happiest man is he who has managed sincerely to admire himself, no matter how.

Schopenhauer felt that existence is a kind of error and love, in particular, interrupted 'at every hour the most serious occupations, and sometimes perplexes for a while even the greatest minds.... It sometimes demands the sacrifice of ... health, sometimes of wealth, position and happiness' (Schopenhauer, ibid., vol. 2, p. 533). According to Schopenhauer, if only we did not strive after happiness we would be less unhappy.

> There is only one inborn error, and that is the notion that we exist in order to be happy ... So long as we persist in this inborn error ... the world seems to us full of contradictions. For at every step, in great things and small, we are bound to experience that the world and life are certainly not arranged for the purpose of maintaining a happy existence ... hence the countenances of almost all elderly persons wear the expression of what is called *disappointment* (Schopenhauer, ibid., p. 634).

They would not be so disappointed by life if they had entered into love with the correct expectations.

> What disturbs and renders unhappy ... the age of youth ... is the hunt for happiness on the firm assumption that itmust be met with in life. From this arises the constantly deluded hope andso also dissatisfaction. Deceptive

images of a vague happiness of our dreams hover before us in capriciously selected shapes and we search in vain for their original ... Much would have been gained if through timely advice and instruction young people could have had eradicated from their minds the erroneous notion that the world has a great deal to offer them (Schopenhauer, 1974, vol. 1, p. 480).

But the young will not be told!

Many seek wealth but for Schopenhauer wealth 'can do little for our happiness' (Schopenhauer, ibid., p. 321). He notes: 'Therefore many wealthy people feel unhappy because they are without any real mental culture, without any knowledge, therefore without any objective interest that could qualify them for mental occupation' (Schopenhauer, ibid.). Indeed, people with a lot of wealth worry about protecting their wealth and their properties. It is not what man has externally but what he has internally that is essential for happiness, according to Schopenhauer. 'Therefore what a man *has in himself* is most essential to his life's happiness' (Schopenhauer, ibid.). La Rochefoucauld had similarly said: 'When we cannot find contentment in ourselves, it is useless to seek it elsewhere' (La Rochefoucauld, 1997, maxim 571). Schopenhauer is against (foolish) extravagance and the (fleeting) pleasures of the sense. He encourages a richness of the inner life. Much depends on one's nature, as is admitted in the *Eudemian Ethics*. Schopenhauer notes: 'What a man is and has in himself, that is to say, personality and its worth, is the sole immediate factor in his happiness and well-being' (Schopenhauer, 1974, p. 323). For Schopenhauer, beauty is akin to wealth – it doesn't really contribute directly to our happiness (see Schopenhauer, ibid., p. 328).

Dissatisfaction with life and frustration can engender weariness and a tendency to suicidal ideation and act. Pain and boredom 'are the two foes of human happiness' (Schopenhauer, ibid.). The more one finds within oneself the sources of pleasure the better and happier one will be. As is enunciated in the *Eudemian Ethics*, happiness belongs to those who are easily contented. This is difficult in old age, according to Schopenhauer, when one is deserted by love, humour and the desire to travel, the delight in horses and the aptitude for social intercourse, as friends and family are taken from the old by death. More than ever, in old age, does it depend on what we have in ourselves. But boredom (a symptom of the existential vacuum, for Frankl) lurks at every corner; wickedness has the upper hand; fate is cruel and man is pitiable (see Schopenhauer, ibid., p. 333). 'In a world so constituted the man who has much within himself is like a bright, warm, cheerful room at Christmas amid the snow and ice of a December night. Accordingly, the happiest destiny on earth is undoubtedly to have a distinguished and rich individuality and in particular a good endowment of intellect' (Schopenhauer, ibid.). Chess, skittles, hunting, painting, horse-racing, music, cards, poetry and philosophy can all help in keeping boredom at bay, he maintains. He is not far removed from Pascal here.

On an Epicurean note (and Schopenhauer cites Epicurus as a great teacher of happiness), Schopenhauer lists three groups of pleasures:

1) The pleasures of reproduction (eating, drinking, digesting, resting and sleeping);
2) The pleasures of irritability (walking, jumping, wrestling, dancing, fencing, riding, hunting, conflict, athletic games and war);
3) The pleasures of sensibility (observing, thinking, feeling, writing, poetry, improving the mind, playing music, learning, reading, meditating, inventing, philosophising).

For Schopenhauer, mere leisure (which he calls 'intellect unoccupied in the service of the will') is not sufficient. He recognises that most people rely on things outside themselves: wife, rank, possessions, children, parties, travel and all the while seeking satisfaction *without*. As he puts it: 'these are the props of his life's happiness' (Schopenhauer, ibid., p. 339). In these cases, the centre of gravity lies outside him and collapses when he becomes disillusioned by these things. How others see us, Schopenhauer feels, is overrated; it is not essential to our happiness.

We should aim at painlessness rather than pleasure, according to Schopenhauer. For this philosopher, the nature of all pleasure and happiness is *negative*, whereas that of pain is *positive*. So, happiness is a state of painlessness and absence of boredom: 'all else is a chimera' (Schopenhauer, ibid., p. 406). Furthermore, setting or constructing *limitations* and restrictions in our environment and position can make us happier. 'The narrower our range of vision, our sphere of action, and our points of contact, the happier we are: the wider these are, the more often do we feel anxious and worried' (Schopenhauer, ibid., p. 416). Schopenhauer is here suggesting that we keep life *simple*. With more cares and desires, terrors increase and are intensified. To banish suffering, we gamble and drink but this leads to ruin and unhappiness. There is no more mistaken path to happiness than the high life, according to Schopenhauer. Simplicity in our relations, even monotony in our living, will make us happy (see Schopenhauer, ibid., p. 469).

In volume two of *Parerga and Paralipomena*, entitled *Short Philosophical Essays* (1974), Schopenhauer says that 'religion affords an inexhaustible source of consolation and comfort in the innumerable sorrows and afflictions of life' (Schopenhauer, 1974, p. 336) but this is simply a 'pious fraud'. Schopenhauer finds some meaning in music and art rather than in religion. He writes: 'Complete satisfaction, the final quieting, the true desirable state, always present themselves only in the picture, the *work of art*, the poem, or music. From this, of course, one might be assured that they must exist somewhere' (Schopenhauer, ibid., p. 416). Schopenhauer was able to find some hope and meaning in beauty. 'What, for a beautiful landscape is the sudden glimpses of the sun breaking through the clouds, is for a beautiful countenance the appearance of its laughter' (Schopenhauer, ibid., p. 421).

Despite his odd moments of hope, Schopenhauer found enough to be depressed about. He calls one chapter 'Doctrine of Vanity of Existence'. He says that 'happiness is not even conceivable' (Schopenhauer, ibid., p. 284). This is what the pessimist in Schopenhauer says: 'In the first place, no one is happy, but everyone throughout his life strives for an alleged happiness that is rarely attained, and even then only to disappoint him' (Schopenhauer, ibid.). In another chapter entitled:

'Doctrine of Suffering of the World', Schopenhauer observes: '*Work, worry, toil and trouble* are certainly the lot of almost all throughout their lives. But if all desires were fulfilled as soon as they arose, how then would people occupy their lives and spend their time?' (Schopenhauer, ibid., p. 293). Suppose everyone went to Utopia and got what they wanted 'then people would die of boredom and hang themselves; or else they would fight, throttle, and murder one another and so cause themselves more suffering than is now laid upon them by nature' (Schopenhauer, ibid.). Happiness, so, in unhappiness or, at least, in stoical contentment.

Schopenhauer reduces happiness to health, nourishment, protection from wet and cold and sexual satisfaction. Happiness is the absence of something rather than its presence. As he says: 'the happiness of any given life is to be measured not by its joys and pleasures, but by the absence of sorrow and suffering' (Schopenhauer, ibid). He contrasts *heaviness* with happiness. 'We always move only under the influence of heaviness which must constantly be overcome ... therefore no happiness on earth can compare with that which a fine and fruitful mind finds in itself at a happy hour' (Schopenhauer, ibid., p. 498).

In a chapter entitled: 'Psychological Remarks', Schopenhauer opines that those who are very happy and who don't suffer can't feel any sympathy (see Schopenhauer, ibid., p. 592). He remarks: 'States of human happiness often resemble certain groups of trees which look very beautiful when seen from a distance; but, if we go up to them and walk among the trees, that beauty vanishes. We do not know where it was and are standing between trees. This is the reason why we so often envy the position of others' (Schopenhauer, ibid., p. 594). Envy, however, is a sign that we are unhappy. According to Schopenhauer, we will never be happy if we compare ourselves to others (see Schopenhauer, ibid., p. 430). He cites Cicero: 'It is impossible for anyone not to be perfectly happy who depends entirely on himself and possesses in himself alone all that he calls his'. But 'all happiness is chimerical, whereas suffering is real' (Schopenhauer, ibid., p. 481).

Schopenhauer speaks of life being a game or jest (as does Freud) and at the end of Book IV in his *The World as Will*, he writes: 'this our world, which is so real, with all its suns and milky-ways – is nothing'. But some modicum of love and hope do manage to break in to Schopenhauer's picture of the world. Life is a dance into the arms of death. 'No rose without a thorn. But many a thorn without a rose' (Schopenhauer, ibid., p. 235). '*Man* Indeed! That passes my comprehension' (Schopenhauer, ibid., p. 65). If, as Aquinas remarks, we can never get to know the essence of a single fly, what chance have we with man himself? Next, we turn to Nietzsche, Schopenhauer's philosophical brother.

Chapter Eight
Nietzsche: Happiness as Power

We take less trouble to become happy than to make others believe that we are so.

La Rochefoucauld

Friedrich Nietzsche (1844-1900), that most poetical of all philosophers, was hugely influenced by the 'dynamic, dismal genius' of Schopenhauer. Nietzsche shared with Schopenhauer the practical wisdom of Aristotle who, in his *Nicomachean Ethics* said: 'The prudent man strives for freedom from pain, not pleasure'. The priority of those seeking happiness or contentment was to recognise the impossibility of its fulfilment and so to avoid all the anxieties we typically encounter in its pursuit. So we shouldn't aim for what is pleasant but seek to avoid what is painful. Like Schopenhauer, Nietzsche too believed that life essentially consisted of suffering and the more we try to enjoy it, the more we become enslaved by it. We must, Nietzsche maintained, avoid pain rather than seek pleasure and 'live quietly'. All Nietzsche really wanted was to do gardening.

Nietzsche was an atheist by instinct – his unbelief was consolidated by reading Schopenhauer's philosophy with its professed atheism. It is God who Nietzsche seeks to destroy with his dialectic. He proudly proclaims that 'God is dead', a position that Kierkegaard, the Danish philosopher, would entirely reject. Where Kierkegaard precipitated himself into the 'either/or' of religious choice, Nietzsche catapulted himself into a full blown war waged against Christianity and plunged into a Dionysian nihilism, euphoria and eventual madness, spending the last eleven years of his life in an asylum for the mentally insane. His sister passed on his philosophy to Hitler who perverted, misinterpreted and misappropriated his thought, to some degree at least.

Nietzsche believed that all human behaviour could be reduced to this basic single drive – the will to power. 'Life is Will to Power' (Nietzsche, 1968, vol. 1, p. 213). Unconsciously, we seek power over others. Jean-Paul Sartre, his twentieth century philosophical heir, took this seriously in his discussion of the *three* options of sadism, masochism and indifference. The 'Superman' lives fully the will to power. 'The vilest is the necessary for Superman's best' (Nietzsche, 1997, p. 322). Nietzsche asserted that the evolution of the human species would lead to the attainment of the Oberman or Superman, who had overcome himself by a radical 'transvaluation of values' – meaning that existing (Christian) values needed to be superseded by a higher set, such as those of power, lordship, domination, arrogance etc. Nietzsche required us to remain faithful to the earth and not to believe those who speak to us of 'otherworldly hopes'. According to Nietzsche, man seeks to become absolutely himself, to possess total freedom, to cease being a creature and to become, instead, a Creator. It is only when he fails in this endeavour does he seek power over others as a substitute. The Superman is the passionate man who is master of his passions, the creative hedonist who lives 'beyond good and evil' and 'to whom nothing is forbidden'. Christians will call him the Antichrist. 'The time has come', Nietzsche proclaims, 'when we have to pay for having been Christians for two thousand years'. For Nietzsche, the God on the cross is a 'curse on life'. And in paragraph 125 of *The Gay Science* , the death of God is proclaimed by the madman – 'God is dead ... We have killed him. You and I all of us are his murderers.... We have bled him to death under our knives'. The death of God leads to the birth of the Superman, who is the 'caesarian creator of civilisation'. His research is creation itself, his word is law and legislation and his will to truth is will to power. For Nietzsche, there are higher and lower men and a single man may, under certain conditions, justify, as he says, the existence of whole millenia. Christianity has waged war on this higher type of man by preaching virtues such as love, meekness, etc. but these are unworthy of the strong superman who must transvalue these, in other words, replace them by a higher set of values, ones more in congruence with the Superman.

Nietzsche's doctrine of the 'Eternal Return' is his equivalent of eternal life. 'And this slow spider which crawls in the moonlight and this moonlight itself and you and I in the gateway, must not all of us have been here before? And return? Must we not eternally return?' He believes that history is in epicycles and that everything that happened before will happen again, not once or twice but over and over again eternally. 'This life, thine eternal life'. And happiness consists in willing that this particular moment happen again and again and again. It involves saying yes to life; it is the greatest test of courage. That said, Nietzsche remained extremely sceptical of the concept of happiness. In *Thus Spake Zarathustra* he writes:

What is the greatest thing ye can experience? It is the hour of great contempt. The hour in which even your happiness becometh loathsome unto you, and so also your reason and virtue. The hour when ye say: "What good is my happiness! It is poverty and pollution and wretched self-complacency. But my happiness should justify existence itself!" (Nietzsche, 1997, p. 7).

We should seek *power* rather than happiness. Happiness is the way to decadence. Only living dangerously is human and gives joy. Perhaps it is true that unless we become as little children we can't enter the Kingdom of Heaven but Nietzsche has no wish to enter the Kingdom of Heaven – 'we have become men and we want the Kingdom of earth'. He wants, not to bury his head in heavenly sand, but to bear it freely. He is of the view that if a higher being exists, then one's humanity becomes degraded, depleted. So, together with Feuerbach, another mystical atheist, he divinises human nature and humanises the Divine. Ultimately, for Nietzsche, *happiness consists in power* but also in affirming life and living each moment as if it were our last. This is what his Eternal Recurrence of the Same is ultimately about. The Eternal Return exhorts us to live life fully and to say to every single moment with Goethe's *Faust*: 'Abide, thou art so fair' or at least to will that it happens again.

Christianity is the great 'no' to life and a flight from reality; it shows contempt for the body and is an enemy of reason and joy, according to Nietzsche. He agrees with Dostoevsky that if God is dead all is permitted and ridicules those superficial atheists who believe that we can rid ourselves of God yet retain morality. 'What guilelessness! As if morality could remain when the sanctioning deity is no longer present!' (Nietzsche, 1968, vol. I, p. 212). For Nietzsche (as it was for Schopenhauer), art remains the great stimulant to life – art rather than religion – to a life in which the question 'why?' finds no answer.

There are some things we need for a 'happy' life even though it is impossible to attain them without feeling miserable some of the time:

> What if pleasure and displeasure were so tied together that whoever wanted to have as much as possible of one *must* also have as much as possible of the other ... you have the choice: either *as little as displeasure as possible*, painlessness in brief ... or *as much displeasure as possible* as the price for the growth of an abundance of subtle pleasures and joys that have rarely been relished yet? If you decide for the former and desire to diminish and lower the level of human pain, you also have to diminish and lower the level of their *capacity for joy* (Nietzsche, 1974, p. 12).

Enjoyment is always coupled with pain, agony with ecstasy, happiness with unhappiness:

> Examine the lives of the best and most fruitful people ... and ask yourself whether a tree that is supposed to grow to a proud height can dispense with bad weather and storms; whether misfortune and external resistance, some kinds of hatred, jealousy, stubborness, mistrust, hardness, avarice, and violence do not belong among the *favourable* conditions without which any great growth even of virtue is scarcely possible (Nietzsche, ibid., p. 19).

Furthermore, anyone who wants to be happy is advised by Nietzsche never to drink alcohol! 'Why this attitude to alcohol? Because Raphael, his favourite painter, had not got drunk in 1504 in Urbino to escape from his envy of da Vinci and Michelangelo and because Stendhal had not drunk in 1805 to escape from his despair but worked instead for seventeen years and finally produced his *De l'amour* in 1822. Nietzsche writes:

> If you refuse to let your own suffering lie upon you even for an hour and if you constantly try to prevent and forestall all possible distress way ahead of time; if you experience suffering and displeasure as evil, hateful, worthy of annihilation and as a defect of existence, then it is clear [that you harbour within you] ... the *religion of comfortableness*. How little you know of human *happiness*, you comfortable ... people, for happiness and unhappiness are sisters and even twins (Nietzsche, ibid., p. 338).

They are two sides of the same coin.

Nietzsche, who reserved his most vehement, righteous rage for religion (a narcotic just like alcohol), also despised the moral bankruptcy of Mill's form of utilitarianism. John Stuart Mill had maintained that actions are 'right in proportion as they tend to promote happiness, wrong as they tend to produce the reverse of happiness. By happiness is intended pleasure, and the absence of pain; by unhappiness, pain and the privation of pleasure' (Mill, 1972, ch. 2, para 2). This type of 'moral philosophy' enraged Nietzsche: 'Man does *not* strive for happiness; only the English do that' (Nietzsche, 1990, 1.9). For Nietzsche, artistic creativity delivered immense personal fulfilment as well as frustration.

The man who loved mountain climbing, almost as much as Frankl did, employed many mountain metaphors in the course of his philosophising: 'The secret for harvesting from existence the greatest fruitfulness and the greatest enjoyment is – to *live dangerously*! Build your cities on the slopes of Vesuvius!' (Nietzsche, 1974, p. 283), which had erupted in 1879, just three years before this statement was penned.

What appealed to Nietzsche was the philosophy of Epicurus and his idea that happiness involved a life among friends but Nietzsche never knew the contentment of human community. Many of his works can be seen as hymns to loneliness. In *Thus Spake Zarathustra* he notes: 'Too long hath solitude possessed me' (Nietzsche, 1997, p. 80). And he observes in relation to the *jouissance* of happiness: 'Wounded am I by my happiness' (Nietzsche, ibid.).

Like Goethe before him, who at seventy-four had fallen in love with a ninenteen-year-old, one of Nietzsche's most painful and passionate experiences of love was with the famous and flirtatious Lou Andreas-Salomé, who was twenty-one and fascinated with his philosophy as she would be with Freudian psychoanalysis later. However, she was more interested in his mind than in marriage. Later, Nietzsche visited a brothel in Cologne and contracted syphilis, though he claimed he had only played the piano there. This was the cause of the many symptoms that plagued him and which finally drove him insane for eleven years before his death in 1900 at the age of fifty-five. He also passionately loved Wagner with a love that was not reciprocated. Nietzsche fought hard to be happy but it seemed to elude him. He remained, though, committed to living life fully. In *Thus Spake Zarathustra* (1883) in Part 1, in a section entitled: 'Of Old and Young Women' he proudly proclaimed: 'The happiness of man is: "I will". The happiness of woman is "He will"' (Nietzsche, ibid., p. 63). This is the will-to-power.

One gets the impression, however, that in Nietzsche's life pain and misfortune far outweighed their supposed opposite number. Like Schopenhauer before him, though far greater, Nietzsche's life was a 'song to melancholy', as he entitled a section in his book, *Thus Spake Zarathustra*. In that section he writes: 'Down nightwards, faded, downsunken – ... Of day aweary, sick of sunshine – Sunk downwards, evenwards, shadow-wards' (Nietzsche, ibid., p. 290). Finally, in *Beyond Good and Evil*, Nietzsche poignantly notes: 'Men of profound sorrow give themselves away when they are happy: they have a way of grasping happiness as if they wanted to crush and smoother it, from jealousy – alas, they know too well that it will flee away'. To employ the title of one of Nietzsche's other works, we are 'human, all too human'. It would seem so.

The question is: Can anyone seriously agree with Nietzsche's verdict that happiness is ultimately *only* about power? Of course there is some truth to this psychoanalytically speaking but as a philosophical theory it is so patently false. Nietzsche is an isightful diagnostician of the human condition and he deserves to be read thoroughly. He is a moralist and a psychologist and was only too aware that if God is dead then all is permitted, as Dostoyevsky put it. Nietzsche noted that morality coud no longer be preserved when the God who sanctions it is dead. Nietzsche acutely and honestly observed the sickness of Western civilisation and European culture. Further, his critique of religion presupposes a criterion of truth (see Walsh, 1990, pp. 20-30). He was psychologically astute in alerting us to the unconscious dimensions of human existence and in this regard prefigures the work of Freud, whom we will next explore, and his eleven paths to happiness. We may note here, *en passant*, that Nietzsche's 'will-to-power' re-emerged in Adler's individual psychology and Frankl criticised both the Freudian 'will to pleasure' and the Adlerian 'will to power' asserting, instead, that man's primary goal is the 'will to meaning'.

Chapter Nine
Freud: Happiness as Neurosis

There is no happiness where there is no wisdom, no wisdom but in submission to the gods.

Sophocles

In 1930 Sigmund Freud wrote his great work on culture, *Civilization and Its Discontents* (1982), in which he deals, amongst other things, with happiness. The original title chosen for it was *Unhappiness in Civilization*. The title says it all, man is unhappy or discomforted in civilisation. The French term *'malaise'* conjures up the point Freud is attempting to put across. The main theme of the book is the conflict and antagonism between the demands of the drives, on the one hand and the restrictions that civilisation imposes to contain and constrain those drives, on the other hand.

Freud begins by saying that people commonly seek *three* things:
1)   Power
2)   Success
3)   Wealth

We admire these attributes and achievements and prize them highly, often underestimating what is of true value in life. The Freudian view is that we are pleasure-seeking beings who fear too much reality. We pursue pleasure and avoid pain. The aim of life, for Freud, is to love and work. That is all but isn't it enough? Life is difficult and in order to cope we cannot dispense with some palliative measures. Freud notes: 'Life, as we find it, is too hard for us; it brings us too many pains, disappointments and impossible tasks' (Freud, 1992, p. 12). There are *three* measures we utilise so as to avoid these hardships:
1)   Powerful deflections, 'which cause us to make light of our miseries',
2)   Substitute satisfactions, 'which diminish it', and
3)   Intoxicating substances, 'which make us insensitive to it'.

Voltaire had concluded his *Candide* with the advice to cultivate one's garden. Hume had ended his *A Treatise of Human Nature* by saying that he prefers to philosophise no longer but rather to join his friends outside for a game of Backgammon. This is what Pascal and Freud mean, Freud calling them *deflections*, Pascal *diversions*. Scientific curiosity is a deflection, art a substitute satisfaction while intoxicating substances, such as drink and drugs, influence the body and alter its chemistry. The question of the purpose of human life has been raised countless times by countless people in every generation and none more so than our own. What is the meaning of life? And why bother?

Freud feels that the idea of life having a purpose stands and falls with the religious system, which he regards as an infantile illusion. Like Pascal, Aquinas and Aristotle before him, Freud too asserts that we want happiness.

> What do they [men] demand of life and wish to achieve in it? The answer to this can hardly be in doubt. They strive after happiness; they want to become happy and to remain so. This endeavour has two sides, a positive and a negative aim. It aims, on the one hand, at an absence of pain and unpleasure, and, on the other, at the experiencing of strong feelings of pleasure. In its narrower sense the word "happiness" only relates to the last (Freud, ibid., p. 13).

What decides the purpose of life, for Freud, is the programme of the 'pleasure principle'. This principle dominates the mind from the beginning but it puts us at loggerheads with 'reality'. There is no chance of it being carried through; the entire universe runs counter to it, according to Freud. Here he stands in marked contrast to Thomas Aquinas. Freud observes:

> One feels inclined to say that the intention that man should be "happy" is not included in the plan of "Creation". What we call happiness in the strictest sense comes from the (preferably sudden) satisfaction of needs that have been damned up to a high degree, and it is from its nature only possible as an episodic phenomenon. When any situation that is desired by the pleasure principle is prolonged, it only produces a feeling of mild contentment. We are so made that we can derive intense enjoyment only from a contrast and very little from a state of things. Thus our possibilities of happiness are already restricted by our constitution (Freud, ibid., pp. 13-14).

According to Freud, there are *three* sources of our suffering:
1) From our body, 'which is doomed to decay and dissolution and which cannot even do without pain',
2) From the external world, 'which may rage against us with overwhelming and merciless forces of destruction';
3) And finally from our relations with others, which 'is perhaps more painful to us than any other'.

Due to all these factors, Freud surmises that we are accustomed to moderate our claims to happiness. Sometimes, Freud suggests, we think ourselves happy merely because we have escaped unhappiness. 'Unhappiness is much less difficult to experience' (Freud, ibid., p. 14).

There are different paths to attain happiness that have been put forward by the various schools of worldly wisdom. In *Civilization and Its Discontents* (1930), Freud summarises *eleven paths* traditionally put forward for achieving happiness. They are:

1) Unrestricted want satisfaction
2) Isolation
3) Participation in the human community
4) Intoxication
5) Asceticism
6) Creativity
7) Illusory escape into fantasy
8) Delusional remolding of reality
9) Mutual love
10) Beauty (aesthetic appreciation)
11) Freedom

Let's explore these eleven paths in more detail.

1) Unrestricted want satisfaction

Firstly, Freud cautions us against having an unrestricted satisfaction of every need. Though this presents itself as the most enticing prospect, it brings its own punishment. Too much pleasure is painful, as the perverse subject knows only too well. The 'pervert' (a term employed in psychoanalysis, to denote a structural category not a stigma) wants to keep on coming but this is painful. Lacan labels this phenomenon *jouissance*. This is the pleasure tinged with pain, the pain that is tinged with (sexual) pleasure. Some people enjoy being unhappy. They get off on it. If too much happiness is bad for us, then misery can sometimes be enjoyable. Perversion involves the attempt to prop up the law so that limits can be set to *jouissance*. The pervert struggles to bring the law into being, to make the Other (the Symbolic order of law and language etc) exist. Consciously, he refuses to give up his pleasure, to sacrifice *jouissance*. His conscious fantasies involve unending *jouissance* – we think of the Marquis de Sade. Unconsciously, he wants the law to be laid down, to limit him, to castrate him and speak a 'no' to his *jouissance*. Perversion (*père version*) is ultimately about the 'father', the paternal function – *le nom/non du père*. The pervert disavows, denies the law. Disavowal is a defense against the father's demand that the child surrender *jouissance*. Perversion testifies to the inadequacy of the paternal metaphor. Anxiety dominates the perverse subject's sexuality. This, according to Lacan.

No one person can fill us up, can fulfil us, can plug up our lack, least of all our lovers in the impossibility of sexual relationships. For as Lacan never tires of telling us: 'there is no sexual rapport'. Spinoza, Hegel and Lacan all insist that we are creatures of desire, as we said earlier, that desire constitutes us in our very being and that it is the nature of desire to be irrepresible, desire being a metonymy. This means that desire can never be fulfilled. Freud says that the 'unrestricted satisfaction of every need' not only puts enjoyment before caution but also brings punishment. We need to understand this and Lacan distinguishes, in his dialectic, between need, demand and desire. We can never get all our desires met and even if we could, would we be happy? No, because desire emanates from lack and if we attained all our desires we would have no lack and thus never desire anymore. We are desiring and desirous subjects.

Our desire finds its meaning in the desire of the Other because all desire is mediated by the Other. And the mother is the first big Other in the child's universe. So if the desire of the mother is the phallus, as a symbol of plenitude, as a monument erected in the place of lack, the child desires to be the phallus for the mother in order to satisfy that desire. There is a division in the heart of desire since the mother will desire something beyond the child – her partner. The phallic signifier is the mark of desire. That's why Lacan keeps repeating: '*Le désir, c'est le désir de l'Autre*' – Desire is always desire of and for the Other.

Love is the reduction of desire to demand. Love kills desire. Love is not ethical; only desire is ethical, according to Lacan. Lacan tells us that the unconscious is ethical on the ontic plane. Love colonises and cannibalises; in love one is a master and one is a slave. A lot of what passes for love rotates around this dialectic. The point of desire is to desire as a subject not as a master or slave. We might be waiting for years for someobody to recognise and acknowledge us. That is the risk of love. Every demand is always a demand for love – 'Thou love me!' 'All speech is demand' (Lacan). We find satisfaction for our demand for love in relationships even though Lacan tells us that in love we give what we don't have to someone who doesn't want it. Desire is metonymical through and through. That means that once we attain our object of desire, we are not satiated. We want more and more. Desire is endlessly deferred. It is never satisfied. Simone Weil says that desire is impossible (see Weil, 1972, p. 86). Our desires ('unrestricted want satisfactions') can never be met, plugged up, fulfilled. What it is you really want is the question of your desire. Desire is a defense against going beyond certain limits in *jouissance*. The person in *jouissance*, like the pervert, is not in his desire. He is divided against himself. Castration governs desire. It also means that *jouissance* be refused. This is the crux: *desire makes happiness impossible*.

Needs are purely biological, physiological, and are satisfied by certain objects such as water and food. But then why isn't the baby happy to be fed by a pasta machine? It wants to be fed by mother. So, behind the need for food is the demand, insatiable as it is, for mother's love. The gap between need and demand constitutes desire – desire is the beyond. Desire is not an appetite; it is insatiable and eccentric, literally. *Desidero ergo sum* is the Freudian equivalent of Descartes's *cogito, ergo sum*. What of the subject who doesn't want to desire? Not wanting to desire, desiring to want not to desire and desiring are the same thing. All Socrates knew about was on the subject of Eros, that is to say, desire but wasn't it enough to know? It cost him his life, after all. Pure hedonism, such as the pervert's, can't explain desire. We desire something we love but don't want. The object that is the cause of desire is the object of the drive. And the Freudian drive designates the paradox of 'wanting unhappiness', of finding excessive pleasure in suffering itself. Love is the subject of desire even though all love operates in the field of narcissism – to love is to want to be loved.

If we all experience ourselves as desire what happens when my desire encounters another's desire? There is a clash, a conflict, seldom a compromise. That is the master/slave dialectic described so well by Hegel and Sartre – the Hegelian 'fight to the death for pure prestige'. Desire culminates in 'Hegelian murder'. Love is an exigency for recognition by the Other. We situate our own desire within the desire of the Other. This is traumatic. It is accompanied by the existential experience of anxiety as we are confronted with nothingness at the heart of desire and being. Human desire is adjusted to a phantasy; the Other is always an Imaginary Other that can bring us into the Real of trauma. We must name and articulate this desire even though speech can never fully do this. There is always something leftover, a surplus. Sometimes we desire what an Other has or desires, simply because they have or desire it. Our desire is always for something else and that something else always brings disappointment. We don't get what we want. We must be grateful for that much. This is summed up in the cliché: 'Be careful what you ask for – you just might get it' and 'too much of a good thing'. This is the very heart of the (psychoanalytical) problem on the subject.

2) Isolation

Some seek solitude to work or to think or to pray or in order to escape the tragedy of a love now over. They isolate themselves from human company and become reclusive. Montaigne withdrew to his estates to search after wisdom, goodness and tranquility of mind. He advises that we should set aside for ourselves a 'room at the back of the shop' (Montaigne, 1925, p. 270). For Montaigne, true solitude is a spiritual withdrawal from the world. This does not mean living as a hermit but it does involve living with detachment. It means being 'alone in a crowd of courtiers', as he puts it (Montaigne, ibid., p. 269). Seneca tells us that once Socrates was told that some man had not been improved by travel, to which he was reported to have said: 'I am sure he was not. He went with himself'! Hence Montaigne's advice: 'That is why it is not enough to withdraw from the mob, not enough to go to another place: we have to withdraw from such attributes of the mob as are within us. It is our own self we have to isolate and take back into possession' (Montaigne, ibid., pp. 268-9). The soul [Freud would say the ego] cannot escape from itself. For Montaigne: 'So we must bring her back, haul her back, into our self. That is true solitude. It can be enjoyed in town and in king's courts, but more conveniently apart' (Montaigne, ibid., p. 269). Tibullus had said: 'in lonely places, be a crowd unto yourself'. And Montaigne concludes thus: 'let us make our happiness depend on ourselves; let us loose ourselves from the bonds which tie us to others; let us gain power over ourselves to live really and truly alone – and of doing so in contentment' (Montaigne, ibid., p. 269) for 'the greatest thing in the world is to know how to live to yourself' (Montaigne, ibid., p. 272). Montaigne was like Horace, who walked in silence through woods, wondering and pondering on questions worthy of the wise and the good. Turning now to another French philosopher for some guidance on this subject.

Jean-Paul Sartre distinguishes between *l'être pour-soi* (Being-For-Itself or Subject) and *l'être en-soi* (Being-In-Itself or slave/ Object), in his *magnum opus, L'être et le néant* (*Being and Nothingness*). In Sartre's ontological dualism, the Being-In-Itself is the self-contained being of a thing. A stone is a stone; it is what it is. The being of a thing always coincides with itself. Being-For-Itself is coextensive with the realm of human consciousness. It is perpetually beyond itself. Consequently, we never possess our being as we possess a thing. One consciousness is always dependent on another consciousness, which makes isolation impossible.

Like Hegel before him, Sartre teaches that man is an unhappy consciousness ('Man is a useless passion') and there is no absolute Being to assuage the sorrow or redeem the striving. Man is nothing other than the drive to be transcendent, the desire for self-divinisation (i.e., Gnosticism). Human subjectivity is an autarchic centre of freedom. Man is unconditionally free. Man is the sole condition of himself. There are no fixed values or laws governing his existence. The only condition is that man act in good rather than 'bad faith' or 'self-deception'. For Sartre, to believe in God is the ultimate form of bad faith for it is to believe in the ultimate lie. It is to hand authority over to an Other and to live an inauthentic life. The only authentic man is the free man. We create our own values – to be is to do and at all times we are free to re-invent ourselves. We make ourselves what we are. Every man is in possession of himself.

But here's the rub: if I am to assert my existential and absolute freedom I can only do so by negating other human being since two freedoms can't co-exist simultaneously. According to Sartre, the first option is sadism: to coerce the Other but the master realises that the slave says 'I love you' simply because he has been forced to, so what joy does the master get? The sadist is only going to get momentary satisfaction. One wants to be approved by another free subject. So sadism is self-contradictory. The next choice is masochism: the masochist says to himself 'I will be all the Other desires me to be' but by becoming that he is becoming an object for the Other, a no-thing. This then fails also. The masochist, as Freud tells us, is a sadist to himself. The final option is indifference and isolation. This option involves the person doing his own thing, going it alone, escaping and taking refuge in solitude. This is individualism as solipsism. And it is also condemned to absurdity because of the fact that, as Dostoevsky showed, when you say 'I'm not thinking of anybody' it means that you are constantly thinking of them. We can't escape from the fact that we are beings-in-the-world. Thoughts and memories are perpetual reminders that other people exist. Hence Sartre's famous cry: *L'enfer, c'est les autres*: 'Hell is other people'. The man who attempts to escape from this situation into isolation becomes a madman: he is always haunted by the memory of the people he has met in his past or by the anticipation of the people he may meet in his future. There is simply no way out. The Carthusian monk is surrounded by other beings in silence and by his God, who perpetually perceives him. We recall Berkeley's *esse est percipi aut percipere*: 'to be is to perceive or be perceived' and God is the eternal perceiver. We are condemned to be in the presence of others. And despite the obvious pain and suffering that belongingness can entail, which one of us would choose utter and complete life-long isolation? Aristotle had told us that solitude befits only beasts and gods. Freud concurs with the Sartrian view: 'But whoever, in desperate defiance, sets out upon this path to happiness will as a rule attain nothing. Reality becomes too strong for him. He becomes a madman' (Freud, 1982, p. 18).

We live in a world with others and so are condemned to a conflict of freedoms. The other always threatens my freedom and makes me aware that the world is not my own. The other steals the world from me and re-writes my script. My existence isn't a soliloquy but a drama of colliding and often hostile subjectivities. Sartre maintains, therefore, that intersubjective relations are doomed to failure by virtue of the ontological division between being and nothingness. The point Sartre is intent on stressing here, and in agreement with Freud (even though he denied the existence of the unconscious, about which Lacan said he would have been a better philosopher if he had accepted the existence of the unconscious), is that we are not Leibnitzean monads but beings-in-relation, as Buber, Levinas and Ricoeur, amongst other philosophers have stressed. No man is an island unto himself. *We are related not isolated*, whether we want to be or not. We are alone but alone *with others*. This is a point of view most fully elaborated by the Spanish philosopher, Ortega y Gasset.

According to Ortega, what is most radically human in man is his radical solitude. Ortega renders Leibnitz's term 'monads' into 'solitudes'. Ortega observes:

The radical solitude of human life, the being of man, does not, then, consist in there really being nothing except himself. Quite the contrary – there is nothing less than the universe, with all that it contains. There is, then, an infinity of things but – there it is! – amid them Man in his radical reality is alone – alone *with* them (Ortega, 1957, p. 49).

Solitude is the recognition of one's absolute difference before an Other. Solicitude is the recognition of one's absolute availability for the Other. Sometimes it is necessary to withdraw, to isolate oneself from an other person, if only for a while, lest we come to invade their space, to overly depend on them, to make incessant demands on them – to risk destroying them. A symbiotic bond is suffocating and stagnant. But the solitude of being separate is difficult to endure. There is also the terror of the absence of dependence. The obsessional can tolerate it better than the hysteric can. In *Daybreak*, Nietzsche wrote: ' That is why I go into solitude so as not to drink out of everybody's cistern. When I am among the many I live as the many do, and I do not think as I really think; after a time it always seems as though they want to banish me from myself and rob me of my soul' (Nietzsche, 1982, p. 201). For Freud, solitude is an absence; for Winnicott it is a presence. We want a life to interpenetrate ours. Friendship is one way we attempt this – the other one being love. And, as Ortega says: 'Genuine love is nothing but the attempt to exchange two solitudes' (Ortega, 1957, p. 49). This is our life. It's the only one we know.

3) Participation in the human community

For Freud, participating in the human community is better than turning away, in dread, from the anguish of the external world. Aristotle, as we have seen, said 'to exist is to act' and take part in the city *polis*, to stake a claim in the Symbolic order. For Heraclitus, change was the only reality. Life is in constant flux and motion and according to Heraclitus, one can't step twice into the same stream because the waters have flown on. 'In the same river we both step and do not step. We are and we are not'. Life is an everliving fire; parts being kindled while other parts are being extinguished. We come into and pass out of existence. Parmenides denied becoming and insisted, instead, on a world of static being. He said what is cannot become because it cannot become what it is. And what is not cannot become because from nothing, nothing can become. Therefore, becoming is impossible. Now, Parmenides got the last part right: nothing can come from nothing, as Shakespeare's King Lear said to Cordelia. But Aristotle took issue with the first of Parmenides's formulations saying what is can become. One can become something other than what one is. Aristotle maintained that being was divisible. Being can be divided into potential being and actual being and becoming is the transition from potential to actual being. To give an example: the acorn becomes an oak tree just as the caterpillar becomes a butterfly. The acorn is potentially an oak tree and the oak tree is an actualised acorn. Change or becoming involves the transition from potency to act. In the order of epistemology potency precedes act but in the order of ontology act precedes potency. For example, a mother gives birth to a baby not an elephant. We can only become what we are (in a sense); we can never become what we are not. I can paint the wall as white as it is. I can't paint it as white as it is not! So the human foetus, to take an example, is not a potential human being but an actual human being with potential.

We are here to *do* something so, to immerse ourselves in the human community, in the world of other people, to act and to change. We are not, as Plato put it, stoical spectators standing on the sidelines. We are, rather, passionate participators in the drama of being. Work, and we hope it is 'meaningful labour' as Marx put it, provides us with a secure place in the Symbolic order – in the human community. If it is freely chosen, work or professional activity, 'is a source of special satisfaction' (Freud, 1982, p. 17), though the vast majority of people work under the stress and strain of necessity. Life is not a spectacle but a happening. Only amongst others do we come into our own. When we are by ourselves we are alone and may experience this aloneness but loneliness always presupposes another. We can only be lonely within community. So though we are called upon to relate and live with others (Freud's 'participation in the human community') we can experience an awful loneliness nonetheless.

The psychoanalyst, Melanie Klein, wrote a paper on this theme entitled: 'On the Sense of Loneliness' in *Envy and Gratitude*, (Klein, 1963, pp. 300-313). Loneliness is here understood not in the sense of being deprived of external companionship but it refers, instead, to an inner sense of loneliness, the loneliness we can feel within community, of 'feeling lonely even among friends or receiving love', as Klein puts it (Klein, ibid., p. 300). For Klein, this loneliness is the result of a yearning for an unattainable perfect internal state. In loneliness we experience anxiety; such anxieties are particularly strong in illness so loneliness is also a part of illness (both of a schizophrenic and depressive nature). To an extent the depressed person and the schizophrenic subject are outside the community, just like the criminal.

A satisfactory bond attachment to mother is crucial for subsequent healthy development. The first object of desire is the breast (the bottle stands for the breast) and this contact between mother and child is the foundation for the experience of being understood and is linked with this preverbal stage. Later, as adults we try, unsuccessfully, to recuperate this magical, primordial, paradisiacal, dyadic relationship ... and never do! Klein observes:

> However gratifying it is in later life to express thoughts and feelings to a congenial person, there remains an unsatisfied longing for an understanding without words – ultimately for the earliest relation with the mother. This longing contributes to the sense of loneliness and derives from the depressive feeling of an irretrievable loss' (Klein, ibid., p. 301).

Paranoid insecuirty is one of the roots of loneliness. Our partners can never be our mothers. Once we leave the breast we feel lonely and deserted. We long to be understood. This gives rise to the phantasy that we have a twin somewhere in the world, a soul's counterpart, who, like our mother before, can utterly fulfil us and understand us. But we never find them, this supposed 'soul-mate'. The 'perfect partner' does not exist. There is no One, only Others – good enough Others. So perhaps we join a group to assuage our sense of loneliness. But we can feel there is no group or person to which we belong. There is a feeling, Klein suggests, that we are not in full possession of ourselves, that we do not belong to ourselves and therefore cannot belong to anybody else, that we are 'strangers to ourselves', as Julia Kristeva memorably put it.

We feel lonely, though there are differences in the way in which we experience loneliness. This can result in withdrawal, in schizoid isolation and paranoid distrust. Participation in community becomes, therefore, problematic. The person here destroys the very thing that might lessen his loneliness somewhat or, at least, counteract it. Loneliness can lead to a diminished capacity for hope. Winnicott felt that a sign of maturity in an infant was in its capacity to be alone in the presence of its mother. Can we, as adults, be alone in the presence of our lovers or others? Being lonely is different. We are never lonelier than when we are with others and experience a missed encounter with them, precisely with those we feel should understand us the most – our close friends and lovers. We feel lonely and let down. There is a failure to establish within us a feeling of fullness and good internal objects, in the Kleinian sense. A secure internalisation of the good breast militates or, at least, mitigates against feeling so lonely. Identification with these good internal objects strengthens feelings of goodness and trust and diminishes harshness and hardness. It opens up sources of enjoyment in the external world, which is another factor in diminishing loneliness. So, for Klein, a happy relation with the first object is crucial to enjoy further good relations with others in society and memories of such happy experiences can compensate for the bad times in that they are bound up with the hope of further happy times. Anger and resentment give way to enjoyment and gratitude. In fact, enjoyment is always bound up with gratitude and 'if this gratitude is deeply felt it includes the wish to return goodness received and is thus the basis for generosity. There is always a close connection between being able to accept and to give, and both are part of the relation to the good object and therefore counteract loneliness' (Klein, ibid., p. 310).

A child who, despite his envy and jealousy, can enjoy the pleasures of other members of his family in old age will be more likely to identify himself with the satisfactions of youth. This becomes possible when there is gratitude for past pleasures without too much resentment that they are no longer present. Thus loneliness may be reduced but never eliminated. Loss, of some sort, dominates our life. Just as some infants use extreme dependency on mother as a defense against lonelinesss so too do some adults in their anaclitic attachments to the object of their desire, which can border, at times, on fixation. Of course, others, in their thrust for independence, which is part of 'maturation', can use this as a defense against loneliness. Some, particularly old people, can become preoccupied with the past in order to avoid the frustrations of the present. Young people idealise the future. Appreciation by others (which Hegel and Lacan call 'recognition'), which originally derived from the infantile need to be appreciated by the mother, can also be used defensively against loneliness. Loneliness is always partly allayed by turning to external objects, which diminish loneliness, to friends and family members, which make the experience of loneliness perhaps more bearable. But in so far as we are alive we will always be prone to experiencing loneliness. Better to accept this than deny it. The presence of loneliness makes full participation in the human community always problematic. In short, loneliness is, I would argue, the awareness of one's absolute difference before the Other.

4) Intoxication

Another option to defend ourselves against the dread in human relationships and in the world is the chemical one of intoxication, which is for Freud the 'crudest, but also the most effective among these methods' (Freud, 1982, p. 15). Foreign substances (the saturated object) in the blood and brain cause us pleasurable sensations, altering the conditions governing our sensibility. Mania can be induced through drugs or drink. Drink, especially in the cultural climate of Ireland, is a profoundly sociable medium. Freud notes: 'The service rendered by intoxicating media in the struggle for happiness and in keeping misery at a distance is so highly prized as a benefit that individuals and peoples alike have given them an established place in the economics of their libido' (Freud, ibid.). We attain an immediate yield of pleasure, a desired degree of independence from the external world. This 'drowner of cares' can, however, be the cause, according to Freud, of a 'useless waste of a large quota of energy which might have been employed for the improvement of the human lot' (Freud, ibid.). We drink or take drugs to escape if only momentarily but flight is of no avail, as Freud reminds us, because the ego can't escape from itself. We are left with the day after the night before, when we experience not happiness but a hangover and the depression to which that can give rise. And sometimes we feel it's just not worth it and vow never to drink again – until the following Friday night! Montaigne observes: 'If a hangover came before we got drunk we would see that we never drank to excess' (Montaigne, 1925, p. 275).

Montaigne despised excessive drinking even though from Ancient times it was associated with higher ecstasies – those of poets, prophets and lovers. In a section in his *Essays* entitled 'On Drunkenness', Montaigne calls drunkeness 'base' and 'stultifying' (Montaigne, ibid., p. 385), a 'vice', 'gross' and 'brutish' too (Montaigne, ibid., p. 382). He cites Lucretius: 'When the strength of the wine has sunk in, our limbs become heavy, we stagger and trip over our legs; our speech becomes slow; our mind, sodden; our eyes are a-swim. Then comes the din, the hiccoughs and the fights' (Montaigne, ibid.). The worst state: 'when he [man] loses all consciousness and control of himself' (Montaigne, ibid.). This is excessive drinking that can lead to anger, about which Montaigne has many interesting things to say.

The true philoospher, who is a stoic, Montaigne contends, should not give way to anger. Anger was believed to be caused by choler, one of the four humours that makes a man irascible. Montaigne also associated it with chagrin – that grievous vexation brought on by melancholy. In a section in his *Essays* entitled 'On Anger', Montaigne describes the effects of anger as 'fire and rage flashing from their [men's] eyes' (Montaigne, ibid., p. 809), as a distemper that distorts the face. Ovid had written of a face swelling with anger, blood darkening the person's veins and the eyes flashing with fire more savage than a Gorgon's. For his part, Montaigne writes: 'No passion disturbs the soundness of our judgement as anger does. No one would hesitate to punish with death a judge who was led to condemn his man as a criminal out of anger: then why is it any more permissable for fathers and schoolmasters to punish and flog children in rage? That is no longer correction; it is vengeance' (Montaigne, ibid., p. 810). Furthermore, 'Faults seen through anger are like objects seen through a mist: they appear large' (Montaigne, ibid.). Anger is a passion that delights in and fawns and feeds on itself. According to Montaigne, it is better, though to show rather than to hide anger because if it is hidden and pushed away into the body, it tears our insides out. 'I would advise you to give your valet a rather unreasonable slap on the cheek rather than to torture your mind' (Montaigne, ibid., p. 814). His other piece of sound psychological advise: 'I would rather make an exhibition of my passions than brood over them to my cost: express them, vent them, and they grow weaker; it is better to let them jab outside us than be turned against us' (Montaigne, ibid., pp. 814-5). Montaigne himself, by his own admission, loses 'control quickly and violently, but not with such turmoil than I go gaily hurling about all sorts of insults at random' (Montaigne, ibid., p. 815). Anger can take us over and 'unfortunately, once you are over the edge, no matter what gave you the shove, you go right down to the bottom' (Montaigne, ibid., p. 816). Of course, as Aristotle realised, anger can sometimes serve virtue and valour as a weapon but more often it 'guides our hand; it gets a hold on us; not we on it' (Montaigne, ibid.).

Sober drinking, in contrast to drinking to excess, renders us not angry but vigorous and lively in our love-making. Warmed with wine, we relax. There is a mid point, Montaigne contends, between Germans who drink virtually anything ['Their aim is to gulp it rather than to taste it' (Montaigne, ibid., p. 385)] and the French who drink much more moderately at meals but who place 'too great a restraint on the indulgence of the god Bacchus' (Montaigne, ibid.). Plato forbade young people to drink before 18 and to get drunk before 40. Only at 40 could the influence of Dionysius be sought and his name invoked. Plato felt that alcohol should be done without on military expeditions and all statesmen and judges should abstain when about to perform their duties. Furthermore, daytime drinking should be avoided and on those nights when we intend to beget children. For Montaigne, alcohol calms and softens the passions of the soul just as iron is softened by fire. However, we can take comfort from the sentiment expressed in Ecclesiasticus: 'What is life worth without wine? It was created to make men happy' (31:33).

5) Asceticism

So if the satisfaction of our instincts spells happiness, severe suffering is caused if the external world allows us to starve and if it refuses to sate our needs. To defend ourselves against suffering we attempt to master the internal sources of our needs – we kill off the instincts, as prescribed by the East and practised by Yoga. But for Freud, such a person has sacrificed his life and achieved only the 'happiness of quietness' (Freud, 1982, p. 16). A less extreme path is to try to control our instinctual life. We don't relinquish satisfaction but secure protection against suffering. Even though the 'feeling of happiness derived from the satisfaction of a wild instinctual impulse untamed by the ego is incomparably more intense than that derived from the sating an instinct that has been tamed' (Freud, ibid.). We can, thus, sublimate our instincts.

Sublimation is a process whereby we redirect our sexual and aggressive drives onto non-sexual sources of satisfaction, ones that are socially acceptable. In sublimation there is a deflection from sexuality. We engage, then, in intellectual work, be it through artistic creativity or the joy the scientist obtains in solving problems or the philosopher in discovering truths. This path is accessible only to a few people, according to Freud, who have the necessary dispositions. Moreover, this method cannot give complete protection from suffering. 'It creates no impenetrable armour against the arrows of fortune, and it habitually fails when the source of suffering is a person's own body' (Freud, ibid., p. 17). Ordinary work, though, is accessible to nearly everybody. It is work which gives man a secure place in his portion of reality, in the human community. Through work we are able to displace our libidinal instincts, whether narcissistic, erotic or aggressive, on to work. Professional work becomes the source of special satisfaction to us, if freely chosen. Work, like sport, is a form of sublimated activity. 'And yet, as a path to happiness, work is not highly prized by men. They do not strive after it as they do after other possibilities of satisfaction. The great majority of people only work under the stress of necessity, and this natural human aversion to work raises most difficult social problems' (Freud, ibid.). Such a necessity goes by the name of *Ananke*.

6) Creativity

Some people turn inward away from reality and engage in the life of imagination. Satisfaction is here obtained from illusions. Freud notes:

At the head of these satisfactions through phantasy stands the enjoyment of works of art – an enjoyment which, by the agency of the artist, is made accessible even to those who are not themselves creative. People who are receptive to the influence of art cannot set too high a value on it as a source of pleasure and consolation in life. Nevertheless the mild narcosis induced in us by art can do no more than bring about a transient withdrawal from the pressure of vital needs, and it is not strong enough to make us forget real misery (Freud, ibid., pp. 17-18).

For Freud, fantasy and daydreaming play a considerable role in the creative process. Being present as a spectator at a spectacle or play does for adults what play does for children, Freud suggests in an article entitled: 'Psychopathic Characters on the Stage' (1905-6). We enjoy the book or play principally by identifying with one of the characters, by imagining all sorts of scenarios and letting off steam. Lyric poetry permits us to vent intense feelings – Aristotle called this *catharsis* or the purgation of the emotions of pity and terror. Epic poetry makes it possible to feel the enjoyment of a great heroic character in his hour of triumph. Drama explores emotional possibilities more deeply. Suffering is the stuff of drama and it is precisely this suffering that gives the audience so much sadistic or sympathetic pleasure. Such is the play of phantasy that pampers us. Creative 'products' of all sorts afford us 'fore-pleasure'.

In his 1908 article, 'Creative Writers and Day-Dreaming', Freud futher explores the sources of creativity and looks for the first traces of imaginative activity as early as in childhood:

The child's best-loved and most intense occupation is with his play or games. Might we not say that every child at play behaves like a creative writer, in that he creates a world of his own, or, rather, rearranges the things of his world in a new way, which pleases him? It would be wrong to think he does not take that world seriously; on the contrary, he takes his play very seriously and he expends large amounts of emotion on it. The opposite of play is not what is serious but what is real. In spite of all the emotion with which he cathects his world of play, the child distinguishes it quite well from reality; and he likes to link his imagined objects and situations to the tangible and visible things of the real world. This linking is all that differentiates the child's "play" from "phantasying". The creative writer does the same as the child at play. He creates a world of phantasy which he takes very seriously – that is, which he invests with large amounts of emotion – while separating it sharply from reality (Freud, 1908, pp. 131-2).

In philosophy, Kant was the first modern philosopher to distinguish between the reproductive and the properly productive power of the creative imagination. The former mimetic model of the imagination is merely representational whereas the latter is actually creative. The movement, in art, from the Greeks (Plato and Aristotle) to Kant was the transition from art as imitation to art as creation (see Kearney, 1988).

For David Hume, the worlds of reason and reality were fictions of imagination – fantasies and falsehoods. Romantics, such as Coleridge, would later distinguish between the merely mimetic function of imagination, which they termed 'fantasy', while the properly productive function is reserved for the term 'imagination'. Wordsworth likewise celebrates the creative power of the human imagination in Book XIV of his *Prelude* where he calls it 'another name for absolute power' and Blake hails it as the 'spiritual fountainhead divine'. With the Romantics, the imagination may be able to form new images but can no longer transfrom reality. Existentialism attempted to return to man's concrete existence in the world. For existentialists, such as Sartre, creativity must lead to social commitment. Depth psychologists, such as Jung, would propose 'active imagination' as a therapeutic tool to access the creative images of the collective unconscious, while Lacan would insist that images be translated into words – the movement from the Imaginary into the Symbolic order of existence, to employ Lacanian terminology.

As Freud says many people who are not creative themselves can obtain immense satisfaction in contemplating works of art. We *attend* to the work of art, be it a painting, a poem, a play or a symphony. We are *arrested* by it. Art can calm the mind and soothe the spirit, can invigorate and purge the emotions. Art is for nothing – it has its end in itself; it exhibits a 'finality without end', as Kant describes it. Ultimately, great art inspires. Gadamer tells us that great art 'shakes us' (Gadamer, 1986, p. 37). It can be a propaideutic to the good, as Kant recognised, though Plato sought to banish the poet from the *polis*. Art can shed light 'upon the miserable human scene, prompting compassion and just judgment', as Iris Murdoch puts it (Murdoch, 1992, p, 9). The beautiful, for Kant and Murdoch, can be a symbol of moral goodness. This is far removed from Freud's position – that art is the fantasy life of the artist stimulating the fantasy life of the viewer/reader but Freud does concede that art can liberate the tensions of the mind. Freud holds to the view that ultimately art is a stimulus to personal fantasy, which means that all art aspires to the condition of pornography. But as Murdoch responds: 'It may be true at least that more does than meets the eye' (Murdoch, ibid., p. 21). But surely it is true to say, also with Iris Murdoch, that a study of good art or literature 'enlarges and refines our understanding of truth' (Murdoch, ibid., p. 86). There is a difference then between (egoistic) fantasy and (transcendent) imagination. The latter permits us to see other non-self things clearly – an exercise, then, in morals. As Murdoch puts it: 'Art, especially literature, has in the past instinctively operated as a form, the most profound generally accessible form, of moral reflection, being in this respect close to ordinary life which is saturated with moral reflection' (Murdoch, ibid., p. 89). Better, Murdoch believes, to have fewer and more worthy readers. With Freud, Murdoch concurs that the charm of poetry and music and art can offer 'some consolation' (Murdoch, ibid., p. 93). But is it enough? For Emmanuel Levinas, art consoles, it doesn't challenge. Ultimately, isn't all creativity a secret bid for love?

7) Illusory escape into fantasy

Winnicott wonders whether the opposite of reality isn't play in his *Playing and Reality*. So there is this contrast between reality and play/fantasy. When the child has grown up and stopped playing he may find himself in a mental situation that once again undoes the contrast between play and reality. We adults never really give up this pleasure of play; we merely exchange it for another thing. What seems to be a renunciation is really the formation of a surrogate or substitute. Instead of playing we phantasise. 'He builds castles in the air and creates what are called *day-dreams*' (Freud, 1982, p. 133). People's phantasies are less easy to observe than a child's play because adults are ashamed of their phantasies; they hide and cherish them as their most private and precious possessions. A child's play is governed by one wish – to be a big grown up. In his games he plays at being grown up. What, then, are the characteristics of phantasying? This is what Freud has to say about it: 'We may lay it down that a happy person never phantasies, only an unsatisfied one' (Freud, ibid., p. 134). Unsatisfied wishes are the motive forces of phantasies and every phantasy is the fulfilment of a wish, a correction of unsatisfying reality. These wishes fall into two main groups: ambitious wishes or erotic ones. These phantasies – 'castles in the air and day-dreams' – are the products of imagination. Our dreams at night are phantasies as well. Freud compares the imaginative writer with the daydreamer and poetical creation with the daydream. Creative writing, like a daydream, is a continuation of and substitute for the play of childhood, according to the Freudian formulation. There is in these imaginative or aesthetic products a yield of pleasure, what Freud calls its 'incentive bonus' or 'fore-pleasure'.

Of course, as Lacan tells us fantasy (spelt 'phantasy' in the *Standard Edition*) sustains desire. Fantasy stages an unconscious desire. Fantasy possesses a protective function. Lacan compares the fantasy scene (the 'other scene' is different from waking life – it is the scene of the unconscious Other) to a frozen image on a cinema screen. Just as the film may be stopped at a point to avoid showing a traumatic scene, so is the fantasy scene a defense against castration, against the lack in the Other.

8) Delusional remolding of reality

There is a difference in degree between the illusory escape into fantasy and the delusional remolding of reality. In the latter case, the person 'regards reality as the sole enemy and as the source of all suffering, with which it is impossible to live, so that one must break off all relations with it if one is to be in any way happy. The hermit turns his back on the world and will have no truck with it' (Freud, ibid., p. 18). But more than that, such a person can also try to re-create the world and try to build another in its stead, one in which the unbearable features will be eliminated. Freud notes: 'But whoever, in desperate defiance, sets out upon this path to happiness as a rule attains nothing. Reality is too strong for him. He becomes a madman' (Freud, ibid.). The psychotic is delusional. Though, to some extent we all behave like paranoics. The personality, for Lacan, is paranoid in its very structure. We all, then, correct the world or some aspect of the world by the construction of a wish. We introduce our delusions into reality. Many people in common attempt 'to procure a certainty of happiness and a protection against suffering through a delusional remolding of reality' (Freud, ibid.) and, for Freud, that is primarily carried out through religion. 'The religions of mankind', Freud writes, 'must be classed among the mass-delusions of this kind. No one, needless to say, who shares a delusion ever recognises it as such' (Freud, ibid.). Religion is a projection, a sublimation, a compensation, a wish fulfillment and an illusion, according to Freud. Here Freud stands in a long line of atheists – Comte, Hume, Feuerbach, Nietzsche and Schopenhauer. But isn't also true to say, that despite the relative validity of many of Freud's insights on the nature of religious belief, that religion has consoled many through its promise of eternal life? For many people, religion offers answers to the ultimate questions about the origins and ends of human existence as prayer and liturgy fill the void of man's being. For the theist, religion is the greatest good as it promises the most complete happiness of which we are capable. It is, however, an uncertain hope, a question that must remain open.

9) Mutual love

Even to speak about love is itself a *jouissance*, just as love is, according to Lacan. La Rochfoucauld said that it 'is difficult to define love' (La Rochefoucauld, 1997, maxim 12). Of course. But we can certainly say that love is one of the most painful and pleasurable aspects of human living. Thousands of poems and songs have been composed celebrating love's ecstasy and capturing its brutality and agony. Love is most clearly and closely connected to our view and vision of human happiness. Spinoza remarked: 'One's happiness or unhappiness, indeed, is made to depend entirely upon the quality of the object which one loves'. It has attracted the attention of philosophers and film-makers, poets and song-writers. In 1774 Goethe wrote his *The Sorrows of the Young Werther*, which achieved huge success across Europe. In this little book, Goethe presented a simple yet seductive view of the nature of love, one that is profoundly popular even to this day – that love is a feeling. The novel tells the tale of Werther's *unhappy love* for Charlotte; Werther's love is one of longing and torment, doubt, rupture and rapture. Unable to obtain the love of Charlotte, Werther shoots himself. And after just one night together, Romeo and Juliet decide to kill themselves. In these two romantic stories, that have gripped the Western imagination, the other person is presented as the key to one's happiness. As the Song of Songs puts it: 'Love no flood can quench, no torrents drown'.

Mutual love is the most common method by which we strive to gain happiness and keep suffering away. Here we don't turn away from the world, from external reality, on the contrary, we cling to certain objects in the world and seek to obtain happiness from an emotional relationship with them. Not content simply to avoid unpleasure – a goal of weary resignation – but insistent on a passionate striving 'for a positive fulfilment of happiness' (Freud, 1982, p. 19) and perhaps, Freud thinks, love comes nearer to this goal than any other method or path. Wittgenstein agrees: 'Man's greatest happiness is love' (Wittgenstein, 1980, p. 77e). This way of life makes love the centre of everything and looks for satisfaction in loving and being loved. Sexual love has given us our most intense experience of an overwhelming sensation of pleasure and has thus furnished us with a pattern for our search for happiness. We first encountered happiness along the path of love, as children. Living on the value of love brings happiness but also a great deal of unhappiness. Freud summarises it succinctly thus: 'It is that we are never so defenceless against suffering as when we love, never so helplessly unhappy as when we have lost our loved object or its love' (Freud, 1982, p. 19). It may perhaps be also true to say, with Rochefoucauld, that there 'are people who would never have been in love if they had never heard of love' (La Rochefoucauld, 1997, maxim 136).

It is said that the eyes are the windows of the soul and surely it is true to say that the eyes of another – their look – can lure us into loving? The Spanish philosopher, Ortega y Gasset, tells us that the eyes show us more of man than anything else. Looks are 'acts that come from *within* as few others do. We see *at what* it is looking and *how* it is looking. Not only does the look come from within, but we observe from what depth the body looks. This is why nothing so delights the lover as the first look' (Ortega, 1957, p. 93). There is, acording to Ortega, *mere seeing*, which he calls 'asthenic' (scarcely a look) and there is a *saturated* look, which is one oveflowing with desire. The body is flesh and expression. We see bodies looking at us as we look at other bodies, desirous. Ortega describes this phenomenon thus: 'I repeat, from the depth of radical solitude that is properly our life, we now and again make an attempt at interpenetration, at de-solitudinizing ourselves by tentatively showing ourselves to the other human person, desiring to give him our life and to receive his' (ibid.).

William Desmond, the Irish philosopher, describes the look and the eyes thus:

> The eyes are strange globes of silence; ... Thus, a glance can be swift or furtive or penetrating or evasive or modest or wrathful or stony or dead. The eyes are called "the windows of the soul": the intimate vulnerable inwardness

of selfness comes from the emergence in the body. Sometimes eyes are the show of troubled spirit, sometimes just a delicate gloss on darkness. This is partly why we experience it as a violence if another holds one's eyes for too long. Eye contact is fraught with ambiguity. It is to show respect for another not to bore into their eyes with one's own, threatening the fragile intimacy with a harsh, brazen look. The intimacy of the eyes is also related to the different mode of looking of lovers. In their look they lose themselves in the other's eyes; the dangerous intimacy is rescued from violence and rendered benign (Desmond, 1990, p. 71).

Man plays with masks, especially in love. One man who played with masks more than most was Oscar Wilde. There was always the very 'real' (understood in the Lacanian sense) danger that he would be unmasked and revealed, despite his disclaimer in the preface to *The Picture of Dorian Gray* (a book that adresses the theme of the look) that to conceal art and reveal the artist is art's aim. Wilde's works are plays of concealment and revealment, self-revelations that are, simultaneously, ostensible and oblique. There is always present deception, half-truths, deceit, double-play, and desire – such desire in those Irish eyes.

Lacan named the look as one of the *objets a*, those partial objects pertaining to an Other that mobilise our desire. We are turned on by the look. Even though, as Lacan says '*You never look at me from the place from which I see you. Conversely, what I look at is never what I wish to see*' (Lacan, 1977, p. 103). So very often is the look the beginning of love. The bridegroom in the Song of Songs says: 'Turn your eyes away, for they hold me captive' and 'you ravish my heart with a single one of your glances'. He says that his bride is beautiful: 'your eyes are doves' and he is sick with love as he beholds a beauty without blemish. As for the bride, she looks for him everywhere: 'Upon my bed at night I sought him whom my soul loves. I sought him but found him not. I called him but he gave no answer. I will rise now and go about the city. In the streets and the squares I will seek him whom my soul loves'. She searches for him but finds him not. Love sickness. Love's sickness.

Oscar Wilde was literally lured to his destruction and doom by the lethal, lovely look of Lord Alfred Douglas. Wilde was so lured by Bosie's forceful yet fatal and very seductive look. As the former gazed at this young aristocrat, poet and (judging by the photographs of the time) incredibly handsome man, he was lured in lust by his deadly look, which would bring about his eventual downfall, his collapse from the Symbolic (where he was a successful and famous playwright) into the Real (where he was deemd bankrupt, got sentenced to two years hard labour and ended his life in poverty, alcoholism and exile). Wilde met Dorian Gray in person when he met Alfred Douglas in 1891; only four years later Wilde would stand trial for him. Bosie seemed to be the incarnate version of those nude and nubile young male bodies depicted in two paintings that so fasinated Wilde: Reni's *The Martyrdom of Saint Sebastian* and George Watts' *Love and Death*. But Bosie was better than these images; he was the Real thing.

Another example – this time taken from fiction: in Thomas Mann's *Death in Venice*, a writer, one Gustave von Aschenbach, arrives in Venice and encounters a young boy with whom he becomes utterly obsessed. He can't take his eyes off him. His pitiful pursuit of the object of his desire reaches its pathetic but inevitable climax. Most of us are like Wilde in this respect – we are unable or unwilling to practise a 'poverty of the eyes', as recommended by St. Benedict to his monks. It is hard to 'look away', to redirect our attention elsewhere, as Iris Murdoch advised. But beauty can also become an occasion for 'unselfing', as our consciousness is consumed by the Other.

The look is sometimes solicited. We cannot *not* see. A visual phenomenology is permanently present. Those eyes! We depend on the visible, on the subject's eyes, lured by his look, captivated, petrified in his gaze. Wilde gives a good example of this captivation by the human look in *The Picture of Dorian Gray*, when the painter, Basil Hallward, becomes aware of Dorian Gray's exceptional personal beauty: 'I suddenly became conscious that someone was looking at me. I turned half-way round, and saw Dorian Gray for the first time. When our eyes met, I felt that I was growing pale' (Wilde, 1995, p. 21). We may note, in passing, that Dorian Gray prioritises beauty over virtue. Dorian Gray is physically beautiful yet morally ugly. Mary Shelley's *Frankenstein* is the opposite: Frankenstein is physically ugly yet virtuous of soul, at least for while.

The dialectic, as the French philosopher Merleau-Ponty recognised in *The Visible and the Invisible*, unfolds in terms of a phenomenological intentionality, between the seer and the seen, between the subject of the look and the object of the gaze. In my bodily being, 'I am looked at from all sides' (Lacan, 1977, p. 72). I am a subject who is subjected to this seeing, as subject of the scopic drive. 'With his subtle smile Lord Henry watched him' (Wilde, 1995, p. 30).

In our relation to the things of this world, which is constituted and constructed by way of vision (a vision, as Iris Murdoch informs us, that is often not very clear), something slips away, is elided, escapes the grasp. This is the gaze that is beyond the pupil of the eye. Our eyes see but if we see ourselves seeing ourselves then we are avoiding the function of the gaze. (This derives from the specular image and the attendant narcissistic structure at the mirror-stage of development which occurs between 6 and 18 months, when the infant begins to (mis)recognise himself in the mirror).

But a look or a sideways glance can so quickly become a bitter, envious glare. St Augustine captured this so vividly in the *Confessions* when he spoke of the envy (*invidia*) he encountered in the jealous baby who, on seeing his brother sharing his mother's milk, at his mother's breast, glared at him with bitterness and hatred: 'I have seen with my own eyes and know very well an infant in the grip of jealousy: he could not yet speak, and already he observed his foster-brother, pale with an envenomed stare'. Wilde relates the incident of the singer, Miss Vane (vain), whom Dorian Gray used to love, crouching at his feet as he glares down at her, his look reducing her to an abject object. 'She crouched on the floor like a wounded thing, and Dorian Gray, with his beautiful eyes, looked down at her, and his chiselled lips curled in exquisite disdain' (Wilde, ibid., p. 76). Behind the pupils of his eyes, which were 'like discs of blue fire' (Wilde, ibid., p. 92), lay the gaze – almost an evil eye. In this example, the gaze reduced Miss Vane to shame.

In *Being and Nothingness*, in a section entitled 'The Look', in part three of the work, entitled, 'Being-for Others', Sartre analyses the emotion of shame. A voyeur, moved by vice, curiosity or jealousy, lends his ear to a door and looks through the keyhole. He is alone and behind the door there is a spectacle to be seen or a conversation to be heard. But suddenly, he discovers that there is someone looking at him. Where before he was only looking, now he is being looked at. The former situation has been radically reversed. He is no longer master of the situation. The voyeur subject or *l'être-pour-soi*, in Sartrean terminology (Being-For-Itself), when he is caught in the perverse act of scoptophilia, is reduced to a shameful object, a *l'être-en-soi* (Being-In-Itself). He now experiences shame, or something similar, which reveals to him the Other's look. This is the recognition of the fact that he is an object, which the other is looking at and judging. He becomes engulfed in his shame and the Other becomes an immense presence who supports and embraces this shame. The act of being looked at signals his alienation. In this case, the Other's look is a look-looking rather than a look-looked-at. 'At each moment the Other *is looking at me*' (Sartre, 1956, p. 257). Every look manifests itself in a sensible form in our perceptive field. A look, of course, mostly manifests itself as the convergence of two ocular globes. But the look is given also 'when there is a rustling of branches, or the sound of a footstep followed by silence' (Sartre, ibid). It is ubiquitous. The eye is the support for the look. 'If I apprehend the look, I cease to perceive the eye' (Sartre, ibid., p. 258). So when eyes are looking at me and I am really seeing them, I cannot say whether I find them beautiful or not. Perception and imagination are not simultaneous for Sartre. 'The Other's look hides his eyes' (Sartre, ibid.).

Dorian Gray's portrait had taught him to love his own beauty. He wondered whether it would teach him to loathe his own soul. 'Yet it was watching him, with its beautiful marred face and its cruel smile. Its bright hair gleamed in the early sunlight. Its blue eyes met his own. A sense of infinite pity, not for himself, but for the painted image of himself, came over him' (Wilde, 1995, p. 78). Dorian Gray's mad desire was to stay forever young and beautiful while the portrait would grow old, the face on the canvas bear the burden of his sins, the painted image carry his dark passions and become seared with the lines of suffering while he remained forever young and retained the bloom of his just conscious boyhood. The narcissist's law of desire is to gaze at his image in the mirror, in the waters of the stream, into which he can gaze more than once. As Basil Hallward informs Dorian Gray: 'You had leant over the still pool of some Greek woodland, and seen in the water's silent silver the marvels of your own face' (Wilde, ibid., p. 94).

None of us can escape from the gaze, even if we wanted to. Lacan quotes Merleau-Ponty as saying: 'We are beings who are looked at in the spectacle of the world' (Lacan, 1977, p. 75). What satisfaction and fascination there is in this fact and what horrible, horrendous frustration too. As Wilde writes about the character

James Vane: 'Jim frowned from time to time when he caught the inquisitive glance of some stranger. He had that dislike of being stared at' (Wilde, 1995, p. 60). This Berkeleyan all-seeing aspect, according to Lacan, can be encountered in the woman 'who knows that she is being looked at, on condition that one does not show her that one knows that she knows' (Lacan, 1977, ibid.). This is the essence of the gaze, containing within it the *objet a* – the apprehension of the gaze in the direction of desire. (It is not for nothing that psychoanalysis is not carried out face to face). Lord Henry Cotton, Epicurean hedonist and Dorian Gray's alter ego, felt 'that the eyes of Dorian Gray were fixed on him ... Dorian Gray never took his gaze off him, but sat like one under a spell, smiles chasing each other over his lips, and wonder growing grave in his darkening eyes' (Wilde, 1995, ibid., p. 45). As desiring beings, we let ourselves, despite ourselves, be lured by the look but Lacan tells us '*You never look at me from the place I see you*' (Lacan, 1977, p. 91). The look is the locus of the missed encounter with the Real. When we look at the same thing we all see different things.

From Plato onwards, philosophers have cautioned against the deceptiveness of perception. Examples one offers to students: the train tracks that seem to converge, the sun which seems to orbit our earth, the pencil in the glass of water or the stick in the stream which appear magnified and crooked, the scarecrow in the distance who resembles our friend. What else is being revealed here except the chasm inherent in the chiasma – a *chiaroscuro*. Lacan relates a story. One day he was on a small fishing boat and one of his companions, a man named Petit-Jean, pointed out to Lacan a small can, which was floating on the surface of the waves under the sun. And he turned to Lacan and said: '*You see that can? Well, it doesn't see you*' (Lacan, ibid., p. 95). The picture of the can was in Lacan's eye but he was not in the picture. With the picture, with mimicry and in the changing colouration of some animals and insects for the purposes of adaptation and survival, we are in the domain or the dimension of deceit, in which something when it is revealed is also concealed. There is camouflage, masquerade, disguise, deception operating in the function of the look. Love is, likewise, deception. Think of photographs, of self-portraits, of your voice on the taperecorder, of your face in the mirror. Is that really me? Does that look or sound like me? How do our lovers mirror us back to ourselves? When Dorian Gray sees himself in the portrait for the first time he draws back. Only later will he want to rip it up with a palette-knife with blades of lithe steel when he sees sodden eyes and his thinning hair where before there was golden hair, beautiful blue eyes and rose-red lips.

At the end of Wilde's moral tale, Dorian Gray, the narcissist becomes Dorian Gray, the murderer. The image in the portrait may have brought some momentary satisfaction so long as it revealed back to him his Adonis-like perfection but it was a perfection he could not possess forever and so, after killing the painter, he takes the carved mirror and 'with wild, tear-dimmed eyes looked into its polished shield ... Then he loathed his own beauty, and, flinging the nirror on the floor, crushed it into silver splinters beneath his heel. It was his beauty that had ruined him' (Wilde, 1995, p. 165). It was the mirror of his soul. Then he seizes the knife and stabs the picture with it. The servants hear a cry followed by a crash. When they enter the room they find a splendid portrait of their master in all the wonder and joy of youth. But 'lying on the floor was a dead man, in evening dress, with a knife in his heart. He was withered, wrinkled and loathsome of visage. It was not till they had examined the rings that they recognised who it was' (Wilde, ibid., p. 167). Such is Wilde's moral message despite his other disclaimer that it 'is only shallow people who do not judge by appearances. The true mystery of the world is the visible, not the invisible' (Wilde, ibid., p. 32).

How do we see? By not looking! As Lacan notes: 'If you wish to see a star of the fifth or six size, do not look straight at it – this is known as the Arago phenomenon. You will be able to see it only if you fix your eyes to one side' (Lacan, 1977, p. 102). In the Japanese martial art of Aikido we are taught to avoid the eyes of our opponent lest we become distracted by their utter beauty and so be rendered impotent in the face of an attack. There are two reasons we do not focus on the eyes. Firstly, if we do we may not see their hands or feet moving in for an attack. The look can distract us from the void and from the still centre, as in the case of Wilde and countless others. It is better to look between the brows and then we will see all. Secondly, if we look into the eyes we may be lured by the look and become distracted from the attack.

So though sight may be the dominant sense, O Sensei, the founder of Aikido, advised: 'Do not stare into the eyes of your opponent: he may mesmerise you. Do not fix your gaze on his sword: he may intimidate you. Do not focus on your opponent at all: he may absorb your energy'. Terry Dobson, a well known Aikidoka, whom we have already mentioned, desribed it thus, in his moving book, *It's a lot Like Dancing*:

> My teacher [O Sensei] used to teach us to look between the eyes instead of into the eyes because you can become enthralled with the beauty of the other person and be unable to deal with his attack. This other person might not be as refined as you. All he will see is a sucker who has fallen into his eyes and he will take your head off. So, if you have the ability to see another person's beauty, you have to avoid becoming a prisoner to it. Look between his brows (Dobson, 1994, p. 120).

The advice of Iris Murdoch, Terry Dobson and Morihei Ueshiba (O Sensei), as well as the example of Oscar Wilde should be enough to alert us all to the dangers inherent in the look that can be so alluring and yet so deadly. But, to return to love.

Wilde asked: 'Who, being loved, is poor?' Love, undoutedly, is one of the foundations of civilisation. Sexual love affords us the strongest experience of satisfaction; it is 'the prototype of all happiness', according to Freud (Freud, 1982, p. 38). Some make genital erotism the central point of life. But depending so much on one's loved object is dangerous when and if that object should be lost either through a break up, unfaithfulness and betrayal or death. Freud says: 'For that reason the wise men of every age have warned us most emphatically against this way of life; but in spite of this it has not lost its attraction for a great number of people' (Freud, ibid.). A small number of people find happiness, despite everything, along the path of love. But some can displace their love away from one particular person and direct it at many people, thus protecting themselves against the loss of the love-object. They thus achieve a state of evenly suspended, steadfast affection. St. Francis of Assisi is an example of someone who benefitted from this inner feeling of happiness. Religions have always insisted on the universal love of mankind.

However, Freud criticises this universal love commandment on two grounds: firstly, it fails to discriminate and thus forfeits a part of its own value, and secondly, not everyone is worthy of love. There are many kinds of love – love of family, friends, neighbours and nations and the love between two sexual partners. Freud opines that such aim-inhibited love (e.g., the love of friends) is still love with a sensual base in one's unconscious. It is intertwined with an erotic aspect.

There is, though, a recognisable rift or rupture between love and the interests of civilisation (e.g., taboos, laws and customs), which threaten love with substantial restrictions. A lot of psychical energy has to be withdrawn from sexuality in order to advance the decrees and designs of civilisation. One such requirement is that there should be a single sexual life for everyone, which, according to Freud, is a source of 'serious injustice' (Freud, ibid., p. 41) but even heterosexual love is restricted by legitimacy and monogamy. But many have revolted against such encroachments upon their sexual liberty. Many transgressions are passed over in silence. Furthermore, for Freud, man is an organism with an 'unmistakenly bisexual disposition' (Freud, ibid., p. 42). Neurotics cannot tolerate such frustrations and therefore create substitutive satisfactions in their symptoms. In any form of intimate relationship, a third party can seem superfluous. A pair of lovers becomes sufficient unto themselves 'and do not even need the child they have in common to make them happy' (Freud, ibid., p. 45). Witness the private languages of two lovers – their 'idiolect' (a dialect of and for idiots). Eros thus betrays the core of his own being – his purpose being to make one out of more than one. Aim-inhibited libido is summoned up in the nature of the bond of friendship to strengthen communal ties. There is the Christic commandment that stands out: 'Thou shalt love thy neighbour as thyself' and 'love thine enemies', a seemingly impossible requirement. How will we achieve it and what good will it do us? Freud asks. Surely, if we are to love someone, then he must deserve it? It is an injustice, Freud opines, to put a stranger who is of no emotional significance to me on a par with my friends whom I love. If I am to love him simply because he is, like me, an inhabitant of planet earth, 'like an insect, an earth-worm or a grass-snake' (Freud, ibid., p. 47), then he will only receive a modicum of my love. It is also a precept that cannot be recommended as reasonable. Probably, the stranger is not only unworthy of my love but actually has more claims to my hostility and hatred, when he insults, harms and injures me. Freud quotes the poet Heine here:

> Mine is a most peaceable disposition. My wishes are: a humble cottage with a thatched roof, but a good bed, good food, the freshest milk and butter, flowers before my window, and a few fine trees before my door; and if God wants to make my happiness complete, he will grant me the joy of seeing

some six or seven of my enemies hanging from those trees. Before their death I shall, moved in my heart, forgive them all the wrong they did me in their lifetime. One must, it is true, forgive one's enemies – but not before they have been hanged (Freud, ibid.).

Men are not gentle creatures but carry within them a fair share of aggression; they want to torture, to humiliate, to kill. Look at the Huns, the Mongols, and the Crusaders. *Homo homini lupus*. Men's passions are stronger than their reason. Such love commandments thus run counter to man's very constitution. The Communists, which Freud cites, believe they have found the way, the path of peace. According to them, man is completely good – it is only the institution of private property that has made him corrupt. Freud makes the point that Communism presupposes a set of psychological premises that are based on an untenable illusion. For example, aggressiveness was not created by property but, on the contrary, has been there since time immemorial and is present in every relation of affection. Man does not feel comfortable without the presence of aggression in some form. The sexual and aggressive drives are important and innate. 'If civilization imposes such great sacrifices not only on man's sexuality but on his aggressivity, we can understand better why it is hard for him to be happy in that civilization' (Freud, ibid., p. 52). There is the immortal battle between the two great adversaries – Eros or love and Thanatos, that force of destruction, that is playing itself out in our species, both onto- and phylogenetically.

Psychoanalysis speaks a lot about love. In 'Why War?' (1933), Freud asserts: 'There is no need for psycho-analysis to be ashamed to speak of love … for religion itself uses the same words: "Thou shalt love thy neighbour as thyself" (Freud, 1933, p. 212). And he likens his concept of libido to the Eros of 'the divine Plato'. For Lacan, love (together with hate and ignorance) is one of the *three* fundamental passions. (For Bion, the British psychoanalyst, it is love (L), hate (H) and knowledge (K)). Lacan devotes his 1972-3 seminar *Encore* to the subject of love.

In St. Paul's thirteenth chapter of his *First Letter to the Corinthians*, he says that love is always patient and kind, never jealous or boastful, rude, selfish or conceited but always prepared to excuse, to trust, to hope and to endure (Paul could be talking about God here). For St. Paul, *three* things endure: faith, hope and love and the greatest of these is love. In *Wuthering Heights*, Cathy speaks to her housekeeper, Nelly Dean, of her great love for Heathcliff:

My love for Linton [her husband] is like the foliage in the woods. Time will change it, I'm well aware, as nature changes the trees. My love for Heathcliff resembles the eternal rocks beneath – a source of little visible delight, but necessary. Nelly, I *am* Heathcliff – he's always, always in my mind – not as a pleasure, any more than I am always a pleasure to myself – but as my own being (Brontë, 1965, p. 122).

Yeats gives poetic voice to this fantasy of fusion too in 'Among School Children', where he writes that 'it seemed that our two matures blent/ Into a sphere from youthful sympathy,/ Or else to alter Plato's parable,/ Into the yolk and white of the one shell'. Later, Yeats cautions thus, in 'Crazy Jane Talks with the Bishop': 'But Love has pitched his mansion in/ The Place of excrement;/ For nothing can be sole or whole/ That has not been rent'. Cathy, for her part, exclaims: 'Whatever our souls are, his and mine are the same'. She is on the side here of Aristophanes. She has found 'the one whom my soul loves' as the Song of Solomon puts it. In *The Twelfth Knight*, Shakespeare's characters – Viola and Sebastian – are portrayed as two parts of one whole. While the metaphysical poet, John Donne, in his poem 'The Good Morrow' writes in the following verse that reflected in the pupils of one another's eyes, lovers possess worlds of their own:

My face in thine eye, thine in mine appears,
And true plain hearts do in the faces rest:
Where can we find two better hemispheres
Without sharp North, without declining West?
Whatever dies was not mixed equally;
If our two loves be one, or thou and I
Love so alike that none do slacken, none can die.

Keats, the romantic, for his part writes of 'Two souls with but a single thought, two hearts that beat as one'. This fantasy of fusion is seductive – to see myself through another and to find that we are identical. What a delicious delirium! But Cathy also recognises that love has its despair, that love is *jouissance*. Her love was obsessive, possessive. (We can ask with Yeats: did excess of love bewilder her till she died?). And when Heathcliff dies Cathy exclaims: 'Take any form. Drive me mad. Only do not leave me in this abyss where I can not find you. I can not live without my life. I can not live without my soul'. Is that the fate of all true love or should we heed the words of Rilke who advised that in a love relation, we should seek to protect the other person's solitude? For Rilke, love is about *privacy*, not *possession*. John Bayley described his relationship with his wife, Iris Murdoch, as a 'solitude in closeness' (see Bayley, 1999). Bayley says his wife was always good whereas he himself is merely nice. Their relationship was the 'closeness of apartness' (Bayley, ibid., p. 137). This approximates to the Rilkean view. Bayley makes the insightful point that when someone says 'my wife doesn't understand me', it usually means that they understand each other only too well! (see Bayley, ibid., p. 49). The Australian poet, A.D. Hope, talks about people who 'move closer and closer apart'. This, I think, is the ideal.

Like Cathy, Christianity speaks of the *two becoming one* 'so that they are no longer two but one flesh' 'bone of my bones', breath of my breath. As Freud writes: 'At the height of being in love the boundary between ego and object threatens to melt away. Against all the evidence of his senses, a man who is in love declares that "I" and "you" are one' (Freud, 1982, p. 3). The so-called unity of love is realised, however, in an existential duality – *if* there is indeed 'unity' at the level of love, there is diversity at the level of existence (i.e., one in love, two in being, according to this formulation).

The most famous myth about the origin of love says that in the beginning each human being was a rounded whole with two faces, two backs, four arms and four legs but Zeus cut them in two to put an end to their strength and pride. Love is seen as the yearning of each part to locate its original partner to return to a completed state of wholeness – the ardent wish to merge and become one. But this dangerous fantasy of fusion ('my other half' or worse 'my better half') is precisely that – a fantasy. But before we critique it from the Lacanian perspective, let's explore the myth that was put into the mouth of Aristophanes by Plato in his *Symposium* in greater detail. It is, after all, our most enduring and romantic myth. Cathy swallowed it whole.

Plato's *Symposium* is a dialogue that details a dinner party given for the literati of Athenian society. A series of speeches are given by the guests on the subject of love. A complex but stimulating philosophy of love emerges from these rich reflections that is playful, profound and provocative. The conversation on love is of universal interest. The direct speakers are only two in number – Apollodorus and an unnamed friend to whom among others Apollodorus reports at second-hand and many years after the event an account which he has had of the party or banquet from a member of Socrates's circle called Aristodemus, who was present at it. Both Apollodorus and Aristodemus are historical persons and were admirers of Socrates. The guests named at Agathon's party are real people. This banquet would have been typical among the upper classes at Athens in 416 B.C. Such a carefree and almost indolent attitude is exemplified by Alcibiades, who only a year later would lead a disastrous Sicilian expedition, one that subsequently led to his ruin, dishonour and disgrace with his betrayal of his country in the Peloponnesian War. In this dialogue, however, he comes across as charming and brilliant, if somewhat shallow and shameless.

To look at the structure of the dialogue: Aristodemus meets Socrates on his way to dine with Agathon, a very handsome tragic poet, who is celebrating a recent success in a dramatic competition. Socrates takes Aristodemus with him but doesn't arrive till the meal is halfway over. Eryximachus, an officious medical doctor, suggests that they be entertained with talk rather than with flute-girls and that each member should give a speech in praise of love. His suggestion is duly adopted and the main part of the dialogue consists of speeches delivered by Phaedrus, a hypochondriacal literary type (who is said to to be the real author of the idea), Pausanias who is Agathon's lover, Eryximachus himself, Aristophanes, the great comic poet, Agathon, a tragic poet, at whose house the party takes place and Socrates. At the conclusion of Socrates' speech a commotion is heard outside and the brilliant but dissolute Alcibiades, who is at the height of his power, enters with some drunken friends and is warmly welcomed. He attempts to give a laudatory speech in praise of Socrates. The party grows less decorous and finally, a fresh crowd of revellers arrive on the scene. Now all restraint is cast aside and some go home while Aristodemus, for his part, falls asleep. When he wakes up early the next morning he finds only Agathon, Aristophanes and Socrates still drinking and talking. Then Agathon and Aristophanes 'succumb' and the still sober Socrates leaves as fresh as when he arrived, with Aristodemus still in attendance, goes to the Lyceum, which was a gymnasium, that was later used by Aristotle in which to teach.

Socrates' speech – there are seven speeches in all, six of which are on love – is the kernel of the dialogue and the love of which they speak is homosexual love. It is assumed that this type of love is alone capable of satisfying man's noblest and highest aspirations and the love of man and woman, when it is mentioned at all, is usually commented on in a derogatory way as altogether inferior, a purely physical impulse whose sole aim is the procreation of children. Homosexuality was quite common among the leisured classes of Athens society. In this dialogue (as distinct from the *Laws*, where Plato becomes more puritanical) Plato holds the view that only a homosexual relationship is capable of being transformed into a lifelong partnership. Furthermore, homosexual love has a range that extends beyond physical passion to incorporate a spiritual marriage of the noblest of minds, one lacking in crude corporeality. The god Dionysus shall judge between the speeches. They settle down and have dinner, pouring libations and sing a hymn to the god of wine. They agree that the party should not be pushed to the point of drunkenness as they compose panegyrics to love.

The first two speakers, Phaedrus and Pausanias, talk about love in a rather platitudinous fashion. Love is personified throughout the dialogue – he is the oldest and greatest of the gods. For Phaedrus, Love inspires honour and self-sacrifice. He cites Hesiod's view that Love came into being after Chaos. Further, Love confers upon us the greatest benefits. Phaedrus says: 'there can be no greater benefit for a boy than to have a worthy lover from his earliest youth, nor for a lover than to have a worthy object for his affection' (Plato, 1985, p. 42). The principle of love ought to guide the whole of one's life, Phaedrus maintains, more than family, position or wealth. Love 'inspires shame at what is disgraceful and ambition for what is noble; without these feelings neither a state nor an individual can accomplish anything great or fine' (ibid.). Phaedrus holds that only lovers will sacrifice their lives for one another and the gods will greatly honour the courage of a lover but 'they admire even more and reward more richly affection shown towards a lover by the beloved because a lover is possessed and thus comes nearer than the beloved to being divine' (Plato, ibid., pp. 44-45). Not only is Love the oldest of the gods but the most powerful 'to assist men in the acquisition of merit and happiness' (Plato, ibid., p. 45).

Pausanias is slightly more subtle and distinguishes between a nobler and baser kind of love, believing that love doesn't have just a single nature. Aphrodite is linked with love and since there are two Aphrodites, it follows there must be two Loves. One is the elder and is the daughter of Uranus and has no mother and is called Heavenly Aphrodite, the other is younger, the child of Zeus and Dione, and is called Common Aphrodite. Firstly, the baser type – Common Aphrodite - aims at sexual gratification and finds the means to this in women and young boys. Secondly, it is physical rather than spiritual. Thirdly, it prefers that its objects should be as unintelligent as possible, because it aims only at the satisfaction of desire. The nobler type – Heavenly Aphrodite – is directed exclusively toward young men and springs entirely from the male. Those who are attracted by this Love are attracted towards the male sex, valuing it as the stronger and more intelligent. Such people 'do not fall in love with mere boys, but wait until they reach the age at which they begin to show more intelligence, that is to say, until they are near growing a beard' (Plato, ibid., p. 47). Its object is a lifelong productive partnership; 'they are not the kind who take advantage of the ignorance of a boy to deceive him, and they are off with a jeer in pursuit of some fresh darling' (Plato, ibid.). He makes the further point that it is good to gratify a lover and to voluntarily sumbit to slavery; 'a lover is allowed the utmost licence by both God and man' (Plato, ibid., p. 50). There is no absolute right or wrong in love; everything depends on the circumstances. The vulgar lover is in love with the body rather than the soul; 'he is not constant because what he loves is not constant; as soon as the flower of physical beauty, which is what he loves, begins to fade, he is gone …. But the lover of a noble nature remains its lover for life, because the thing to which he cleaves is constant' (Plato, ibid.). Pausanias discredits two things: first, to give in quickly to a lover; 'time, which is the best test of most things, must be allowed to elapse – and second, to give in on account of his wealth or power' (Plato, ibid., p. 51).

The pompous and pedantic Eryximachus comes next (Aristophanes has hiccups) and further distinguishes between a good and bad kind of love, basically plagiarising Pausanias. He views love as a cosmic principle and distinguishes between the love that takes beautiful boys as its objects and the love that has many other objects such as the love of animals and plants and all existing things. He believes that love 'is the author of all our happiness' (Plato, ibid., p. 57). And he concludes with the invitation to Aristophanes to fill in any caveats he may have created in his discourse.

Aristophanes's speech (or at least the one assigned to him by Plato that is responsible for our most enduring myth) is stimulating and original in a Rabelaisian way. According to Aristophanes, men are halves of original wholes, which were of three sexes, male (who sprang from the sun), female (who came from the earth) and hermaphrodite (who came from the moon), and were bissected by Zeus as a punishment for their pride. For Aristophanes, love is the cure that 'constitutes the greatest happiness of the human race' (Plato, ibid., p. 59). It is man's attempt to regain his former happy state by reuniting with his lost, other half. The two long to be one. Aristophanes treats homosexual and heterosexual love as being on the same level though he does describe as the best those individuals who are halves of male wholes and, consequently, homosexual. The men who are halves of hermaphrodite are lovers of women (adulterers and sexually promiscuous women who are mad about men fall into this class). The women who are halves of the female whole are lesbians. Those who are halves of a male whole love men and physical contact with men. 'Such boys and lads are the best of their generation, because they are the most manly' (Plato, ibid., p. 62) and 'cleave to what is akin to themselves' (Plato, ibid., p. 63). He maintains that 'the soul of each has some other longing which it cannot express, but can only surmise and obscurely hint at' (Plato, ibid.). *Love is the desire to be whole.* It is 'the name for the desire and pursuit of the whole' (Plato, ibid., p. 64), as the lover seeks to melt into his beloved so they can be no longer two but one flesh. Those whose wounds are thus healed are happy; 'the way to happiness for our race lies in fulfilling the behests of Love, and in each finding for himself the mate who properly belongs to him; in a word, in returning to our original condition' (Plato, ibid., p. 65).

For Aristophanes, love is a need, a want, a lack, whose satisfaction is more than physical, the universal nature of which will be described to Socrates by Diotima. Love is a longing to regain a lost happiness (*à la* Platonic metaphysics). The ultimate object of love is the vision of absolute beauty that the soul experienced and enjoyed prior to its incarnation and incarceration.

An interlude follows before the vain but handsome Agathon speaks. He begins by making the point that so far in the discussion everyone has concentrated on the happiness that is conferred by the god of Love rather than on the type of being he is. Agathon says that Love 'is the most happy' of all the gods not least because, far from being the oldest, he is in fact the youngest and flees before old age 'which moves fast, as we know' (Plato, ibid., p. 68). Love hates old age – such is its nature. 'His whole life is passed in the company of the young, for there is truth in the old saying that like clings to like' (Plato, ibid.). He thus disagrees with Phaedrus that Love is of antediluvian antiquity. Love is young, sensitive to hardships, possesses a supple form, is beautiful in complexion and good, endowed with self-control because Love is master of all the passions, and is wise and clever. 'Love is in the first place supreme in beauty and goodness himself' (Plato, ibid., p. 71). Love bestows good-humour, banishes surliness. Love's gift is the gift of good-will. It is 'contemplated by the wise, admired by the gods; coveted by men who possess him not' (Plato, ibid., p. 72).

He loads on Love all desirable qualities and virtues. For Agathon, the object of love is beauty. And since the object of Love (*Eros*) is beauty, Love cannot be beautiful nor, as the good is the same as the beautiful, can he be good (which does not mean that Love is ugly or bad). The transition to Plato's Socrates involves a trajectory from sophistic rhetoric to philosophical wisdom. Socrates embarks on his views, which take the form of a reported debate between Socrates and a woman of Mantinea called Diotima, who is a fictitious personage and Socrates' instructor in the art of love.

Socrates professes to be reduced to 'the speechlessness of a stone' (Plato, ibid., p. 73) and proposes to give a 'plain statement of the truth about Love' (Plato, ibid., p. 74). First, though, he asks whether Love is Love of something or Love of nothing and makes the point that 'one desires what one lacks, or rather [that] one does not desire what one does not lack' (Plato, ibid., p. 76). So, firstly, Love only exists in relation to some object. Secondly, that object must be something of which one is at present in want. And thirdly, Love will be the Love of beauty. It is not itself beautiful or good.

In terms of mythology, Love's mother was Poverty, who lives in want, but from his father Contrivance Love has inherited boldness, daring and resoluteness in pursuing his object. Love is not a god but a spirit who interprets and conveys messages to the gods from men and to men from the gods. Love was begotten on Aphrodite's birthday. So Socrates says that Love is always poor, 'is hard and weather-beaten, shoeless and homeless' (Plato, ibid., p. 82) and lives in want though he schemes to secure for himself whatever is beautiful; he is bold, strenuous and sly, full of cunning resource, a lover of wisdom, a skilful magician and an alchemist. The aim of Love is 'to attain possession of beautiful things' (Plato, ibid., p. 84), thus gaining happiness, which consists in possessing the good and the beautiful. Socrates' Diotima defines Love thus: 'love is desire for the perpetual possession of the good' (Plato, ibid., p. 86). There is something divine about Love as it progresses from physical love to moral beauty and beauty of soul to absolute Beauty. Once such an Ideal has been attained 'you will not value', Diotima tells Socrates, 'it in terms of gold or rich clothing or of the beauty of boys and young men, the sight of whom at present throws you and many people like you into such an ecstasy' (Plato, ibid., p. 94).

To conclude the *Symposium*: Socrates and Plato are philosophers (lovers of wisdom) because wisdom is beautiful and beauty is the object of Love. For Plato and the Platonists, life is a struggle for a far away and dimly discerned Good, the attainment of which is happiness. Love is desire for the Good – is attracted by the magnetism of Good. To love, therefore, is to will the good of the other. But the ascent is always upward, in the Platonic pilgrimmage, from the senses to the spirit. Platonic love is wholly spiritual, involving the soul rather than the senses. The stages are: from the physical love of particular forms to physical beauty in general: thence to beauty of soul (though not necessarily beauty of body), to moral beauty and then to the beauty of knowledge, to the vision of the Form of Beauty. Such a being who attains this apex no longer lives in the shadows of the Cave but is emancipated from the bondage of the senses and lives in the world of the really real. The crowning achievement of the philosophical quest is a marriage with the real, which is the Good. The Platonic hope is that beauty can inspire a common search for truth and goodness. This is made more probable by two persons of the same sex inspired by mutual affection and admiration. The philosopher searches for wisdom and truth just as the mystic searches for his God. An amount of sublimation is required before the gradual attainment of the beatific vision – the Good (for the Platonist) or God (for the Christian). Plato exemplified human nature at its metaphysical highest: the philosopher in love.

In Plato's *Phaedrus* (his other dialogue on love), Phaedrus informs Socrates that Lysias has written a speech designed 'to win the favour of a handsome boy for someone who is not in love with him' (Plato, 1973, p. 22). Lysias depicts the supposed superiority of the man not in love to the man in love. Love is portrayed as an aberration or as a form of madness – the lover is not a man in his sober senses but is like one possessed. Love makes one neglect one's own interests and lovers 'themselves admit that they are mad, not sane' (Plato, ibid., p. 27). Those who are in love are to be pitied rather than admired. For Socrates, sensual love is the irrational desire for the enjoyment of physical beauty and the lover is a person in whom this irrational desire has get the better of rational judgement. Socrates had rejected the advances of Alcibiades in the *Symposium*. The man in love is under the sway of desire and a slave to pleasure and passion. An unknown quotation is cited: 'As wolves for lambs, so lovers lust for boys'. Socrates's recantation or palinode is welcomed by Phaedrus and Socrates describes love as a form of divine possession. The lover is taken up in a 'flood of longing'; he is in a frenzy; cannot sleep at night or remain still by day; he is full of pain and pangs; 'he is ready to be a slave and to make his bed as near as he is allowed to the object of his passion' (Plato, ibid., p. 59). This 'sickness' men call Eros. And the lover desires 'to see, to touch, to kiss him, and to share his bed' (Plato, ibid., p. 64). Love, in short, literally consumes the lover with burning, heart-wrenching passion and desire.

The most profound antithesis to this prevailing (Barbara Cartland) view of love is the one adumbrated by Freud and especially by Lacan, though as we have just seen it was first touted by Plato using Socrates as a mouthpiece for his own views. For Lacan, the two can never become one. $1 + 1 = 2$ is a truth, not of mathematics, he suggests, but of the psychoanalytic (Lacanian) insight that there is no sexual rapport, between man and woman, man and man or woman and woman. Our lovers cannot fill us up or fulfil us *because desire is insatiable*. Simone Weil says something similar: 'Lovers cannot be one' (Weil, 1972, p. 86). This is not a cause for worry, but rather of celebration since if they did satisfy our lack we would stop desiring them since all desire springs from lack, as Lacan, for one, repeatedly says. Love is an attempt at de-solitudinising ourselves. There is a loneliness, so, in love – a lack. Lack fuels love just as it creates desire. What we're looking for in the 'good enough' partner (there is no such person as Mr. Right) are all the qualities that we lack in ourselves (i.e., we *identify*), that, or we look for ourselves in others. Love is imaginary – it addresses itself to a semblance. Woody Allen caricatures this latter idea in 'Husbands and Wives': 'Spencer was searching for a woman interested in golf, inorganic chemistry, outdoor sex and the music of Bach. In short he was looking for himself, only female'. But there is an element of incompatibility in every relationship, especially between the sheets, as Lacan and countless lovers have shown. We can't just 'fit into' another person; we aren't jigsaws. Psychological lack, according to the Lacanian view, drives us.

If fantasy sustains desire, love kills it, according to this psychoanalytic perspective. 'In loving someone, we love something in them that is more than them (the *objet a*) and so we mutilate them. While I am loving you I am all the time destroying you in (unconscious) fantasy'. Othello 'loved not wisely but too well'. He strangled Desdemona because he loved her too much. 'I hate you out of love for you'. People say 'I love you *to bits*' and 'I could just eat you up'. Indeed. In 'The Ballad of Reading Gaol', Wilde gives poetic utterance to this perspective:

Some kill their love when they are young,
And some when they are old;
Some strangle with the hands of Lust,
Some with the hands of Gold;
The kindest use a knife, because

The dead so soon grow cold.

Some love too little, some too long,
Some sell, and others buy;
Some do the deed with many tears,
And some without a sigh:
For each man kills the thing he loves,
Yet each man does not die.

Seldom is it possible to find both love and desire in the same person. According to Lacan, in love we give what we don't have (the phallus) to another who doesn't want it – better if we don't understand this! According to George Bernard Shaw, love means greatly exaggerating the difference between one person and another. And Neil Simon remarked that there is only one thing worse than a hopeless romantic – and that's a hopeful one!

In the Hegelian perspective, we can say that love is wanting to be known – Hegel had said that desire desires *recognition*. The Bible talks about carnal *knowledge*. They *knew* one another. Love is a lure. Love is ambivalent – we love to hate. There is no love without hate – it is important to be able to hate those we most love. Love is narcissistic – to love, as Freud and Lacan note, is to want to be loved, even though for Aristotle love is sustained volition, in other words, to love is to will the good of the other. Love is, therefore, connected to kindness. Aristotle places altruism at the centre of love. For Aristotle, friendship is a form of love – love without wings. Aristotle felt that the good of the other related to happiness. Happiness is the goal and aim and end of life, as he makes clear in his *Ethics*. To seek the other's good is to seek their happiness but Lacan questions this by asking: what exactly is the Good? And perhaps seeking the good for someone else is actually not as moral as we are led to presume. In fact, Lacan feels that there is an aggressivity underlying the most Samaritan of aid – encountered in the activities of the philanthropist, the pedagogue and reformer. By being good to somebody, we feel good ourselves. Morality may be a reaction-formation. There is usually something in it for us. Iris Murdoch suggested: *we must be good for nothing*. Perhaps we need to love for nothing too – in an austere and unconsoled love? So when a friend goes to hug us after a prolonged period of painful absence there must be nothing in it for us – it must not console. Simone Weil: 'That is why we read in the Gospel: "I say to you that these have received their reward." There must be no compensation' (Weil, 1972, p. 22). *One must love for nothing.* Courtly love is the ideal because it is unrequited and unhappy. Courtly love is sublime rather than sexual. The troubadours were sick with desire and mourned unto death. Their love object remained inaccessible and impossible – just like the deisre of the obsessional. The courtly lover demands to be deprived. Such was the madness of their love.

Lovers say 'I missed you'. Of course. We miss each other all the time in love because of this fantasy of fusion and our unwillingness to accept the utter difference and aloneness of our partners. Love, then, is the locus, like speech and sex, of the missed encounter. In fact, far from being one at the moment of ejaculation, we are never so lonely – hence the post-coital *angst* and *tristesse* of separation after sex. In the arms of my lover I wonder: 'how long is this going to last'? The happiness here is so near to becoming quiet, resigned or desperate despair – a case of too much of a good thing. Coitus confirms solitude. Two spasms, two solitudes. *Post coitum omne animal triste*. Lucretius says: 'From the very fount of our delights there surges something bitter which gives us distress even among the flowers' (Lucretius, 1994, 1130-1).

The moment we obtain what we desire, we move on. Desire is based on continuous deferral. In her novel *A Fairly Honourable Defeat*, Iris Murdoch's character says the following:

> Human beings are roughly constructed entities full of indeterminacies and vaguenesses and empty spaces. Driven along by their private needs they latch blindly onto each other, then pull away, then clutch again. Their little sadisms and their little masochisms are surface phenomena. Anyone will do to play the roles. They never really see each other at all. There is no relationship ... which cannot easily be broken and there is none the breaking of which is a matter of any genuine seriousness. Human beings are essentially finders of substitutes (cited by Conradi, 2001, p. 502-3).

Desire is organic – it grows; the more one feeds it, the stronger it gets. Desire precludes satisfaction. There is something in the nature of human desire itself that makes total fulfilment or happiness impossible. We will always feel unsatisfied. We can never be truly happy in this picture. Happiness is fleeting. But we love to love. Love, so, is impossible. And it is impossible, too, not to play the game of love. Someone once said that love is a disease invented by poets who but for them we would never have caught the infection. La Rochefoucauld says something similar in his celebrated maxim no. 136, cited earlier: 'There are people who would never have fallen in love if they had never heard others talking about it'.

But is this all we can say about love? Is this type of love the only one that exists? Both Freud and Lacan address a certain type of love, what the Greeks called Eros. But is there a love beyond the love we have been discussing, a love beyond love as an *egoisme-à-deux*? Iris Murdoch concurs with the Freudian picture, *to an extent*:

> What seems to me ... true and important in Freudian theory is as follows. Freud takes a thoroughly pessimistic view of human nature. He sees the psyche as an egocentric system of quasi-mechanical energy, largely determined by its own individual history, whose natural attachments are sexual, ambiguous, and hard for the subject to understand or control. Introspection reveals only the deep tissue of ambivalent motive, and fantasy is a stronger force than reason. Objectivity and unselfishness are not natural to human beings (Murdoch, 1970, p. 51).

But ... Murdoch insists on the sovereignty of the Good, of the Good as sovereign concept over love because love 'can name something bad' (Murdoch, ibid., p. 102). For Murdoch, human love 'is usually self-assertive' (Murdoch, ibid). Murdoch holds the view that a refined, purified love can be identical with goodness. But is there such a love? According to the Greeks and the Scholastic metaphysicians, there is indeed such a love.

Traditionally, a distinction has been made between *concupiscent love* (loving another for one's own personal benefit) and *benevolent love* (loving another for his or her own benefit). Pure love is pure. It is benevolent love. It is loving without hope, without reward, without consolation – loving for nothing. Such is *philia* and *agape*. The Greeks, in contradistinction to Freud and Lacan, distinguished between three types of love: 1) *Eros* – understood as lust or sexual and passionate love; 2) *Philia* – friendship; and 3) *Agape* – selfless love of one's fellowman (translated into Latin as *caritas*). Christ's love is the paradigm of *caritas*. It is the love that forgives one's enemies even as one is hanging on a cross. It is a love that forgives 'seventy times seven'. It is a love without preconditions and prerequisites. Is it possible? Christians are called to this type of love, to participation in the Divine Life. It is a theological virtue. Of course, the attempt can never be fully possible. 'Be ye therefore perfect just so as your heavenly Father is'. If the Buddha's message was compassion, Christ's was love. And if you can't love, at least cease to hate or 'love and do as you want'. It is a love that does not possess and is not possessive; it is the love of which St. Paul beautifully and most movingly spoke. As Simone Weil says: 'To assume power over is to soil. To possess is to soil' (Weil, 1972, p. 58). She continues: 'to love purely is to consent to distance' (Weil, ibid.) and distance is 'the soul of the beautiful' (ibid., p. 136). This is love as non-possession. *To love is to lose*. A familiar adage runs: 'If you love someone let them go. If they come back to you, they are yours. If they don't, they never were'. It is a risk, certainly. Conversely, 'to love purely', to quote Weil again, 'is to consent to distance'. Such a love is a joyful, disinterested, non-possessive acceptance. It is willing the good of the other, as Aristotle defined it as. Spinoza defined love as *joy*. 'Love is a joy, accompanied by the idea of an external cause' (Spinoza, 1994, p. 189). Cesare Pavese wrote in his diary: 'You will be loved the day when you will be able to show your weakness without the person using it to assert his strength'. Such a love is strong in its fragility and vulnerability (read Wilde's long lovely love letter to Bosie – *De Profundis*). He obeyed Rilke's advice: 'Seek the depths of things'. Love seeks out the depths of things.

'Love and do as you wish' (see *Matthew* 5: 17), which Augustine quotes, does not mean endorsing Nietzsche's suggestion that that 'which is done out of love always takes place beyond good and evil' (Nietzsche, 1964, p. 98). No. It is not love beyond good and evil but love beyond duty. Of course love has its roots in the sexual, as Freud and Lacan suggest, and as I believe, but it cannot be reduced to the simply sexual. Kant called love an 'ideal of holiness' (Kant, 1948, p. 176). This is love functioning as *agape*. This type of love is the alpha and omega of all virtue.

We have seen Eros defined in Plato's *Symposium*. Love is the philosopher's subject *par excellence* – indeed the only subject Socrates said he knew anything about – 'I claim that love is the only thing in the world I understand'. Iris Murdoch also said: 'Like Socrates, perhaps, love is the only subject on which I am really expert?' (cited by Conradi, 2001, p. xvii). The most pressing view: love's fulfilment is the prerequisite for happiness. Aristophanes' answer is seductive: love finds for each his proper mate. Then we can become one again; Freud speaks of a 'fusional cannibalism' but one doesn't have to be a cannibal to exist. There is no happier fate, in this picture, than in locating and merging with one's true love. But the *reality* of love is somewhat different, I would contend, as we see in the works of Plato, Lucretius, Pascal, Spinoza, Nietzsche, Freud, Rilke, Proust and Lacan. Love is not a fusion but a search, a quest. 'Love', as Plato says, 'is the love of something which [one] hasn't got, and consequently lacks'. For Plato, all love is want; love is the son of *Penia* and *Poros*. As Diotima observes: love is always barefoot and homeless, in pursuit of the beautiful and the good, always searching, craving, hunting, seeking. It is 'ever insatiable', as Plotinus says of *Eros* in his commentary on Plato (see Plotinus, 1956, p. 197). This is the love that starves, that tortures one and imprisons, that is solitary and full of anguished longing and ardent pining. It is love as seizure and love as sin. If, in this Platonic picture, we desire only what we lack, what we do not have, how could we have what we desire? We can't! There are, thus, *no happy loves*. Love, in fact, is the very lack of happiness. Of course, there are some solutions. One common (and sometimes selfish) solution, which is not a salvation, is procreation – to perpetuate oneself and so partake of immortality. This was Unamuno's one passion and obsession. Religion offers another solution – religion can save love. Religion promises that love can be fully and completely satiated in *post mortem* existence but is it still love if it lacks nothing?

Three views: 1) Love as fusion (Aristophanes), 2) love as lack (Socrates/ Plato as well as Lacan), 3) love as faith in transcendence (Diotima). (C .S. Lewis talks of the four loves – affection, friendship, eros and charity). We have been here considering one type of love, which goes by the name of Eros, whose essence is want and whose climax is passion. Such wanting entails suffering and possession. I love you means I want you (in Spanish, *te quiero* means both 'I love you' and 'I want you'). This is concupiscent love, one which Plato describes in the *Phaedrus* – love as jealous possession, one that does not rejoice over the loved one's happiness but suffers when that happiness threatens its own. Love here is a gluttony of appetite (one of the seven deadly sins): 'as wolf to lamb, so lover to his lad' (see the *Phaedrus*). Eros is a jealous god and this form of 'love' (which, it has to be said, is an apt description for most of what goes by the name of love) wants to possess the beloved. If he or she is happy with someone else, you would rather see that person dead. Better for him to be unhappy with me than happy with someone else! This is the reality of the love that dare not speak its name. It pays homage to the dark god. Love has been described as 'a normal obsessional syndrome' (Allendy, 1962, p. 144). Further: 'It is the essence of love to profess to love forever but in fact to love only for a time' (Rosset, 1988, p. 54). In this picture, love can't last if it is happy.

If we desire what we can't have, we can never have what we desire and so can never be happy. Our very desire for happiness, it would seem, hinders us from attaining it. Fine but, let us ask again, is there a love beyond the love we have been talking about? Is love always doomed to frustration and failure? Or can there be a love that stems from plenitude perhaps, rather than possession or poverty? Such, according to the Greeks, is *philia* – the love of friends, which we devoted a section to earlier and, again there are different forms of friendship. Far too frequently we say 'I love you' in order to hear back the inverted echo 'I love you too'. But we should say 'I love you' for nothing and want not to hear it back. This is love as fullness, not love as lack, which always wishes to possess for that which it longs. Here love is a lightness not a heaviness; it is air and space not darkness. It is love as expansiveness not constriction. It is love as joy, freedom, and happiness. It is love as gift and grace. It cannot be summoned only attended. It is love as presence not possession. It is love as pleasure (should it exist at all). It proclaims: 'I do not love because I lack. I love and that which I love I sometimes lack' (Comte-Sponville, 2002, p. 253). *Philia* is love as joy, in the Spinozist sense – the model being, as Aristotle noted, the delight and joy mothers take in loving their children. Whereas *Eros* is love as passion and want in the Platonic sense. (Surely it is not a matter of choosing between the two?) Of course, it is easy to *fall* in love; the question is: can we stay *in* love – 'till death us do part'? Should we? Can love last the course (curse) of time? – 'I have run the race. I have kept the faith'. I don't intend to answer these questions. Suffice to say that we can all be in love even if not everyone is capable of loving. To adopt a maxim from Serge Gainsboug: we love a person for what he is not and leave him because of what he is. Love, that *egoisme à deux*: two solitudes, each sustained and inhabited by the other one. But not always. For Freud, all love was transference but the scholastic philosophers distinguished between a covetous or concupiscent love (a Freudian kind) and a benevolent love, as Aquinas called it, which is *philia* or the love of friendship. Covetous love is faithful to Plato; benevolent love is faithful to Aristotle. And of course, I agree with Freud that *philia* doesn't preclude sexuality (it can do though).

What is, of necessity, omitted in the Freudian (and Lacanian) picture is the third form of love, that is love as *agape*. Agapic love does not feature in the Freudian account of love (I am not saying it should). What is agapeic love? 'You have have heard it say, 'You shall love your neighbour and hate your enemy'. But I say to you, love your enemies and pray for those who persecute you' (*Matthew* 5: 43-44. See also *Luke* 6: 27). St. Paul calls this a stumbling block to Jews and folly to Gentiles (1 *Corinthians* 1: 23). Christic love is a love beyond love, beyond *eros* and *philia*. It is love as charity (*caritas*). It is a disinterested and selfless love, one simply not recognised in psychoanalysis. It is what the Greek of the Scriptures calls *agape* and which, in the Vulgate is rendered as *caritas*. It is divine love – the love of the Cross and of Creation. It is the love that lacks nothing but is not full of itself. It lacks nothing because it has relinquished everything. It is gratuitous and groundless, and perfectly pure. It is unconditional, like God's love. Agapeic love involves a decentering, a decreation (*décreation*), as Simone Weil calls it. Along with faith and hope, it is a theological virtue, because it has God as its ultimate object.

Three degrees of love, therefore: want, joy, charity. The ascent is from *eros* to *philia*, then perhaps as a possibility (however difficult) of moving from *philia* to *agape*. This journey is the Christian's pilgrimmage. Indeed, it is his very calling.

Lacan once remarked that all love is love of a name. Think of your lover calling you by name – it is different from the way your mother calls you. In the Song of Songs the bride, speaking of her bridegroom, says this: 'Let him kiss me with the kisses of his mouth. Your love is more delightful than wine; delicate is the fragrance of your perfume, your name is an oil poured out'. In May 1997 Iris Murdoch's response to one particular name, to the name of someone she once loved, was to say: 'His name shudders me with happiness' (cited in Conradi, 2001, p. xxi). Sometimes when night falls and one is alone in the dark of one's room one whispers into the night a name – a name that fills one not with happiness but with *jouissance*. 'You are my everything'.

10) Beauty

Yeats asked: 'Who dreamed that beauty passes like a dream?' In 1942 Albert Camus wrote: 'Beauty is unbearable, drives us to despair, offering us for a minute the glimpse of an eternity that we should like to stretch out over the whole of time'. And Rilke similarly captures the torment to which beauty can give rise in the Second Duino Elegy: 'And those who are beautiful/ oh who can retain them?'

Some seek happiness in the (sometimes agonising) enjoyment of beauty, in aesthetic appreciation. This occurs whenever beauty presents itself to our senses and judgement. It consists not only in the beauty of human forms and gestures but natural objects and landscapes and in artistic and scientific creations. Though this path to happiness cannot protect against suffering, it can compensate for it. Freud observes:

> The enjoyment of beauty has a peculiar, mildly intoxicating quality of feeling. Beauty has no obvious use; nor is there any clear cultural necessity for it. Yet civilization could not do without it. The science of aesthetics investigates the conditions under which things are felt as beautiful, but it has been unable to give any explanation of the nature and origin of beauty, and, as usually happens, lack of success is concealed beneath a flood of resounding and empty words. Psycho-analysis, unfortunately, has scarcely anything to say about beauty either. All that seems certain is its derivation from the field of sexual feeling. The love of beauty seems a perfect example of an impulse inhibited in its aim. "Beauty" and "attraction" are originally attributes of the sexual object. It is worth remarking that the genitals themselves, the sight of which is always exciting, are nevertheless hardly ever judged to be beautiful (Freud, 1982, pp. 19-20).

There is, as Gadamer, said 'something in our experience of the beautiful that arrests us and compels us to dwell upon the individual appearance itself' (Gadamer, 1986, p. 16). The beautiful is something that 'enjoys universal recognition and assent' even if it 'serves no purpose' (Gadamer, ibid., p. 14).

John Ruskin (1819-1900), the English writer makes a similar point about the uselessness of art in his *The Stones of Venice* when he says: 'Remember that the most beautiful things in the world are the most useless; peacocks and lillies for instance'. Wilde had said that all art is quite useless. Beauty first comes through the senses – it is *phenomenal* (!). As Shakespeare put it in *The Rape of Lucrece*: 'Beauty itself doth of itself persuade the eyes of men without an orator'. The nineteenth century Irish novelist Margaret Hungerford in her *Molly Bawn* opined that: 'Beauty is altogether in the eye of the beholder'. And Saki (Hector Hugh Munro, 1870-1916), the English novelist, in *Reginald's Choir Treat* mused: 'I always say beauty is only sin deep'. This is far removed from Plato's position in the *Lysis* where he says that: 'The good is the beautiful'. But Iris Murdoch says: 'The good is compulsory, the beautiful is not' (Murdoch, 1992, p. 311). For Kant, the beautiful is aesthetic, the sublime is moral. For Plato, though, beauty is the only spiritual thing we love instinctively; the beautiful could act as a starting-point for the good life. 'Plato allowed to the beauty of the lovely boy an awakening power which he denied to the beauty of nature or of art' (Murdoch, 1970, p. 88).

How wrong Helena *seems* to be in Shakespeare's *A Midsummer Night's Dream* when she opines that 'Love looks not with the eyes, but with the mind; And therefore is wing'd Cupid painted blind'. In 'As kingfishers catch fire', Gerald Manley Hopkins writes: 'Lovely in limbs, and lovely in eyes not his/ To the Father through the features of men's faces'. From Beauty to Goodness.

The lure of the look captures and captivates, ensnares. Beauty is a lure. Whether we imagine beautiful buildings or beautiful bodies on a Bermuda beach, each one of us has been affected by the phenomenon of beauty and caught in its snare, sometimes encountering the mad Medussa herself who freezes us still and strikes us dumb, beholden as we are to the face of the Other. The doomed Oedipus plucked out his eyes just as the dying Socrates shielded his eyes from his philosopher friends as he drank down the poisonous hemlock. And Padraig Pearse, the great Irish poet and patriot, penned a poem 'Fornocht do conach thu' in which he said: 'Naked I saw thee O beauty of beauty, And I blinded my eyes, For fear I should stare'. But we are touched, not just by the eyes, but by the graceful form, by the arms and legs and lips, by the voice, the gesture, the turn of phrase or nod of the head as much as by the elegant composition, sad sonnet, or lovely leaf. Philosophers from Plato up to contemporary thinkers like Lacan and Iris Murdoch have attempted to plumb the secrets, mysteries and manifold manifestations of beauty.

Pablo Picasso (1881-1973), the great Spanish painter, had this to say, as reported in *Life with Picasso*: 'I hate that aesthetic game of the eyes and the mind, played by those connoisseurs, those mandarins who "appreciate" beauty. 'And what *is* beauty anyway?' There's no such thing. I never "appreciate", any more than I "like". I love or I hate'. In the *Greater Hippias*, Plato makes a similar point when he says that though we know what a beautiful horse or man is, we can't say what 'Beauty', unattached to any object, is. The particular beauty of faces and flowers, poems and pots are somehow less problematic than the abstract concept 'Beauty'. But let us ask with Picasso and Augustine: *What is beauty*? Augustine had also asked: 'And what is beauty? What is it which charms and attracts us to the things we love?' (Augustine, 1992, p. 64). Augustine describes the distractions that beauty provided him with as they kept him away from his God:

> Late have I loved Thee, beauty so old and new: late have I loved you. And see, you were within me and I was in the external world and sought you there, and in my unlovely state I plunged into those lovely created things which you made. You were with me, and I was not with you. The lovely things kept me far from you, though if they did not have their existence in you, they had no existence at all. You called and cried out loud and shattered my deafness. You were radiant and resplendent, you put fight to my blindness. You were fragrant, and I drew in my breath and now pant after you. I tasted you, and I feel but hunger and thirst for you. You touched me, and I am set on fire to attain the peace which is yours' (Augustine, ibid., p. 201).

Symmetry, proportion, unblemished skin, luxuriant hair, cleanliness, youth, and absence of deformities are attractive in all cultures. The equation of youth and beauty is understandable in terms of evolution: teenage women have larger eyes, fuller and redder lips, smoother skin and firmer breasts. Age and pregnancies coarsen women's facial bones. Men's looks don't decline as quickly when they age. Among women, a low waist-to-hip ratio has been found to correlate with youth, health, fertility and never having being pregnant. La Rochefoucauld said this about youth: 'Youth is perpetual intoxication; it is the fever of reason' (La Rochefoucauld, 1997, maxim 271) – to love somebody who is young then. Statistical evidence has shown that the vast majority of heterosexual males find a ratio (of waist to hip size) of .70 or lower the most attractive. This is the old idea of the hourglass figure. Such is the geometry of beauty. Eye make-up enlarges the eye; lipstick enlarges the mouth. Such is beauty's masquerade. Both sexes purchase products that increase the lustre of the body generally and diet, exercise and sunbathe in order to look more beautiful. The beauty industry is big bucks. We admire the beautiful in all things, from persons to poems and paintings, from furniture to faces, from seascapes to sculptures, from buildings to Byzantine architecture.

Is beauty skin deep, soul deep or 'sin deep', as Saki, the English novelist felt? Is beauty in the eye of the beholder, as Margaret Hungerford, the Irish novelist fancied? Is it subjective or is there a 'biology' of beauty, as some evolutionary psychologists have theorised? The theme of beauty has attracted much philosophical comment from Plato and Aquinas, through to Burke, Kant (his *Third Critique*), Schopenhauer, Nietzsche, Gadamer and Iris Murdoch, amongst others.

Beauty invites, inspires, incites, excites. As Kant recognised, the pleasure we take in beauty is inexhaustible. It prompts new creations: infants, epics, sonnets, philosophic dialogues, as well as madness, melancholia, murder – 'in his gaze my ruin was writ', as Slavoj Zizek, the Lacanian commentator put it. I died in his eyes. Wittgenstein says that when the eye sees something beautiful, the hand seeks to draw it. We want to reduplicate the beautiful object. When something beautiful enters our perceptual field, our sensory horizon, our scopic vision, it causes us to gape and gaze, to suspend all thought, to stare; stunned, arrested by the beautiful object that we behold we succumb. So something *happens* when suddenly a beautiful object becomes present to us, be it a new poem or when a new student arrives on the scene. It carries a physical concomitant – tremors, paleness, palpitations, butterflies in the stomach.

In the *Phaedrus*, Plato gives an account of the destabilising effects of beauty when a man beholds a beautiful boy: he spins, shudders, shakes, shivers, sweats; he worships, makes sacrifices to the boy; feathers appear on his back and shoulder blades and his plummage lifts him up to the eternal realm. The homely Socrates meets the handsome Phaedrus and is rocked to the core. Dante trembles before the beautiful Beatrice in the *Vita Nuova*. Wilde, who said that beauty can fill a man's eyes with tears, looked into the eyes of Bosie and became beholden. Which of us can't recall a moment in time when we were transfixed, riveted, rooted to the spot on suddenly seeing someone in all their sensuous delight, in the loveliness of their countenance and attempted anything just to retain them in our field of vision? Some have died for beauty. Some have lived by banishing beauty from their midst, by sacrificing their senses.

Plato, Plotinus, Pseudo-Dionysius and Dante all speak of beauty as a 'greeting'. It is an epiphany. It calls, summons, greets us. Beauty quickens, adrenalises, makes life more animated, vivacious, alive. Sometimes, a face no longer now seen as ravishing is turned away from and even turned upon. There is beauty beheld and beauty banished. There is beauty witheld. The badness and bloom of beauty – its moral and political ambiguity (see Scarry, 1999).

The beautiful preoccupies our attention; some suggest that it diverts and distracts us from more serious social, ethical or political engagements. Some say that when we stare with sustained regard at the object of our desire or attraction, that this look is destructive to the object, harmful to the person we are admiring. Some say that they do not deserve such attention because they were 'born' with it and it's boring. People come to conclusions. How can someone so beautiful be intelligent, just, good? Beauty should not be beloved. But surely the moment of the look or the admiring gaze confers life on the object perceived? The vulnerability and ethical availability of the looker is greater, perhaps, than the person looked at. But a look or a glance can become a glare carried out in envy. We recall Augustine's comment in the *Confessions*, that once he had observed a brother glaring at his foster-brother suckling at his mother's breast – he was pale with an envenomed stare.

But beauty can lead to justice, as Iris Murdoch and Simone Weil have argued. Beauty is allied, though not identical, with truth, justice and goodness. Beauty can lead to an enlargement and alteration of the self, to the ego's transformation. It can come as a wake up call to perception – vision leading to ethical action. Plato requires the move from *eros* to *caritas*, from beauty to care. When we see something beautiful standing there, shimmering forth before our senses we undergo a decentering; we cede ground to the Other. Iris Murdoch calls this change in consciousness an 'unselfing'. According to Murdoch in *The Sovereignty of Good*, the most 'obvious thing in our surroundings which is an occasion for "unselfing" and that is what is popularly called beauty'. This is the moral benefit of beauty, its ethical alchemy. The beautiful can ignite ethical behaviour and bring us into the presence of the just, the good and the true (*à la* Iris Murdoch and Emmanuel Levinas). A brush with beauty can come as a carrion call to a conversion of consciousness. Murdoch observes: 'The apprehension of beauty ... seems to us like a temporally located spiritual experience which is a source of good energy .... Beauty appears as the visible and accessible aspect of the Good' (Murdoch, 1997, pp. 356-7). Murdoch is here, as elsewhere, a modern Platonist. In 'The Sovereignty of Good Over other Concepts', she writes of Plato: 'Plato held that beauty could be a starting point of the good life' (Murdoch, ibid., p. 372). In 'The Fire and the Sun: Why Plato Banished the Artists', Murdoch similarly writes: 'Beauty gives us an immediate image of good desire, the desire for goodness and the desire for truth. We are attracted to the real in the guise of the beautiful and the response to this attraction brings joy .... The proper apprehension of beauty is joy in reality through the transfiguring of desire' (Murdoch, ibid., p. 425). We will see shortly that Lacan says something quite different.

Simone Weil defines the beautiful 'as that which we can contemplate. A statue, a picture which we can gaze at for hours. The beautiful is something on which we can fix our attention' (Weil, 1972, p. 135), such as Gregorian music, for example. Though the beautiful is a carnal attraction we must resist possessing it. We must keep our distance, according to Weil. 'We want to eat all ... objects of desire. The beautiful is that which we desire without wishing to eat it' (Weil, ibid., p. 136). Later on, she notes: 'Beauty: a fruit which we look at without trying to seize it' (Weil, ibid., p. 137), nor should we draw back either. Perhaps the beautiful is the real presence of God in matter. If this were the case, contact with beauty would be a sacrament. But, Weil wonders, 'how is it that there are so many perverted aesthetes?' (Weil, ibid., p. 138).

In a Kantian vein I believe that beauty is not purely in the eye of the beholder, that it is not merely subjective but that it possesses a 'quasi objective reality', in Kant's words. Aquinas proffered a threefold division of beauty, taken up by Joyce in the conversation between Stephen Dedalus and his friend Lynch in the *Portrait of an Artist as a Young Man*: integrity (*integritas*), proportion or harmony (*consonantia*) and clarity (*claritas*). Symmetry (proportion of the parts) is the attribute most steadily singled out in philosophical discussions on beauty. In *De Musica*, Augustine notes: 'Beautiful things please by proportion'. He talks about the 'body's soft, smooth surface, *corpora, leniter mollia*'. Aquinas had observed that 'the beautiful is that which when seen pleases' (Aquinas, *S.T.*, pt. I, q. 5, art. 5). Edmund Burke defines beauty thus: 'By beauty I mean, that quality or those qualities in bodies by which they cause love, or some passion similar to it' (Burke, 1958, p. 91). And Schopenhauer remarks: 'Everything is beautiful only so long as it does not concern us' (Schopenhauer, 1969, p. 374). For Schopenhauer, the beautiful (especially in art) calms the will; it counteracts sexual interest. Kant had spoken of the three kinds of delight – in the beautiful, the agreeable and the good, calling the taste for the beautiful the one and only free and disinterested delight. Stendhal:'The beautiful is a *promise* of happiness'. For Stendhal, the function and effect of the beautiful is to *arouse* the will. The beautiful does not free us from torture. Oh no. It can induce it.

Beauty *arrests*. And I think there is something more going on, apart from this physical phenomenality. There is a metaphysics of beauty. It is not just all show, sentience and sensuousness. There is beauty's seriousness, a place, perhaps, where ethics may meet aesthetics? In the *Tractatus*, Wittgenstein went so far as to say that these two terms were identical: 'Ethics and aesthetics are one and the same' (proposition 6.421 of the *Tractatus*).

Traditionally, the beautiful is placed near to the good (we have seen this in Plato and Iris Murdoch) but Lacan interstingly says, though he doesn't elaborate, that 'the beautiful is closer to evil than to the good' (Lacan, 1992, p. 217). It certainly occupies the centre of moral experience. Beauty is desire made visible. Lacan defines the beautiful as an element that occupies the field of the 'beyond-the-good-principle' (Lacan, ibid., p. 237). There is a strange and ambiguous relationship between beauty and desire. Beauty disarms desire. The beautiful has the effect of lowering and suspending desire. 'The appearance of beauty intimidates and stops desire' (Lacan, ibid., p. 238). Beauty is insensitive to outrage. Beauty keeps us awake. Beauty is a bait, a lure. There is a beauty that mustn't be touched. Saint Thomas insists on the tempering or extinction of desire through the effect of beauty but the effect of beauty on desire is one of instinctual excitement, but more, it makes you lose the head. Perhaps that is why Lacan placed beauty nearer to evil than goodness. Plato's *Phaedrus* is a dialogue on the beautiful and its effects, which we have already cited. There is a link between the phenomena of beauty and the play of pain. It is painful to behold the beautiful. Lacan opines that grace is beauty's finest flower (see Lacan, ibid., p. 261). Kant's *Critique of Judgement* treats of nothing else. Perhaps the function of the beautiful is to reveal the relationship of man to his own death, and in a flash that is not brilliant? (see Lacan, ibid., p. 295). The French philosopher, Michel Foucault, died for beauty and, when discussing the risk of AIDS, which he got, said: 'Besides, to die for the love of boys: what could be more beautiful?' (cited in Rodgers and Thompson, 2005, p. 223). I end this section with a question, one posed by Henry James: 'To whom do you beautifully belong?' Now that is a question.

11) Freedom

In the sentence that begins chapter one of his *Contrat Social* Rousseau famously said: 'Man was born free, and he is everywhere in chains'. He also opined:

'Obedience to a law which one prescribes to oneself is freedom'. In *Man and People* José Ortega y Gasset (whom Camus calls 'the greatest European writer after Nietzsche') opines: 'We are forced to be free' (Ortega, 1957, p. 58). This Spanish philosopher makes a number of points: firstly, that life is personal, secondly, that one's life is lived in view of circumstances, thirdly, we are obliged to exercise our freedom, and fourthly and finally, life is untransferable – it is my responsibility. These are the attributes Ortega accords to life: personal, circumstantial, untransferable and responsible. According to Ortega: 'I am free *by compulsion*, whether I wish to be or not' (Ortega, 1961, p. 203). To be free is to be able to be other than what one was. For Ortega, man is infinitely plastic. He elaborates a non-Eleatic conception of being, as others have elaborated a non-Euclidean geometry. As Ortega puts it: 'The time has come for the seed sown by Heralcitus to bring forth its mighty harvest' (Ortega, ibid.). Freedom, so, consists in that compulsory choice among possibilities. Man is, thus, necessarily and constitutively free but he is not completely or forever free. He does not have the freedom to renounce his freedom. Man is the novelist of himself. We seem not to possess a fixed or static being. Our being is freedom to be. We can always be different from what we have been. Life is change, as Heraclitus held, and endless becoming. Only death frees us from change and renders us eternal.

Of course, the French Revolution with their catchcry of *liberté, fraternité*, and *egalité* proudly proclaimed freedom or liberty. Leisure, as Aristotle first noted, is freedom from necessity. In *The Politics* he describes it as a total pleasure involving the cultivation of the mind. Democracy holds that all 'men' (!) are freeborn citizens and are the subjects of rights (and responsibilities). Hobbes makes the point in his *Leviathan* that liberty (the absence of external impediments) is a 'right of nature' and inheres in man as such. This is the freedom to exercise one's own reason in one's own way according to the dictates of one's own nature. It was one of the dreams of the Enlightenment. For John Locke (see his *The Second Treatise of Government*) liberty and equality are as close as identical twins. If all are equal, all are free from one another. In short, equality *is* freedom. And freedom is the cardinal feature, according to these thinkers, of man's being. Simone Weil speaks of liberty being an essential and vital need of the soul in her book *The Need for Roots*, posthumously published like all her works. For Weil, liberty consists in the ability to choose. She observes: 'Only the human being is fit to be free' (Weil, 1987, p. 31). So liberty or freedom is one of the fourteen needs of the soul; the others are order, obedience, responsibility, equality, hierarchism, honour, punishment, freedom of opinion, security, risk, private property, collective property, and truth – the need for truth being more sacred than any other need.

The question is: how free are we? Freud is often seen as a determinist. Undoubtedly, there is some determinism present in psychoanalysis. Indeed, Freud speaks of 'the illusion of Free Will' in his *Introductory Lectures on Psycho-Analysis* (Freud, 1916-17, p. 1919) and asserts in *Five Lectures on Psycho-Analysis* that 'psychoanalysts are marked by a particularly strict belief in the determinism of mental life' (Freud, 1910, p. 38).

Determinism is the view that every action in the universe, including human actions, is caused and therefore fixed by some prior events. Events, thus, couldn't have happened otherwise – there is a chain of prior causes that determines every action. If determinism is true, it would seem to preclude freedom. *Strict* determinism holds that human beings are in no sense free while *soft* determinism (i.e., compatibalism) attempts to make some place for free will. Most critics and defenders too attribute hard determinism to Freud. There are only eight references to determinism in the twenty-four volumes that comprise the *Standard Edition*. Freud suggests a 'psychic determinism' but implies that freedom (*Freiheit*) is one of the main goals of psychoanalytic praxis. In the early, more mechanistic Freud of 1883-1890 there is evidence of his embracing a strong determinist doctrine, which seems to have waned somewhat in the middle period of 1900-1919, and the later Freud asserts that the ego has some control over the id, the demands of the drives and has a capacity for freedom of choice. One of Freud's aims was to increase his patients' freedom – freedom from neurosis. In *The Ego and the Id*, Freud maintains that making a person aware of conscious and unconscious factors is giving 'the patient's ego freedom' (Freud, 1923, p. 50) and 'On Psychotherapy', he talks of 'conscious will-power' (Freud, 1905, p. 266). It would seem that Freud had a 'thin' view of freedom and a 'soft' view of determinism *à la* Hobbes and Hume. In other words, some determinism is compatible with some freedom. The ego acts in a relatively free manner but *within* a psychologically determinist context.

However, the great philosopher of freedom is Jean-Paul Sartre, so we will see what he says on the subject.

It was Sartre, though, who made man absolutely and unconditionally free. He is the philosopher of freedom *par excellence*. For Sartre, man is *condemned* to be free. In his essay, *Existentialism and Humanism*, he writes:

We are left alone, without excuse. That is what I mean when I say that man is condemned to be free. Condemned, because he did not create himself, yet is nevertheless at liberty, and from the moment that he is thrown into this world he is responsible for everything he does (Sartre, 1987, p. 34).

Even the choice to have no choice is itself a choice. We make our own identity and make ourselves whatever we choose to be. We are free because we define who and what we are. As he puts it: 'Man is nothing else but that which he makes of himself' (Sartre, ibid., p. 28). Man is what he does. So despite the conditioning limits of our past or present, our future offers itself to us as a '*tabula rasa*', as a blank slate waiting to be filled in. Sartre puts every man in possession of himself and places the responsibility for his existence squarely on his own shoulders. He gives the example of Paul Valéry. Paul Valéry was indeed a petit bourgeois Parisian but he succeeded in becoming one of the greatest poets France had ever produced. His class and backgroud etc dictated that he becomes a plumber or plasterer but he recreated and fashioned himself anew. So we are free and not free not to be free. Sartre's philosophy entails a philosophy of freedom, choice and responsibility as well as anxiety. The realisation of the inescapability of choice is accompanied by the experience of anxiety. Man 'cannot escape from the sense of complete and profound responsibility' (Sartre, ibid., p. 30). Sartre is opposed, therefore, to all forms of determinism including what he perceives to be the determinism of Freudian psychoanalysis. He states that 'there is no determinism – man is free, man *is* freeedom' (Sartre, ibid., p. 34). We make our moral choices in spite of our environmental factors to become heroes or cowards, great or small. Sartre's philosophy is an appeal to total freedom. Those who hide or attempt to escape from this freeedom commit an act of 'bad faith' – *mauvaise foi.*

Sartre gives the example of a student coming to see him to ask him his advise as to whether he should fight in the war for the Allies or stay at home with his ailing mother. Sartre says: 'You are fee, therefore choose' (Sartre, ibid., p. 38) and makes the interesting point that he has already probably made up his mind and only wants Sartre to confirm him in his decision. And even if he chooses to ask someone else for his or her advice, for example a priest, he still has to choose which priest to ask. An army chaplain will more than likely tell him to fight, a priest friend of the family's will more than likely tell him to stay and look after his sick mother (see Sartre, ibid., p. 35). Sartre observes: 'That is what 'abandonment' implies, that we ourselves decide our being. And with this abandonment goes anguish' (Sartre, ibid., p. 39). He continues: 'In life, a man commits himself, draws his own portrait and there is nothing but that portrait' (Sartre, ibid., p. 42). Sartre feels that his existentialist ethic is alone compatible with the dignity of man (see Sartre, ibid., pp. 44-5). What is at the heart of his existentialism is the character of the absolute free commitment. Man is a free being who cannot but will his freedom. He reproaches those who try to escape from such a freedom, thus:

> Those who hide from this total freedom, in a guise of solemnity or with deterministic excuses, I shall call cowards. Others who try to show that their existence is necessary, when it is merely an accident of the appearance of the human race on earth, - I shall call scum' (Sartre, ibid., p. 52).

But are we really this free? For those of us who believe that there are unconscious mental proceeses it is impossible to accept Sartre's doctrine. However, the man who said that man was a 'useless passion' devoted himself to the problem of freedom with a passion that wasn't entirely useless.

Aquinas, like most of the mediaevals, devoted a lot of his time to the free will debate and wonders whether human beings choose their actions freely or whether such choices are compelled. Will, like mind, is an immaterial power; Aquinas opined that will's love moves us more ardently than mind's knowledge (see Aquinas, 1993, p. 173). If knowledge assimilates, love transforms, as Pseudo-Dionysius says. If it is true that nothing causes its own existence, will must be moved by something else but what is moved by something else is placed under compulsion, so will must will under compulsion and not freely. Augustine says that unless one resists habit, it compels one. However, in Ecclesiasticus 15 we read: 'God made human beings in the beginning, then left them to their own deliberations'. This means that they had free choice, which Aristotle defines as a 'deliberated desire'. Will is a power in reason. For Aristotle, we are able to act or not to act but this is because we can freely choose. Some have suggested that human will is compelled to choose what it does, though not coerced (not all compulsion is violent) but Aquinas rejects this opinion as being 'philosophically anarchic', as it opposes faith and destroys the foundation of ethics. If we are not free to will but compelled, everything that comprises ethics vanishes – exhorting, commanding, punishing, praising etc. Habit doesn't compel one totally since however habituated one is we can go against a habit – difficult granted, but not impossible. For Ortega too, life 'is at the same time freedom and fatality' (Ortega, 1960, p. 241). And again, 'life is fate in freedom' (Ortega, ibid., p. 222). So, free to a certain extent. Free enough. Fearing freedom too, as Fromm suggested. Free so, but free for what? Isn't that the more interesting question? This brings us to the end of our philosophical account of Freud's eleven paths to happiness.

Despite the acknowledged incompleteness of Freud's enquiry and enumeration, he concludes *Civilization and Its Discontents* by saying that the 'programme of becoming happy, which the pleasure principle imposes on us cannot be fulfilled' (Freud, 1982, p. 20) even if we seek pleasure (the positive aspect) or seek to avoid pain (the negative aspect). 'By none of these paths can we attain all that we desire' (Freud, ibid.). Happiness is a problem and there is no golden rule. 'Every man must find out for himself in what particular fashion he can be saved' (Freud, ibid). Much will depend on one's psychical constitution. The erotic individual will give his preference to emotional relationships with others; the narcissist will gain satisfaction from his own internal mental processes while the man of action will commit to the external world. Freud advises: 'Just as a cautious business-man avoids tying up all his capital in one concern, so, perhaps, worldly wisdom will advise us not to look for the whole of our satisfaction from a single aspiration' (Freud, ibid., p. 21). Success in happiness is never certain and it depends on the convergence of many factors, not least environment and on one's psychical constitution. 'The man who sees his pursuit of happiness come to nothing in later years can still find consolation in the yield of pleasure of chronic intoxication; or he can embark on the desperate attempt at rebellion seen in a psychosis' (Freud, ibid.).

So, for both Aristotle and Freud, the goal of life is happiness. Happiness is not just about maximising agreeable feeling. Happiness, according to the Freudian formulation, is an 'inclusive' rather than 'dominant' end. In other words, the activities through which happiness is sought are not instrumental means but parts of a whole. As one commentator summarises:

> To pursue happiness as an inclusive goal through such activities as artisitic creativity, intellectual work, sensuality, love, and aesthetic appreciation is to enjoy each of these activities as contributing something qualitatively unique to a life plan. Insofar as these activities are "means", it is the sense of being "constitutive of" the comprehensive end of happiness in life as a whole. It is only through such activities that genuine happiness in the sense of a "positive fulfilment" is possible (Wallwork, 1991, p. 133).

All kinds of factors are involved in determining how a given person finds happiness in life, from innate endowments to environmental opportunities and sheer luck. But the eleven paths that Freud mentions are recommended by various philosophical and religious schools and practised by ordinary people everywhere. Happiness, we can say, is the supreme goal of human life.

That said, some of the paths are negative while others are more positive. Freud does evaluate them. The negative paths to happiness seek an absence of pain and unpleasure while the positive paths aim at procuring strong feelings of pleasure. Freud designates six of the paths as being negative: 1) unrestricted want satisfaction, 2) isolation, 3) intoxication, 4) asceticism, 5) illusion, and 6) delusion. Though these six may be undesirable, most people will make modest use of some of these defense strategies for living. Unrestricted want satisfaction is self-defeating because it puts enjoyment before the caution required to attain one's basic needs. Isolation is rejected because there is a better way: 'that of becoming a member of the human community'. Intoxication can be injurious to one's health. Alcoholism wastes a large portion of energy, which might have been better employed elsewhere. Asceticism reduces the pressure of modern life so that non-satisfaction is not felt as much but it diminishes the potentialities of enjoyment. Illusory satisfactions in fantasies and delusional remoldings of reality are both criticised for their lack of truthfullness. In *The Future of an Illusion*, Freud argues against the wish-fulfilling nature of religious belief, which makes people believe themselves to be happier in this world than they are in reality.

In contradistinction, Freud endorses the five remaining paths to the alleviation of man's misery: 1) participation in the human community (and the value inherent in freely chosen productive work and social solidarity), 2) sublimation (as in the pursuit of knowledge and artistic creativity), 3) mutual love, 4) aesthetic enjoyment, and 5) freedom. Each of these embodies a distinct enjoyment that is valuable not only in itself but also for the contribution it can make to society as a whole (societal as well as individual happiness). These are the paths then, the eleven paths. As Freud recognises: 'There are ... many paths which *may* lead to such happiness as is attainable by men, but there is none which does so for certain' (Freud, 1982, p. 22). Even with all the advances in medicine and technology that our civilisation has enjoyed 'man does not feel happy in his Godlike character' (Freud, ibid., p. 29). Despite all our philosophical, artistic and scientific achievements, '*inter urinas et faeces nascimur*' ('we are born between urine and faeces' – see Freud, ibid., p. 43).

Freud finds two urges in men: the egoistic and the altruistic one. The 'development of the individual seems to us to be a product of the interaction between two urges, the urge towards happiness, which we usually call "egoistic", and the urge towards union with others in the community, which we call "altruistic"' (Freud, ibid., p. 77). We selfishly want to be happy, but don't we deserve to be? The urge to happiness is a strong one; it is *urgent* and each man must pursue his own path in life. Some people, like Aristotle and Aquinas, will admire the order in the universe and see the hand and love of God; others like Freud will look upon the same universe and see only chaos and disorder. To Freud's 'dull eyes' (Freud, ibid., p. 78), the play is an eternal struggle between Eros and Thanatos – love and hate and 'it is this battle of the giants that our nurse-maids try to appease with their lullaby about Heaven' (Freud, ibid., p. 59). Freud says that he has found his way to these 'deepest truths' through 'tormenting uncertainty and with restless groping' (Freud, ibid., p. 70). The struggle is between the individual and society, Eros and Thanatos and the two urges – one individual, the other cultural. 'So, also, the two urges, the one towards personal happiness and the other towards union with other human beings must struggle with each other in every individual' (Freud, ibid., p. 78). But this struggle is the very stuff of life. Religion promises a better, happier life in Heaven but, according to Freud, 'so long as virtue is not rewarded here on earth, ethics will, I fancy, preach in vain' (Freud, ibid., p. 80). Freud concludes *Civilization and Its Discontents* by asserting that he can listen to the person who says that 'the whole effort is not worth the trouble' (Freud, ibid., p. 82) 'without indignation' (Freud, ibid., p. 81). Freud writes: 'I have not the courage to rise up before my fellow-men as a prophet, and I bow to their reproach that I can offer them no consolation: for at bottom that is what they are all demanding – the wildest revolutionaries no less passionately than the most virtuous believers' (Freud, ibid., p. 82).

Freud died within a decade of writing these lines. We can only wonder about Freud's last agony of the mind and how he contemplated his own impending death, his last days, but he probably did it with the philosophical stoicism and resilience with which he had approached life. In *Metamorphoses* (III, 135), Ovid wrote: 'You must await a man's last day: before his death and last funeral rites, no one should be called happy'. Solon similarly says that no one can be called happy until they have passed through the last days of their life on account of the uncertainty of fate. According to Montaigne, Solon intended to tell us that 'happiness in life (depending as it does on the tranquility and contentment of a spirit well-born and on the resolution and assurance of an ordered soul) may never be attributed to any man until we have seen him act out the last scene in his play, which is indubitably the hardest' (Montaigne, 1925, p. 87). In all the other scenes we wear an actor's mask but there is no more feigning in the last scene as it plays itself out between death and ourselves. The mask is ripped off and truth emerges. All of man's actions, all his deeds, dastardly or daring, must be judged and tried on the touchstone of the final deed and death should be borne well, 'in a quiet and muted manner' (Montaigne, ibid., p. 88). For we are only properly named, as Lacan remarked, at the hour of our burial.

In *Studies on Hysteria*, Freud had told us that the aim of psychoanalysis was to replace suffering by (common) human unhappiness. If this is so, isn't happiness ultimately, in this picture, a neurosis? We now turn to Freud's famous French follower, Jacques Lacan, who takes up the logic of the Freudian position on the subject.

Chapter Ten
Unamuno and Lacan: Happiness as *Jouissance*

We are sometimes less unhappy in being deceived by those we love than in being undeceived by them.

La Rochefoucauld

In this chapter I wish to explore the idea of happiness as *jouissance* as this features in the thought of two very different Continental thinkers: Jacques Lacan (1901-1981) and Miguel de Unamuno (1864-1936).

Lacan

Lacan, Freud's faithful French follower, informs us: 'Certainly Freud leaves no doubt, any more than Aristotle, that what man is seeking, his goal, is happiness' (Lacan, 1992, p.13). Everyman 'aspires to happiness. The truth than man seeks happiness remains true' (Lacan, ibid., p. 187). However, though Freud concurs with Aristotle (he studied Aristotle under Brentano with his class-mate, Husserl), Freud differs from Aristotle and from the humanistic psychologies of Maslow, Rogers and Fromm in his views about the relation of natural human capacities to the ideal of happiness. In contrast to the classical theory of human happiness, represented by Aristotle *par excellence*, Freud's idea of the happy person is not someone who actualises innate potentialities within a particular social milieu but someone who has also come to terms with his intrapsychic vicissitudes. Any number of the eleven paths may lead to this elusive goal of happiness but none can do so for certain. 'There is no golden rule which applies to everyone'. In fact, Freud goes further in *Civilization and Its Discontents*, as we have seen. Lacan summarises the Freudian position on happiness thus, in relation to the human subject: 'If there is indeed something that can be called his good or happiness, there is nothing to be expected in that regard from the microcosm, nor moreover from the macrocosm' (Lacan, ibid., p. 34). Moreover, if I wish for the happiness of my lover, I sacrifice my own. But who knows if my lover's happiness is not dissipated too (see Lacan, ibid., p. 187).

Aristotle makes pleasure central in his *Ethics*. As Lacan asks: 'What is happiness if it doesn't contain the bloom of pleasure?' (Lacan, ibid., p. 27). But Freud shows us that at the level of the pleasure principle there is no Sovereign Good – 'that the Sovereign Good, which is *das Ding*, which is the mother, is also the object of incest, is a forbidden good, and that there is no other good. Such is the foundation of the moral law as turned on its head by Freud' (Lacan, ibid., p. 70). *Das Ding* is the object of desire; it is the lost object; it is the mother, the forbidden object of incestuous desire, which is what the subject desires as the key to his happiness. The Thing is the subject's Sovereign Good but if the subject attains this

Good by transgressing the pleasure principle, it is experienced as suffering or evil (*mal*). The subject 'cannot stand the extreme good that *das Ding* may bring to him' (Lacan, ibid., p. 73). The Thing pertains to the register of the Real. Happiness belongs to the pleasure principle. The beyond-the-pleasure-principle, that is to say, the death drive, as well as desire, subverts happiness, makes us less happy. If happiness happens, it surprises us, breaks in on us – it's a rupture, an interruption, made possible fortuitously.

Lacan says that happiness is demanded by those who have had an analysis. 'In the first place, is it the end of analysis that is demanded of us? What is demanded can be expressed in a simple word, *bonheur* or "happiness", as they say in English. I'm not saying anything new in that; a demand for happiness is doubtless involved here' (Lacan, ibid., p. 292). But this goal is always indefinitely postponed, due to the nature of desire, as we have said. Happiness, as Saint-Just says, has become a political issue – 'there is no satisfaction for the individual outside of the satisfaction of all'. The analyst receives a demand for happiness, but like all demands, this one can wait. Moreover, the analyst cannot give the patient this; he cannot make him happy. Happiness is problematic, analytically speaking, in a way it wasn't for Aristotle. From Aristotle to Freud is a long trajectory. The unconscious buts in. 'Since Aristotle's time we have experienced a complete reversal of point of view' (Lacan, ibid., p. 13). Lacan observes: 'There is in Aristotle a discipline of happiness. He shows the paths along which he intends to lead anyone who is willing to follow him in his problematic, paths which in different spheres of potential activity lead to the realization of one of the functions of virtue' (Lacan, ibid., p. 292). But there is nothing similar in psychoanalysis. Happiness is not to be found in love, in genital satisfaction, nor in adjustment to reality (social engineering) - good heavens, no! Perhaps sublimation comes close – the sublimation of a drive without necessitating repression. Psychoanalysis insists, instead, on realising one's desire rather than setting out on a search for happiness. And for Lacan, the only sin of which we can be guilty is surrendering that (analysed/informed/experienced) desire. Desire has the force of a Last Judgement – 'have you acted in conformity with the desire that is in you?' Desire makes happiness impossible, psychoanalytically speaking, and one always pays a price for access to desire. Desire makes life difficult. Lacan admits: 'things don't always seem to me to be that much fun' (Lacan, ibid., p. 296). He reminds us of the story of the individual who emigrated from Germany to America and who was asked, 'Are you happy?' 'Oh yes, I am very happy', he answered, 'I am very, very happy, *aber nicht glücklich!*' ['but not happy'] (Lacan, ibid., p. 13). Happiness is not a category of truth but, to put it in the philosopher, Alan Badiou's terms, a category of mere Being and hence, inconsistent and confused, as in the above story. Happiness is not man's Sovereign Good because there is no Sovereign Good at the level of pleasure, but only at the level of *jouissance*. Lacan wryly notes:

> That's something to remember whenever the analyst finds himself in the position of responding to anyone who asks him for happiness. The question of the Sovereign Good is one that man has asked himself since time

immemorial, but the analyst knows that it is a question that is closed. Not only doesn't he have that Sovereign Good that is asked of him, but he also knows there isn't any. To have carried an analysis through to its end is no more nor less than to have encountered that limit in which the problematic of desire is raised (Lacan, ibid., pp. 299-300).

Desire sustains itself by not being satisfied. Love is supposed to fill up the hole, the lack, introduced by desire. Desire is always directed at something other and more than the object demanded. Happiness is demanded but not desired. The 'realisation of desire', of which Lacan speaks in the *Ethics*, does not mean 'the fulfilment of desire'. Desire never ends. To realise one's desire is to realise the (impossible) infinite, the infinite of desire. As Lacan notes, in relation to Kant: 'The moral law, looked at more closely, is simply desire in its pure state' (Lacan, 1977, p. 275). Happiness, as the Real Thing, represents the subject's pathology that prevents him from acting ethically.

Now according to Lacan: 'Psychoanalysis makes the whole achievement of happiness turn on the genital act' (Lacan, 1992, p. 300). Hap-penis. What are we to make of this? Let's continue with the quotation, which puts it in context:

It is, therefore, necessary to draw the proper consequences from this. It is doubtless possible to achieve for a single moment in this act something which enables one human being to be for another in the place that is both living and dead of the Thing. In this act and only at this moment, he may simulate with his flesh the consummation of what he is not under any circumstances. But even if the possibility of this consummation is polarizing and central, it cannot be considered timely (Lacan, ibid.).

We are not the Thing for the other in the non-sexual relationship, in the impossibility of union. *Happiness is to come*, indefinitely. Here's the rub: at the moment of ejaculation we are most alone. One plus one makes two. One cannot overcome one's separation, one's castration, one's lack. Desire springs from lack; fantasy sustains it and love kills it. It is fortunate that our sexual partners cannot fulfil our desire because if they did, we would cease to desire them. We want what we don't have. Love *is* lack, for the Lacanian but for the Christian a question will always remain and a doubt will always linger – is there not a love beyond love, a love stemming from a source of superabundance like the one proclaimed by Saint Paul, a love perhaps beyond the ego? Lacan:

What the analyst has to give, unlike the partner in the act of love, is something that even the most beautiful bride in the world cannot outmatch, that is to say, what he has. And what he has is nothing other than his desire, like that of the analysand, with the difference that it is an experienced desire. What can a desire of this kind, the desire of the analyst, be? We can say right away what it cannot be. It cannot desire the impossible (Lacan, ibid.).

It's a question, so, of desire rather than (impossible) happiness. The 'promise of analysis grants no other' (Lacan, ibid., p. 301). As Lacan later puts it: 'There is no other good than that which may serve to pay the price for access to desire – given that desire is understood here, as we have defined it elsewhere, as the metonymy of our being' (Lacan, ibid., p. 321). In religion, the good is sacrificed for (sublime) desire. The laws of heaven are the laws of desire.

Because of the Fall (to draw on the religious register of human existence) and because of the fact that we can never return to the bliss enjoyed at the breast (to employ psychoanalytic language), we are condemned to being in a state of what I have called 'divine discontent'. Our home is elsewhere. There is something uncanny (*unheimlich*) about our exiled life on earth. Desire is always caught up in saying 'this is not that', 'that's not what I wanted'. When we obtain what we think we want, what we assume will make us happy, what happens? We go on wanting; we go on desiring to death. Desire thrives in the gap that eternally 'separates the *obtained* satisfaction from the *sought-for* satisfaction' (Zizek 2001, p. 90). There is a constant distance and dehiscence between the subject and the object of one's desire (a lost object) and a continual displacement onto substitute objects that attract us by occupying the place left desolate and empty by the lost object.

Due to the divine within us (however we conceive this to be), we can never be fully human or completely happy. Our Now looks always to the Beyond of its ultimate fulfilment. Furthermore, unconsciously and due to the death drive, we sometimes subvert our happiness for all sorts of psychological reasons, not least out of the belief that we don't deserve to be happy. Speaking of the drive, Zizek, the Slovenian Lacanian philosopher, notes: 'The Freudian drive, however, designates precisely the paradox of "wanting unhappiness", of finding excessive pleasure in suffering itself' (Zizek, 2003, p. 23). Happiness is elusive; it will always escape us. It elides the grasp – it may be approached but never appropriated. Happiness is, as Freud felt, episodic in nature. That is all but maybe it's enough. To paraphrase a passage from the Song of Songs, we sought happiness but found it not.

But let's not totally despair: the human subject is always getting off on something even if it is dissatisfaction. *We are happy in our unhappiness.* We are content in our misery and suffering. We are happier, so, than we think, according to the Lacanian view. Our symptoms afford us with endless pleasure. Freud found that people didn't really want to get better, to be cured. La Rochefoucauld noted: 'Those who have had great passions find themselves during the whole of their lives both happy and unhappy at being cured of them' (La Rochefoucauld, 1997, maxim 485). Our passions and symptoms are a constant source of *jouissance*. It would seem, therefore, that we are always happy but because we are more familiar with unpleasure and pain, we are unable to tolerate too much happiness. Too much happiness is a burden, is injurious, is bad for us – harmful to our (psychic) health. Too much happiness is a kind of death. The French call sexual orgasm *le petit mort* – the little death. Moreover, happiness, like suffering, is subjective. Montaigne also held that too much joy is overbearing – we simply can't endure too much pleasure. Ovid opined that there is a certain painful pleasure (*jouissance*) in our tears. And La Rochefoucauld had said that 'we weep to be wept over' (La Rochefoucauld, ibid., maxim 233). Our unhappiness is not simply the result of not getting our desires fulfilled but rather of a surplus of *jouissance*, an excess, that is shameful to us, one which we don't want to acknowledge as providing us with pleasure and happiness. It is in our symptoms and suffering that we find our favourite forms of enjoyment (a masochistic *jouissance* but a *jouissance* nonetheless). This is the Good News: that we are a lot happier than we thought with these endless sources of painful pleasures. We are, so, justified in speaking of happiness in this context, or in its guise, as *jouissance*. Unhappiness and happiness are not absolute opposites, then, but simply two sides of the same coin and the result of our submersion in life, this life. As Beckett said: 'You're on earth; you're on earth. There's no cure for that'. The notion that the goal of life is to be happy is pure paganism. The idea of living 'happily ever after' is the Christianised version of a pagan concept, as Zizek notes, in his *Welcome to the Desert of the Real* (Zizek, 2002, p. 59).

It is tempting to see happiness as an American construct, the febrile search for which may become destructive or futile or both, as it so easily slips away – the American, anarcho-capitalist dream dispensed with. After all, Thomas Jefferson held that the pursuit of happiness was an inalienable *right* (a right?). It is enshrined in the Declaration of Independence. Lacan launched a blistering critique of the 'American way', which guides Americans towards happiness, seeing it as a subtle and not so sibtle form of social engineering. Slavoj Zizek, describes America thus: 'the USA., the ultimate empire of the (pursuit of) happiness' (Zizek, ibid.). Maybe we need to go to America in order to be happy!

The 'American way of life' revolves around such signifiers as 'happiness'. This is part of the culture of the United States. In 1950, Lacan coined the term 'factor *c*' (*facteur c*), which may be defined as the constant characteristic of any given cultural milieu. *C* stands for culture. It is part of the Symbolic order; it is that which defines the featues of one's culture as opposed to another. Lacan gives 'ahistoricism' as an example of the *c* factor of the culture of the USA

In Lacanian terms, *happiness is the betrayal of desire* (see Zizek, ibid., p. 58). This is the key psychoanalytic insight. Zizek observes that happiness:

> ... relies on the subject's inability or unreadiness fully to confront the consequences of its desire: the price of happiness is that the subject remains stuck in the inconsistency of its desire. In our daily lives, we (pretend to) desire things which we do not really desire, so that, ultimately, the worst thing that can happen is for us to get what we "officially" desire. Happiness is thus inherently hypocritical: it is the happiness of dreaming about things we do not really want (Zizek, ibid., pp. 59-60).

Understood thus, we shouldn't aim at being happy but at locating the Real Cause of our desire. The bad news is that there is no happiness pill. The good news, as we have said is that we're happier than we think – happy being unhappy. As La

Rochefoucauld observed: 'We console ourselves for being unhappy by a certain pleasure we find in appearing so' (La Rochefoucauld, 1997, maxim 573). Happiness is a double-edged sword. Our state: divine discontentment. Ortega defines divine discontent thus: 'like loving without being loved, like a pain we feel in parts we do not have' (Ortega, 1960, p. 94). This aptly describes the state that is the human condition.

However, the *hope* for (eternal) happiness is a supernatural virtue, bestowed by grace, according to Christian thinkers as diverse as Aquinas and Paul Ricoeur. Faith, hope and charity (agapeic love) are not acquired; they are *infused*. 'Faith is the assurance of things hoped for, the conviction of things not seen' (Hebrews 11: 1). The believer believes against hope even as he walks in the shadow of death. Though Lucifer is happy in Hell ('better to reign in hell than to serve in Heaven') we would not be. Of course, as Milton said, 'the mind in its own place can make a heaven of hell and a hell of heaven'. Wilde tells the tale of a man who, when he died and went to Judgement, announced that he could neither go to hell, because in hell he had always lived, nor to heaven because he was not able to imagine it. This was met with silence in the House of Judgement. Our lives are lived in solitude amidst all the others with the fantasy always of the One. 'The element of which I am made, the thread of which I am woven, is solitude' (Ortega, ibid., p. 161).

Unamuno

Miguel de Unamuno, the Spanish philosopher, who also considers happiness to be a form of *jouissance*, and whom I want to consider here, gives an account of Byron's poem regarding Cain and Lucifer: 'Cain, in Byron's poem, asks of Lucifer, the prince of the intellectuals, "Are ye happy?" and Lucifer replies, "We are mighty". Cain questions again, "Are ye happy?" and then the great Intellectual says to him: "No, art thou?"' (Unamuno, 1954, p. 102). Was Unamuno happy? And you reader, are you happy? In his magnum opus, *The Tragic Sense of Life*, Unamuno exclaims: 'Unhappy man! And unhappy fellow men!' (Unamuno, ibid., p. 7) and also: 'Unhappy men that we are!' (Unamuno, ibid., p. 47), while recognising, though, that 'from the depth of unhappiness springs new life' (Unamuno, ibid., p. 57). He asks: 'What if some other people are better than our own? Very possibly, although perhaps we do not clearly understand what is meant by better or worse. Richer? Granted. More cultured? Granted likewise. Happier? Well happiness ... but still, let it pass!' (Unamuno, ibid., p. 11). For Unamuno, suffering, the suffering that love entails, is the stuff and substance of life and the root of what he calls 'personality'. And anguish is more spiritual than suffering. It is worth quoting the text in full:

> We are wont to feel the touch of anguish even in the midst of that which we call happiness, and even because of this happiness itself, to which we cannot resign ourselves and before which we tremble. The happy who resign themselves to their apparent happiness, to a transitory happiness, seem to be as men without substance, or, at any rate, men who have not discovered this substance in themselves, who have not touched it. Such men are usually

incapable of loving or of being loved, and they go through life without really knowing either pain or bliss.

There is no true love save in suffering, and in this world we have to choose either love, which is suffering, or happiness. And love leads us to no other happiness than that of love itself and its tragic consolation of uncertain hope. The moment love becomes happy and satisfied, it no longer desires and it is no longer love. The satisfied, the happy, do not love; they fall asleep in habit, near neighbour to annihilation. To fall into a habit is to begin to cease to be. Man is the most man – that is, the more divine – the greater his capacity for suffering, or, rather, for anguish.

At our coming into the world it is given to us to choose between love and happiness, and we wish – poor fools! – for both: the happiness of loving and the love of happiness. But we ought to ask for the gift of love and not of happiness, and to be preserved from dozing away into habit, lest we should fall into a fast sleep, a sleep without waking, and so lose our consciousness beyond power of recovery …. Love dies as soon as it touches the happiness towards which it reaches out, and true happiness dies with it (Unamuno, ibid., pp. 205-6).

Mathematicians call it the problem of maxima and minima – it is the law of economy. It goes like this, in the words of Unamuno:

Either to obtain the most happiness with the least love, or the most love with the least happiness. And it is necessary to choose between the one and the other, and to know that he who approaches the infinite of love, the love that is infinite, approaches the zero of happiness, the supreme anguish. And in reaching this zero he is beyond the reach of the misery that kills (Unamuno, ibid., pp. 206-7).

There you have it. The choice is stark but simple: happiness or love, for Unamuno. Your happiness or your desire, for Jacques Lacan. Stendhal, whom Herbert Marcuse evokes, defined beauty as the '*promise* of happiness' rather than its possession. Well, love is not even the promise of happiness, for Unamuno.

Unamuno chose love and so suffered; he suffered sweetly. His was a *dolor sabroso*. The question is: 'Is it possible to be happy without hope?' (Unamuno, ibid., p. 244). Do we not hope for Heaven and eternal happiness? We will consider this question from a Kantian perspective in the next chapter. 'Is not eternal happiness an eternal hope, with its nucleus of sorrow in order that happiness shall not be swallowed up in nothingness?' (Unamuno, ibid., pp. 244-5). Unamuno's soul longs for such a hope, for the immortality of his soul; it longs for a hope that is an eternal lack of something and 'an eternal suffering', as he himself admits (ibid., p. 256). He is talking in all the above quotations about happiness in its guise of *jouissance*, though he doesn't mention this French (Lacanian) term throughout.

In 'Love and Death'. Woody Allen would seem to endorse this Unamunian and Lacanian sentiment thus:

To love is to suffer. To avoid suffering one must not love. But then one suffers from not loving. Therefore to love is to suffer, not to love is to suffer. To suffer is to suffer. To be happy is to love. To be happy then is to suffer. But suffering makes one unhappy. Therefore, to be unhappy one must love, or love to suffer, or suffer from too much happiness. I hope you're getting all this down.

Turning to another film: In "Iris", which is based on the life and death of Iris Murdoch as recorded by John Bayley in his books, the character of Dame Iris Murdoch, played by Judi Dench, has this to say about happiness at the beginning of the film:

Education doesn't make you happy. And nor does freedom. We don't become happy just because we're free, if we are or because we're educated, if we have but because education may be the means by which we realise we're happy. It opens our eyes, our ears. It tells us where delights are lurking, convinces us that there is only freedom of any importance whatsoever, that of the mind. And gives us the assurance, the confidence to walk the path our mind – our educated mind – offers.

And a little later: 'Human beings love each other in sex, in friendship and when they're in love. And they cherish other beings – humans, animals, plants, even stones. The quest for happiness and the promotion of happiness is in all of this and the power of our imagination'. Iris Murdoch's biographer tells us that on September 18th Iris Murdoch wrote that happiness was to be utterly absorbed in at least six other human beings (Conradi, 2001, p. 515). She had asked herself the question: 'why should I be cheated of happiness?' (Conradi, ibid, p. 401). Why indeed? In 'The Horatians', Auden advised: 'Look at/This world with a happy eye'. And Iris Murdoch, who had made the concept of vision central to her philosophy, looked out into the same world as Auden looked, and had her moments of happiness and grace. In *Metaphysics as a Guide to Morals* Iris Murdoch has this to say about our search for happiness here below: 'Happy love can be an ingenious moral cheat. Happiness is not our business, and speculations about what God might do about it are not only empty, but likely to mislead us into giving it a value' (Murdoch, 1992, p. 438). Murdoch does, however, believe in the Form of the Good as 'a sign or symbol of the possibility of spiritual happiness' (Murdoch, ibid.). Iris Murdoch again: 'Happiness "in spite of" the misery of the world.' A brave young man might well believe that it could be achieved' (Murdoch, ibid., p. 54). Well he might.

We mortals, despite all this, will continue in our quest for happiness without, I fear, finding it in fame or fortune, in knowledge, power or pleasure, in culture or capitalism. With love's brutality and beauty, tenderness and tragedy, we cannot conceive of finding happiness in love either, as love does not understand what love is. Perhaps, at the end, the divine laughter will fill our souls with eternal happiness. Yes, perhaps.

In *That They May Face the Rising Sun*, John McGahern observes intelligently, with a soft wisdom:

> They were discussing the sale and transfer of the business. As he listened to the two voices he was so attached to and thought back to the afternoon, the striking of the clocks, the easy, pleasant company, the walk round the shore, with a rush of feeling he felt that this must be happiness. As soon as the thought came to him, he fought it back, blaming the whiskey. The very idea was as dangerous as presumptive speech: happiness could not be sought or worried into being, or even fully grasped; it should be allowed its own slow pace so that it passes unnoticed, if it ever comes at all (McGahern, 2002, p. 192).

Chapter Eleven
Wittgenstein: Happiness as Meaning

We are never so happy, or so unhappy, as we imagine.
La Rochefoucauld

For Ludwig Wittgenstein (1864-1936), happiness is not pleasurable satisfaction; it is not quantitative hedonism (aka Bentham), nor is it Aristotle's *eudaimonia*. Happiness is a metaphysical or transcendental state, not a psychological one. It may come to us, if it is linked to *meaning*. Strictly speaking, however, it is ineffable. It most resembles Schopenhauer's description of the state of those undergoing aesthetic or mystical experiences. A 'happy life' – its nature and causes – can be best described in contrast with an unhappy life. Unhappiness, for Wittgenstein, is connected to *three* ideas: frustration, fear, and meaninglessness and to two others indirectly: desire and will. Unhappiness is produced by the frustration of desires. All wants/desires seek to attain their fulfilment. Death may intervene between desire and its fulfilment. Fear of death is another cause of unhappiness, so. Even if the eternal life of maximum desire-satisfaction could be guaranteed, such a seemingly happy life could be transformed into its opposite by the intuition that such a life is meaningless. So, if one is to lead a happy life it is essential to understand the meaning of life. Surviving does not put a stop to the riddle of life. Eternal life is just as much a riddle as our present life. For Wittgenstein, something about the world is problematic and that is its meaning, which lies outside the world (see Wittgenstein, 1979, 73e). 'The meaning of life, i.e, the meaning of the world, we can call God' (Wittgenstein, ibid.). And, 'To pray is to think about the meaning of life' (Wittgenstein, ibid.). The world waxes or wanes as a whole, by 'accession or loss of meaning' (Wittgenstein, ibid.). So, it seems that Wittgenstein is saying that the sense of the world, its meaning, lies outside it in transcendental reality, what Frankl calls 'super-meaning'. Indeed, he is very close to Frankl in relating happiness to meaning. To this end he quotes Dostoyevsky who says that man is happy when he is fulfilling the purpose of existence. His purpose is to live. If he can do that he is content.

In the Wittgensteinian perspective on the subject, as set out by Wittgenstein aphoristically in his *Notebooks 1914-16*, happiness relates to meaning and meaning relates to God. 'To believe in a God means to understand the question about the meaning of life' (Wittgenstein, ibid., 74e) and, 'To believe in God means to see that life has a meaning' (Wittgenstein, ibid.). Such a person does not fear death; a happy person – and, according to Wittgenstein, 'I am either happy or unhappy, that is all' (Wittgenstein, ibid.) – is one who has no fear, in that he lives eternity. 'Only a man who lives not in time but in the present is happy' (Wittgenstein, ibid.). Because there is no death for a life in the present – death is not an event in life nor a fact of the world. He who lives in the present has no fear and also no hope.

A happy person ultimately, according to Wittgenstein, is someone who lives in harmony or in agreement with the world. The happy life seems to be in some sense more *harmonious* than the unhappy, he contends. Is it harmonious because it is not rent by conflicting desires, so? No, says Wittgenstein. 'What is the objective mark of the happy, harmonious life? Here it is again clear that there cannot be any such mark, that can be *described*. This mark cannot be a physical one, but only a metaphysical one, a transcendental one' (Wittgenstein, ibid., 78e). For Wittgenstein, ethics is transcendental (see Wittgenstein, ibid., 79e).

So a harmonious life is not a life in harmony with some physical or psychological state of affairs. 'In order to live happily, I must be in agreement with the world. And that is what "being happy" *means*' (Wittgenstein, ibid., 75e). How do we know when we are in agreement with the world? When we are doing the will of God; when we are acting according to our conscience (here again Wittgenstein shows some remarkable similarities with Frankl who likewise stressed the importance of conscience). 'When my conscience upsets my equilibrium, then I am not in agreement with something' (Wittgenstein, ibid.). 'Conscience is the voice of God' (Wittgenstein, ibid.). So, 'Act according to your conscience whatever it may be' and 'Live happy!' (Wittgenstein, ibid.). 'Good' conscience is the 'happiness that the life of knowledge preserves' (Wittgenstein, ibid., 81e).

It depends on seeing the world aright – seeing its order (*logos*) which is revealed in mystical experience. Happiness transcends desire. 'How can man be happy at all, since he cannot ward off the misery of this world? Through the life of knowledge ... The life of knowledge is the life that is happy in spite of the misery of the world' (Wittgenstein, ibid., 81e). It is 'mystical' knowledge of the world-as-a-whole. How can this mystical vision lead to transcending desire? We may here cite the first three of the Buddhist four Noble Truths: 1: Life is suffering; 2: The cause of suffering is found in our attachments to the things of the world; 3: Suffering can be ended by overcoming this attachment. How one does this is in the Eightfold Noble Path of right views, intention, speech, conduct, livelihood, effort, mindfulness and concentration.

For Wittgenstein, the only way to gain true happiness is to *see* the world in a correct way; he rejects the view that moral conduct can lead to happiness. That said, moral behaviour is the result (not the condition) of attaining the proper mental state. 'Or is only he happy who does *not* will? ... not wanting is the only good' (Wittgenstein, ibid., 77e). Wittgenstein is advocating personal transformation through mystical experience with its attendant moral consequences. He is a practical mystic. This effect could also arise from an aesthetic experience. In the *Tractatus*, Wittgenstein had said that ethics and aesthetics are one and the same. And in the *Notebooks*, Wittgenstein has this to say: 'The work of art is the object seen *sub specie aeternitatis*; and the good life is the world seen *sub specie aeternitatis*. This is the connection between art and ethics' (Wittgenstein, ibid., 83e). Aesthetic and mystical experiences both may lead to moral metanoia. It all depends on how we perceive the world: 'the world of the happy is a *different* world from the world of the unhappy' (Wittgenstein, ibid., 77e). The essence of aesthetics is to look at things with a happy eye. 'Life is grave, art is gay' (Wittgenstein, ibid., 86e). The end of art is the beautiful; 'And the beautiful *is* what makes happy' (Wittgenstein, ibid.). To a certain extent, I am my world. 'Man *is* the microcosm' (Wittgenstein, ibid., 84e).

In both the *Tractatus* and the *Notebooks*, Wittgenstein is concerned with whether life has meaning and how to be happy. Ethics is about the attitude or orientation to the world as a whole.

In his 'Lectures on Ethics', Wittgenstein endorses Moore's views of ethics: the enquiry into what is good. It is an enquiry into what is good and valuable, of what makes life worth living, of happiness, so. In *Philosophical Investigations* Wittgenstein puts forward the view that there is not one philosophical method – there are different methods, like different therapies. His intent, so, is therapeutic-ethical. Ethics enables us to clarify happiness and unhappiness. If the 'self' has a correct view of the world, a correct *attitude*, then it inhabits a happy world. A self is aware there is no meaning or value in the facts of the world. This awareness is the problem of life. This problem is removed when the self views the world *sub specie aeternitatis*. It depends on one's attitude to the world (again we may note here further similarities with Frankl and with his insistence on the importance of attitudinal change), one that does not change with changes in circumstances. Agreement or attunement with the world is the meaning of happiness. Wittgenstein's therapeutic trajectory: from puzzlement to peace, from confusion to clarity. And health is the capacity to bring about minimal happiness and its absence the incapacity to bring about happiness. Ethical health, so, is being happy with the world no matter what. Wittgenstein opines that he keeps coming back to this: that the happy life is good and the unhappy bad. The happy life justifies itself – it appears as the only right life (see Wittgenstein, ibid., 78e).

If Wittgenstein relates happiness to meaning, Ricoeur links it to hope and Lacan, to desire. This will occupy our attention in the following chapter.

Chapter Twelve
Lacan and Ricoeur: Happiness, Hope and Desire

*In our crazy separated ways we were almost happy, able at
any rate to enjoy the kites, the boats, the dogs, the birds.*
Iris Murdoch

Paul Ricoeur (1913-2005), the French hermeneutic phenomenologist, said a number of things about what he might have called (but didn't), a 'hermeneutics of happiness', in a conversation that took place in Taizé, the ecumenical religious community, during Holy Week of 2000. Ricoeur felt happiness could come in *three* main ways:

> I like the word happiness a lot. For a long time I thought that it was either too easy or too difficult to talk about happiness, and then I got beyond my scruples, or rather I deepened those scruples with respect to the word happiness. I take it in all its various meanings, including that of the beatitudes. The formula of happiness is "Happy the one who…" I greet happiness as a "re-cognition" in the three meanings of the word. I recognise it as mine; I approve of it in others, and I am grateful for the happiness that I have known, the small experiences of happiness, which include the small experiences of memory, in order to heal me of the great unhappiness of forgetting. And there I function both as a philosopher, rooted in the Greeks, and as a reader of the Bible and the Gospel where you can follow the trajectory of the word happiness. It seems that there are two levels: the best of Greek philosophy is a reflection on happiness, the Greek word *eudaimon*, for example in Plato and Aristotle, and on the other hand I am very much at home with the Bible. I think of the beginning of Psalm 4: "Ah, who will teach us happiness?" It's a rhetorical question, but it finds its answer in the beatitudes. And the beatitudes are the horizon of happiness of an existence placed under the sign of kind-heartedness, because happiness is not simply what I do not have and what I hope to have, but also what I have tasted.

For the believer, the beatitudes are the answer to happiness. They are the great hope. Beatitude is the uncreated good – God – who alone fills the heart by His love. As Aquinas notes: 'Human blessedness resides in God alone' (Aquinas, *S.T.*, 1-2. 3.1). And: 'God is beatitude' (Aquinas, *S.T.*, 1.26). *Beata vita hominis Deus est*. It is through Christ's humanity that we are drawn into the destiny of beatitude. Through God's grace we share in the beatitude laid open for us in the Incarnation. Happiness is the focus of 'Christian ethics'. Such an ethics is motivated by *anticipated* happiness. The beatitude that is God is the beatitude that is the ultimate fulfilment of the human heart and mind. For this we were made. For nothing else and for nothing less, according to this picture. Ricoeur, as we have noted, talks about *three* figures of happiness:

> I was reflecting recently on the figures of happiness in life. With respect to the created universe, the beautiful landscape in front of me, happiness is admiration. Then, a second figure, with respect to others: recognising others and, according to the nuptial model of the Song of Songs, it is a jubilation. Then, a third figure of happiness, turned towards the future, is expectation: I still expect something from life. I hope to have courage to face the misfortune I am not aware of, but I still expect happiness. I use the word expectation, but I could use another word that comes from the First Epistle to the Corinthians, from the verse that introduces the famous chapter 13, on "love that understands everything, that excuses everything". The verse says: "Aspire to the greatest gift". "Aspire": that is the happiness of aspiring that completes the happiness of jubilation and the happiness of admiration ('Taizé –Liberating the core of goodness'. Internet source).

Happiness, so, as admiration, jubilation, expectation, aspiration and hope too. In *Critique and Conviction*, which is a book of interviews with Ricoeur, Ricoeur talks of the 'call to love' that comes from on high – the Kerygma of glad tidings, that Ricoeur himself, as a practising Protestant, never ceased to hearken to and hope in, obedient as he was to the Word, to the 'apprentice' theologian, as he called it, that moved within him. Ricoeur asks us to practise Eckhartian detachment, to bracket, in the Husserlian manner of phenomenology, any concern about our own personal resurrection and belief in an imaginary 'afterlife'. For 'afterlife' still connects us to 'life' but 'Heaven' is wholly Other; it is that dimension of otherness beyond ourselves, the kingdom of the 'not yet'.

This is possible only when everything has been given up. We must let go of those things we fear to lose. Such love. In contradistinction to the Heideggerian notion of beings-towards-death, Ricoeur perfers and proposes as an alternative 'beings up until death'. He himself expressed this wish to remain living until death. One survives in the memory of the Other (though we desire the One). And the Resurrection of the dead? In this the believer *hopes*, for this he prays. Yes, it's possible.

Ricoeur considered life eschatologically as an unveiling in the face of dying. He never let himself become fascinated by the possibility of the *post mortem* future of the person. He practised a personal and professional asceticism (see Ricoeur, 1998, ibid., p. 161). He lived in the *hope* of the Kingdom. *Beatitudo* is a blessing and for Ricoeur we can only 'hope to tend in this direction. We catch glimpses of it, in brief flashes' (Ricoeur, ibid., p. 163). Ricoeur himself, like Brother Roger of Taizé whom he much admired, both died after I completed writing this work. I was reminded of what Ricoeur had said a few years earlier: 'Let God, at my death, do with me as he wills. I demand nothing. I demand no "after". I cast upon others, my survivors, the task of taking up again my desire to be, my effort to exist, in the time of the living' (Ricoeur, ibid., p. 158) – a Spinozistic, joyous affirmation of the power to be.

In the wake of Ricoeur, we are enjoined, exhorted even, to admire happiness in others, aspire to and hope for it ourselves and rejoice if and when we receive this blessed gift, beloved of the gods, even if the philosopher whom Ricoeur admired most in the philosophy of religion, Immanuel Kant, opposed what he termed 'happiness theory'. Kant suggests that 'we should renounce the claims to happiness; it requires only that we take no account of them whenever duty is in question' (Kant, 1993 [1956], p. 97). For the relation between happiness and (Kantian) duty is usually seen as one of indifference (see Zupancic, 2000, p. 21).

We are not only much more unhappy than we believe, but also much happier than we know. According to the Lacanian position, by contrast, if you travel the path of happiness, you end up an addict. The road to happiness is the road to addiction (I owe this insight to Charles Melman, Lacanian analyst, in a private conversation with the author). Such is the happiness that puts pleasure centre-stage. But what of (one's duty towards) the Other? The only happiness we should be concerned about (I am tempted to invoke Kantian duty here) is the happiness of the Other, even though he (like us) can't be 'happy-happy', to use Lacan's phrase (Lacan, 1988, p. 236). Lacan notes: 'During the time it took me to realise that the main thing is that the other be happy, I persisted in my non-happiness' (Lacan, ibid.). This is truly an ethical stance despite Lacan's insistence that *il faut pas céder sur son désir*. But desire is always desire of/for the Other. Not one's own happiness, but the happiness of the Other – a Lacanian position which, I would suggest, Kant, Levinas and Ricoeur would surely endorse. Of course, for Lacan, desire is ethical, unlike love.

In a letter to Fliess, Freud, for his part, wrote: 'Happiness is the belated fulfilment of a prehistoric wish. For this reason wealth brings so little happiness. Money was not a childhood wish' (Freud, 1984, p. 294. Letter dated 16 January 1898). Money equals excrement. Capitalism, so, can't make us happy, with its greed, commodification of culture, fetishisation of goods, materialism, with its pure pursuit of profit and with its endless, empty promises. 'All things solid melt into air' (Marx) and happiness melts away too. Capitalism: the wish for more and more; an excess that can never be satisfied.

By contrast, the psychoanalytic view of love is that love is the wish that one be given something for nothing. In Lacan's definition, love is the gift of something that one does not have, so according to this view 'we are to be given a nothing that is something', as John Forrester, the British Lacanian philosopher, puts it (Forrester, 1997, p. 159). If money can't make us happy, some people admit that they have a *gift* for being happy, even if, psychoanalytically speaking, happiness is determined by the age of five. Perhaps, as Forrester suggests, our deepest desires are for something that is 'as gratuitous, as full of grace, as happiness. The gift of something for nothing' (Forrester, ibid., p. 171). Gift and grace, for Ricoeur and Frère Roger; luck and good fortune, for Lacan.

Happiness, should it exist, comes to us as a lucky *chance*, if it comes to us at all. This is the Lacanian position (or *a* Lacanian position) as I read it and I take the risk of reading it thus. Let's explore it in more detail. In his seminar of 1964, *The Four Fundamental Concepts of Psycho-Analysis*, Lacan draws on Aristotle's distinction between two kinds of chance, what Aristotle calls *automaton* and *tuché*, in order to illustrate the distinction between the Symbolic (order of language) and the Real order, which is outside language and symbolisation. In the *Physics*, Aristotle discusses the role of 'chance' and 'fortune' in causality, though Lacan tells us that these two terms have been mistranslated in English (see chapter 5 of his *The Four Fundamental Concepts of Psycho-Analysis*). The two types of chance are *automaton*, which refers to chance events in the world, and *tuché*, which refers to chance in so far as it affects moral agents. The former may be located in the Symbolic order and designates those phenomena that seem to be chance. The latter – *tuché* – is in the Real and is beyond the *automaton*. *Tuché* is the encounter with the Real, with the incursion of the Real into the Symbolic. *Tuché* is extrinsic to signification and is purely arbitrary. (Footnote: Woody Allen's film, 'Matchpoint', brilliantly explores this game of luck/chance). *Entuchia* is a happy encounter while *dustuchia* is an unhappy encounter, a mis-fortune. *Bonheur* or 'happiness' is what contingency brings us (I owe this last point of insight to Cormac Gallagher, Lacanian analyst, in a private conversation with the author). To repeat: for Ricoeur, so, happiness is *gratuitous*; for Lacan, it is *fortuitous*.

Now Freud has been dismissed by some as being a determinist with his view that no slip, or blunder, may be ascribed to chance. But Freud writes this: 'I believe in external (real) chance, it is true, but not in internal (psychical) accidental events' (Freud, 1901, p. 257). Chance (in the sense of *tuché*), does not exist in the Symbolic; in the Symbolic order there is no such thing as pure chance. Chance in the sense of pure contingency, alluded to above, exists only in the Real. For the Lacanian, happiness is *tuchic* (not a sneeze!) (See Lacan, 1977, p. 80). *Tuché* designates this encounter with the Real; the former is purely arbitrary. We *miss* being happy and are justified, therefore, according to Lacanian theory, in saying that happiness in its guise of *jouissance* pertains to the order of the Real.

However, isn't this the root of the problem, that, just to take two examples, when Aristotle is talking about happiness he means human flourishing and when Lacan is talking about happiness he means something else entirely, that there is a missed encounter between these two thinkers because each one is talking of happiness from within their own reference-frame, that, in other words, each thinker we have explored is using the term 'happiness' differently according to their own particular usage? Happiness means quite different things to the Aristotelian and to the Lacanian.

But we are living in the wake of Freud and Lacan and postmodernism and this changes things. We have to take other things into account that Aristotle did not, such as unconscious mental processes, the (postmodern) Other, the Lacanian Real and modern movements in philosophy such as hermeneutics, structuralism, phenomenology, deconstruction etc.

Understood hermeneutically, happiness may only be glimpsed or glanced, like the Promised Land for Moses, to use Ricoeur's image. We may tend in the direction of happiness. Just that. Not impossible but difficult. So certainly, Ricoeur is no naive optimist. His philosophy is not a 'how to be happy' one. But... and there are many 'buts' in this tense relationship between Ricoeurian hermeneutics and Lacanian psychoanalysis, which I have explored in my book, *Hermeneutics and the Psychoanalysis of Religion* (2010).

And here a key word, in the Kantian and Ricoeurian lexicon, would be hope – *hope* for happiness. Up until now, we had been taking about happiness from within the register of *desire* but Kant talks of happiness from within the domain of hope, which is under the sign of promise and Ricoeur adopts this Kantian line. Kant *adds* this hope-ful dimension to the debate. As Ricoeur explains, hope 'is the anticipation, the expectation, of a connection between the purity of heart and satisfaction of our most intimate desire' (Ricoeur, 1995, p. 214).

Hope is an eschatological response to Heideggerian being-towards-death – hope 'in spite of' death, to use Ricoeur's category. Isn't hope an answer to the Real (enigma) of evil? Could happiness remain hidden within hope? Is hope the hint of happiness? We can't absolutely know happiness or be absolutely happy but we can hope. *'Il n'y a pas une vie heureuse. Il n'y a que des heures heureuses'*. As Hopkins puts it: 'There is a happiness, hope, the anticipation of happiness hereafter: it is better than happiness, but it is not happiness now' (Hopkins, 2002, p. 303).

The end is a *promise*, promised through symbols of the sacred. But this promise is as precarious as it is uncertain. Kant distinguishes and develops a division between duty, which is obedience to the moral law, and happiness, which is the satisfaction of desire. And what Kant has torn asunder, Lacan brings together. This connection is necessary, demanded even if it is not given. Can't we say, therefore, that hope resides in the possibility of reconciling morality with happiness, and duty with desire?

We can concur with Kant that happiness is not our accomplishment: 'it is achieved by superaddition, by surplus', as Ricoeur puts Kant (Ricoeur, 2004, p. 412). Hope is the movement from demand (the demand for happiness that Lacan rightly criticised) to expectation (the expectation of happiness that Ricoeur emphasises but one that Freud and Lacan deny) and this movement, if we want to make it, enables us to pass from ethics (where the question of happiness is traditionally posed) to religion. It was Kant, after all, who defined the religious question as: 'what may I hope for?' Happiness is what we may hope for, according to the religious register of existence, but a happiness beyond this life. For Kant, God is the highest good. Kant's trajectory, so: from *morality* to *immortality*. For Kant, 'morals is not really the doctrine of how to make ourselves happy but of how we are to be *worthy* of happiness. Only if religion is added to it can the hope arise of some day participating in happiness in proportion we endeavored not to be unworthy of it' (Ricoeur, ibid., p. 416).

Hope is hope of resurrection from the dead. This is the joyous 'how much more' than *this*. This belongs to the law of superabundance and agapeic love, such as one finds articulated in St. Paul. Ricoeur wishes to reconcile what Kantian rigorism has separated: virtue, as obedience to pure duty, and happiness, as satisfaction of desire. 'This reconciliation is the Kantian equivalent of hope' (Ricoeur, ibid., p. 434). (Totalitarianism is the pathology of hope). Ricoeur maintains that:

> The much more of the law of superabundance cannot go without the in spite of, the in spite of death, which gives to hope its lucidity, its determination. For my part I should say that freedom is the capacity to live according to the paradoxical law of superabundance, of denying death and asserting the excess of sense over non-sense in all desperate situations (Ricoeur, 1995, p. 207).

This 'much more' is the much more of grace, of the excess of sense over nonsense. Ricoeur: *Spero ut intelligam*: 'I hope in order to understand'. And between (irrational) hope and absolute knowledge, for Ricoeur, we must choose. 'Irrational' because hope confronts the limits of reason (just as evil does). The Kantian dialectic, unlike the Lacanian one, has more (obvious) affinity with a theology of hope (*à la* Jürgen Moltmann and Ernst Bloch, to an extent) and the Christian tradition in general.

The object of the entire quest, as Aristotle, Aquinas, Lacan and Ricoeur (and Ricoeur is a disciple of Aristotle, Kant and Hegel, with a dash of Nietzsche) know, merits, in Ricoeur's words in *Memory, History, Forgetting*, 'the beautiful name of happiness', a name that is problematic for the Freudian-Lacanian. There is no happy ending for us only the apostrophe of the Hebraic psalmist: 'Who will make us see hapiness?' (Psalm 4: 7). That is the question. Hope, which the Christian tradition sees as a supernatural or theological virtue, advances the Kingdom of God. Hope means the superabundance of meaning as opposed to an abundance of senselessness. Hope opens up what gnosis closes. Yes, but *IF* all this is to happen, it can only happen outside our experience of time and space (to be Kantian about it), outside the macro- and microcosm (to be Freudian about it).

If happiness is viewed under the sign of hope, then isn't *acedia* the worst temptation, even happiness's opposite? By *acedia* the mediaevals understood choleric discord and complaisance toward sadness. Here we touch on the (Freudian) moral ground of melancholia. Sadness without a cause tends in the opposite direction to hope, if we conceive this to be Kierkegaard's sickness-unto-death or Marcel's 'no hope' (*inespoir*). Isn't the missing piece in the panopoly of Freud's metapsychology a sadness that can be sublimated into joy, as Ricoeur suggests? Aren't there missing pieces everywhere (thankfully) in what has been a long detour, from Aristotle to Ricoeur, on the quest-ion of human happiness, and one that hasn't yet finished but which is nearing its end? Ours has been a roundabout, arduous path. This is as it should be. Reflection is carried out only by degrees and none too suddenly. They have been tracks in the forest, in the field, that have carried conceptual risks along the way and who knows, we may have hit on some answers or may have gone shamefully astray: paths leading nowhere? Or we may have stumbled upon the work of the woodsmen in this the dark of the world's night (to mix Ricoeur's idiom with Heidegger's). 'Streaks of light, shafts of light, which ... may be only talking shadows' (Ricoeur, 2004, p. 194).

Prometheus's gift was hope (even if this means hoping against hope). Prometheus, so, and Hermes, a definitely wounded hero, who accompanies the hermeneuticians on their journey. But here we must also mention and spare a thought for Ulysses. When Ulysses returned from Troy on his hazardous 'journey home' to Ithaca, he was confronted with a choice, faced with a decision about which way to go forward. He could attempt to circumnavigate a way between the sheer rock-faced cliff of Scylla and the deadly whirlpool of Charybdis or he could make his way through wandering rocks. We, too, have wandered over difficult terrain. Happiness, as we have seen, may be said in many ways. But ultimately, from within a Christian register, it is an uncertain promise not a presense or a possession, one that involves hope rather than having, and aspiration rather than accomplishment and appropriation. It involves signs, signals, signposts, sentinels, cyphers, tracks, traces.

G. K. Chesterton, the English Catholic writer, suggests that we let the melancholy of *acedia* be an innocent interlude and that we let praise rather than pessimism be the permanent pulsation of the soul (see G.K. Chesterton, 2001, p. 118), what Ricoeur calls 'hope' and 'love of Creation'. As Chesterton observes: 'joy is the uproarious labour by which all things live' even if this 'laughter of the heavens is too loud for us to hear' (Chesterton, ibid., p. 119). Chesterton mentions a figure who fills the Gospels, as an example:

His pathos was natural, almost casual. The Stoics, ancient and modern, were proud of concealing their tears. He never concealed His tears; He showed them plainly on His open face at any daily sight, such as the far sight of His native city. Yet, He concealed something. Solemn supermen and imperial diplomatists are proud of restraining their anger. He never restrained His anger. He flung furniture down the front steps of the Temple, and asked men how they expected to escape the damnation of Hell. Yet He restrained something. I say it with reverence; there was in that shattering personality a thread that must be called shyness. There was something that He hid from all men when He went up a mountain to pray. There was something that He covered constantly by abrupt silence or impetuous isolation. There was some one thing that was too great for God to show us when He walked upon our earth; and I have sometimes fancied that it was His mirth' (Chesterton, ibid.).

The Greeks, such as Plato and Aristotle, and Chesterton was a follower of Aristotle (and Aquinas), connected the soul with the city-state, the personal with the political, ethics with politics, joy in the soul with justice in society. They related happiness to virtue; happiness was virtue's reward.

For St. Thomas, the 'natural' desire for happiness is of divine origin, placed in the human heart by the One who alone can fulful it. God calls us to His own beatitude. He is the end just as our end is to reach the Kingdom that has no end. For Freud and Lacan, the aim and end is to bring the human subject to an awareness of his desire, not his happiness. For the Freudian-Lacanian, between desire and happiness one must choose. For the Aristotelian-Thomist, and the theist in general

– be he orthodox, 'anonymous' (in Rahner's phrase) or radical – restless desire seeks its repose in God, our final hope, in Whom is found the full and final happiness of humanity.

For the psychoanalyst, the question of *earthly* happiness is closed. There is no Sovereign Good. That is to say, *in this life*. But the question of *eternal* happiness is an open question. Both are open questions – the 'next life' and the notion of complete happiness. The question is: should we be concerned about this? Perhaps. Perhaps not. That, perhaps, is God's business (should He exist), not ours. Maybe we should think little of it. For Ricoeur, the question of happiness in 'Heaven' is suspended, phenomenologically speaking.

For Lacan, it is suspended on earth. Desire relates to death. Desire takes us beyond pity and fear, as we move away from the register of demand with its promise of false goods and into the domain of *Atè*. Our aspiration to happiness implies 'a place where miracles happen' (Lacan, 1992, p. 303). A miracle or a mirage? To guarantee the possibility that a subject will find happiness, be it earthly or eternal, is 'a form of fraud', according to Lacan (Lacan, ibid.). The demand for happiness is nothing other than a bourgeois dream. The point, instead, is to realise one's being-for-death (subjective destitution/absolute disarray), for Lacan. This touches the end of what man is and what he is not. *Le dur désir de durer*: the difficult desire to endure: this is the desire to desire. Such is the tragic sense of life. And action must catch up with desire, with its array and disarray. 'Heaven', as a concept, can be (mis)used to postpone both desire and action.

Giving ground relative to desire, to use Lacan's famous formula, is always accompanied by some betrayal – be it happiness or honour or such like. Happiness is sacrificed for ethical desire. Isn't a saint's goal to access sublime desire? And wasn't that the real goal of Saint Thomas (*sinthome*), the trace of his *jouissance* that allowed him to live especially after encountering the God of the Real, about Whom all his previous signifiers and symbolic systems appeared 'like straw', in the name of the father? His desire, we can speculate, crossed pity and fear through that cathartic, because traumatic, experience. No, 'all is not a bed of roses' (Lacan, ibid., p. 323), but one's eyes are opened. Thomas, the Dominican mystic, was motivated by mysterious desire: desire for God rather than happiness and for what he perceived was God's desire for him. Isn't that why Lacan can write that the laws of Heaven are the laws of desire? (see Lacan, ibid., p. 325). Perhaps 'Heaven' is not a 'place' of Paradise understood as eternal happiness but the eternalisation of desire as it takes us *à Dieu*? Perhaps it is through desire that man's end finds its meaning in the Last Judgement, where the Word absolves or condemns him.

Perhaps the true meaning of Christianity is that we should be prepared to give up the totality of our life for nothing? Perhaps there is no guarantee, only the Kierkegaardian leap of faith in 'infinite resignation' or in Lacanian 'subjective destitution'? This would mean giving it all up for nothing rather than for some Thing, where the former is only truly ethical and the latter merely moral. And isn't this how we can understand the sentence, that it is only by losing our lives that we can save and find them, that it's not about peace but the sword? And (worldly) hate.

'If anyone comes to me and does not hate his father and his mother, his wife and children, his brothers and sisters – yes even his own life – he cannot be my disciple' (Luke 14: 26). Is this divine (diabolic?) desire, in so far as *diabolos* means 'to tear apart'? Perhaps it is also a desire that rents happiness asunder? Perhaps.

For Ricoeur, by contrast, happiness involves living the beatitudinal life. The Sermon on the Mount taught the following eight beatitudes (if we are to follow St. Matthew's Gospel): Happy the poor in spirit, for theirs is the kingdom of heaven; happy are the meek, for they shall inherit the earth; happy are those who mourn, for they shall be comforted; happy are those who hunger and thirst for righteousness, for they shall be satisfied; happy are the merciful, for they shall obtain mercy; happy are the pure in heart, for they shall see God; happy are the peacemakers, for they shall be called the sons of God; happy are those who are persecuted for righteousness' sake, for theirs is the kingdom of heaven. The beautides, for both Thomas and Ricoeur, are a response to the question of happiness. We can, according to Servais Pinckaers, the Dominican theologian, discern three levels operative here: at the sensible level, happiness is sought in pleasures and tangible goods; at the active level, in the exercise of virtues; at the spiritual level, in contemplation and love (see Pinckaers, 1998, p. 196). Pinckaers summarises the Thomistic teaching thus:

> The first three beatitudes correspond to the first level. The beatitude of the poor runs counter to a concept of happiness based on the pursuit of sensible goods, riches and honors. The beatitude of the meek countervails the idea that happiness is to be found in the gratification of the irascible passions, anger and the instinct to dominate. Thirdly, the beatitude of those who mourn reverses the theory that happiness consists in pleasure and sensual delight. The next two beatitudes deal with the active life, in which the virtues of justice and liberality or generosity are exercised. This form of life certainly contributes to happiness, but does not constitute it. The final two beatitudes relate to the contemplative life. They prepare us for it, although it must of necessity remain imperfect in this world. This preparation is effected through purity of heart and peace, which have to do with our relationships with our neighbor. The eighth beatitude subsumes the others and confirms and demonstrates them (Pinckaers, ibid., pp. 196-7).

St. Thomas follows the hierarchy of the virtues. At the sensible level we have detachment, courage and temperance; in the order of willing, justice and liberality; and in the order of contemplation, wisdom and love. These are Scripture's answer to the question of happiness, which is inextricably linked with virtue. It is the Catholic Thomas's and the Protestant Ricoeur's too, in their different ways. But it is far removed from Lacan's more atheistic understanding. In sum, for Lacan *desire* renders happiness impossible in this life; he doesn't comment about the next life. Interestingly, Levinas is more on the side of Lacan when, in *Totality and Infinity*, he opines that 'desire is the misfortune of the happy' (Levinas, 1969, p. 62) – a luxurious need. So desire spoils happiness; it interrupts it and puts it into question.

Desire is surplus, though, for Levinas; happiness is satisfaction, the satisfaction of a need. For Schopenhauer, happiness is the absence of suffering, as we saw. However, for Levinas, suffering is the absence of happiness. The love of life, for Levinas, is primordial (likewise with Ricoeur) just as joy is edenic. There is enjoyment even amid suffering, sin and suicide. The *taedium vitae* is steeped in the love of the life it rejects. 'The happiness of enjoyment is stronger than every disquietude' (Levinas, ibid., p. 149), but disquietude can trouble it. 'One minute more, Mr. Hangman'! So our relation to the world is on the side of enjoyment. We are basically happy creatures, according to Levinas. To take an example: starvation is tied to the possibility of satisfaction (unless, of course, there is a famine but this confirms Levinas' position that unhappiness is an interlude). Happiness is pagan, primordial, paradisal and proto-ethical; happiness is not ethical as such. The Other interrupts my happiness without necessarily destroying it, asserts this Jewish former priosner of war. Without happiness there would be no ethics but happiness itself is not ethical, is Levinas' position on the subject.

For his part, Ricoeur *hopes* and wagers on happiness happening, both in this and the next life. 'I do not aim at "my" personal idea of happiness and honour but happiness and honour *per se*' (Ricoeur, 1965, p. 94). My character, as Ricoeur calls it, is finite; it is determined by my being born; it is constant. And there is a disproportionate relationship between happiness and character, which is the disproportion between infinitude and finitude. Happiness is an example of the infinite. Ricoeur asserts that 'happiness is the horizon from every point of view' (Ricoeur, ibid., p. 100). Happiness is that towards which we all aim. The ethical question, for Frankl, as we shall see in the final chapter, is: should we aim at happiness? Happiness is the 'infinite end' (Ricoeur, ibid., p. 104). I have a character but the ultimate aim of everything I do is happiness. Happiness, for Ricoeur, is happiness *per se*, not *my* happiness and so it is infinite (and ethical): 'no act gives happiness, but the encounters of our life which are most worthy of being called "events" indicate the direction of happiness' (Ricoeur, ibid., pp. 104-5). Happiness may be acquired, so, as we accumulate events. Ricoeur hopes, at least, for that much.

Chapter Thirteen
Aquinas Again: Heavenly Happiness

What are you thinking, my love, my darling? About
you. I was wondering if you could make me happy. It would
be fearfully difficult. I'm fearfully clever, and I love you
fearfully much.

Iris Murdoch

We have seen in the last chapter that Ricoeur situates happiness within hope, believing that happiness to be possible however difficult and that Lacan relates happiness to desire, believing happiness to be impossible. My contention, no, Christian wager, in this concluding chapter is that happiness relates to both desire and hope and that while perfect happiness is impossible in this life, there is a happiness to come, based on such hope and desire. As such, I am proposing here to return to St. Thomas one final time to help me here. My intention is to go 'back' to Thomas in order to go 'beyond' both Lacan and Ricoeur. For it is Aquinas who draws on both desire and hope in relation to the question of happiness and, further, opines that complete happiness is impossible in this life (Lacan's position) but achievable in the next (closer to Ricoeur's position). Thus, his theological reflections complement both Ricoeur's philosophical ones and Lacan's psychoanalytic ones, while surpassing them both.

St. Thomas Aquinas, as we saw in chapter five, was a Dominican friar. By all accounts he was very happy, thus living the reality of Pascal's dictum that 'nobody is as happy as a real Christian'. A phrase that crops up on lives of Thomas is 'O happy teacher' (*'O felix Doctor'*). Blessed Jordan of Saxony, St. Dominic's first successor as Master of the Order, was said to be the most good-humoured and exuberant of friars. These mendicants were different from their more monastic confrères. St. Benedict had forbidden 'talk leading to laughter' in his Rule. These three friars had one thing in common: they learned the 'secret' of happiness from the wisdom contained in the Beatitudes. Theirs was an evangelical joy grounded in a supernatural faith. St. Thomas, in his commentary on Psalm 34, speaks of a joy which is an expansion of the heart. Further, it is a joy to God to pour forth His being. For Thomas, those who devote themselves to the contemplation of truth (the motto of the Dominican Order) are 'the happiest anyone can be in this life' (cited in Murray, 2006, p. 67). Affability and cheerfulness are defended by Thomas throughout the *Summa*. (For Wittgenstein, as we saw in chapter eleven, humour is not a mood but a way of looking at the world). We, of course, share in the joy and hope (*gaudium et spes*) of the world but also in its grief and anguish (*luctus et angor*). Happiness is the great task – a duty, in fact, for Alain.

We have seen in chapter five that for Aquinas beatitude or happiness is the reward of virtue and that this beatitude belongs to God in a special way. Beatitude is the perfect good of an intellectual nature but God's beatitude is not acquired by merit. It is assigned to God in respect of His intellect; it is the supreme good absolutely. God, according to Thomas, possesses a certain and continual happy contemplation of Himself. God possesses joy in Himself and all things are ordered for His delight and delectation (see Aquinas, *S.T.*, q. 26, art. 1, pt. 1).

In contrast to God, we, His creatures, merit happiness chiefly through charity. Spiritual joy is caused by charity. For Thomas, joy is the effect of hope and caused by love (see Aquinas, 'Of Joy', ibid., pt. 11-11. q. 28. art. 2). However, the spiritual joy that proceeds from charity cannot be filled in this life because of desire. Here Thomas' thought is in complete acccord with Lacan's. 'But as long as we are in this world, the movement of desire does not cease in us' (Aquinas, ibid., art. 3). But when perfect happiness is attained, there will be nothing left to be desired. Aquinas argues that 'desire will be at rest, not only our desire for God, but all our desires' (Aquinas, ibid.). Desire is not a virtue for Thomas; nor is joy. Both desire and hope follow on from love. 'Hope proceeds from love even as joy does' (Aquinas, ibid., art. 4).

All things desire peace, which is the 'tranquility of order' in Augustine's memorable phrase. For Thomas, man 'desires to obtain what he desires' and peace can only reign when all our desires are fulfilled. Peace provides calm and concord and is the effect of charity. Peace is our last end.

It is charity that unites us to God; charity is friendship with God. It is a theological virtue and is included in the definition of every virtue – indeed it is the most excellent of all the virtues. Without charity, there is no true virtue. Charity is caused by infusion and is founded on the fellowship of everlasting happiness. Charity is a gratuitous gift. It can increase, strengthen and be perfected in this present life and is expressed in the desire to be dissolved, in union with God.

As for hope, hope is a supernatural/theological virtue like charity. Its object is a future good that is difficult but possible to obtain (see Aquinas, ibid., q. 17, art. 1, pt. 11-11). Hope is a habit of the mind; it is not a passion. For Thomas, we hope to obtain happiness by means of merit and grace. The object of such hope is heavenly happiness. Such an eternal life of happiness consists in the enjoyment of God Himself.

According to Thomas, we can hope for another man's eternal happiness as a friend is another self. 'A man can hope and desire something for another man, as for himself; and, accordingly, he can hope for another's eternal life, inasmuch as he is united to him by love' (Aquinas, ibid., art. 3). Prayer is the expression of such hope. Hope, so, is a kind of expectation; its object is something arduous. Hope expects happiness. And God, so, is the object of such hope. Through hope man tends to God. Through hope we trust in God for our obtaining happiness. Hope and faith (another theological virtue) are related. Faith is expressed in the very act of hope. Faith begets hope; it also precedes hope (just as hope precedes charity). Hope is the entrance to faith itself.

For Thomas, hope is in the will not in the memory or the intellect (see Aquinas, ibid., 'Of the Subject of Hope', pt. 11-11. q. 18. art. 1). The will is rational desire, for Thomas. By virtue of hope we can hope for happiness, both for ourselves and for others. There is a question we must pose: is there hope in the Blessed? Aquinas answers in the negative. The Blessed have no hope as they enjoy the sight of God. 'Therefore hope has no place in them' (Aquinas, ibid., art. 2). When happiness is no longer future but present, then it is incompatible with the virtue of hope. There is no faith or hope in heaven; both are voided. 'The happiness of the saints [who neither have joy nor faith] is called eternal life' (Aquinas, ibid.). The Blessed in heaven don't hope for the continuation of their happiness because they are in possession of it. If they hope for the happiness of others they do so, not through the virtue of hope, but through the love of charity.

The Blessed have this in common with the damned: none of them have hope. It is a condition of happiness that the will should find rest. Perfect happiness requires that we should be certain of being happy forever, else the will would not rest. The damned can't apprehend or comprehend happiness as a possible good, just as the Blessed can't apprehend it as a future good. However, hope, Thomas opines, can reside in those in Purgatory as they apprehend happiness as a future possible possession. Here Thomas differs in his theology of hope from Ricoeur. For Thomas, in contrast to Ricoeur, hope tends to its end with certainty. '*Hope is the certain expectation of future happiness*' (Aquinas, ibid., art. 4). That said, some who have hope fail to obtain happiness.

In 'Of Those Things in Which Man's Happiness Consists' (Aquinas, ibid., pt. 1-11. q. 2. art. 1), Thomas asserts that since happiness is man's last end, it must consist in that which has the greatest hold on man's affections. He rules out honour, wealth and glory. What we desire above all other desires is happiness; it is our true and perfect good. Happiness endures; it is for ever. Aquinas opines that 'it is the nature of happiness to *satisfy of itself*' (Aquinas, ibid., art. 4). Man is ordained to such happiness. Just as the First Cause (God) flows into all things, so the last end is that which attracts the desire of all things. Desiring good is the same as desiring delight, which is the appetite's rest in good; it is rest in the thing desired. Happiness, so, is the perfection of man. And that which constitutes the life of happiness is to be loved for its own sake, according to both Augustine and Aquinas. Man attains this happiness through his soul. But, even though we say that happiness is something belonging to man's soul (it is an inherent good of the soul), its source (that which constitutes it) is outside the soul. It is not found in any creature but in God alone. No created good can constitute man's complete happiness. It lulls the appetite completely and once attained nothing more is desired. Indeed, in this regard, the summit of man touches the base of the angelic nature. Happiness is the infinite good and is the same as God; '*God is happiness itself*' (Aquinas, ibid., q. 3). Here Thomas concurs with Boethius. Happiness is man's last end, as we have said, 'to which man's will tends naturally' (Aquinas, ibid., q. 3, art. 1). The last end is the uncreated good, God, who alone can satisfy man's will. Men are happy by participation whereas God is happy by His essence. 'His Being is His Happiness'

(Aquinas, ibid., art. 2). (Just as there are degrees of participation so too are there various meanings applied to happiness). The question is: will everyone in heaven be equally happy? Aquinas' answer is in the negative. Some people will be happier than others in Heaven on account of their fuller participation in the Divine happiness. Perfect happiness cannot be attained in this present state of life. We await it in heaven, in the resurrected life, and such as the angels have. This heavenly happiness consists in the knowledge of God, according to Thomas, which is an act of the intellect. Delight is its proper accident. To explain this: the essence of happiness consists in an act of the (speculative rather than the practical) intellect but the delight resulting from happiness pertains to the will. Augustine had summed this up beautifully and succinctly: happiness is joy in truth. Joy is the consummation of happiness. Only when man has attained his last end is his desire at rest and he remains in peace. 'He who has whatever he desires, is happy, because he has what he desires' (Aquinas, ibid., art. 4).

Happiness consists in the contemplation of divine things. The last and 'perfect happiness, which we await in the life to come, consists entirely in contemplation' (Aquinas, ibid., art. 5). The contemplation of God makes man supremely happy but a certain imperfect happiness may be achieved through contemplating the angels. Angels minister to men and as such help us to attain happiness but they are not the object of our happiness. Final happiness culminates in the vision and knowledge of the Divine Essence. While on earth, man is not perfectly happy because there is something more for him to hope for and desire.

Perfect happiness is the good desired and hoped for. Happiness is our Sovereign Good and comes by concomitant delight, caused by the sight of God Himself. Delight consists in this vision and in a certain repose of the will. Man is ordered to an end and happiness consists in gaining that (last) end. Man hopes while on earth and this causes the search for the end. The 'presence of the end corresponds to the relation of hope; but delight in the end now present results from love' (Aquinas, ibid., q. 4, art. 3).

Three things must concur in happiness, according to Aquinas: vision (the perfect knowledge of the intelligible end); comprehension (presence of the end); and delight or enjoyment, 'which implies repose of the lover in the object beloved' (Aquinas, ibid.).

In terms of the happiness of this life, Aquinas agrees with Aristotle, that the happy man needs friends but in our heavenly Fatherland, the fellowhsip of friends is not essential to happiness since man has the entire fullness of his perfection in God. That said, 'the fellowship of friends conduces to the well-being of happiness' (Aquinas, ibid., art. 8). Friendship is thus concomitant with complete happiness.

In 'Of the Attainment of Happiness' (Aquinas, ibid., q. 5), Thomas asserts that our intellects apprehend the perfect good and our wills desire it. Happiness brings rest to our desire even though there are different degrees of happiness. Happiness is not equally in all, as we stated earlier. 'Happiness is one in its object. But the many mansions signify the manifold Happiness in the diverse degrees of enjoyment' (Aquinas, ibid., q. 5, art. 2). There are degrees of happiness in this life too – different degrees of participation in God's triune life. Such an imperfect happiness is attained by knowing and loving God, albeit imperfectly. But man born of woman lives for a short time and is filled with many miseries (Job xiv. 1). Thus man cannot be happy in this life as happiness excludes such misery. Only a certain participation of happiness can be had in this life. Real happiness excludes every evil and fulfils every desire. We are saved by hope (Rom. viii. 24). The happiness of hope is bestowed on us by sanctifying grace. Once gained true happiness cannot be lost because what is eternal ceases not, though in this life happiness is transitory. In this life man may be potentially happy but he can become actually happy in the hereafter. Man has the assurance, Thomas opines, of never losing the good that he will possess in the heavenly paradise. As such, happiness is consummate perfection and endures forever. Happiness has a beginning but it has no end. In *Love Alone is Credible*, Hans Urs von Balthasar concludes the controversy over whether eternal beatitude consists in vision or love: 'it can consist only in the loving "vision" of love, for what else but love is there to see in God, and how else can it be seen except from within love?' (Balthasar, 2004, p. 146). This, I think, says it all.

We desire and hope for happiness. And perfect happiness awaits us. This assurance is given to us by the Word who died for us, despite the travails we have to endure in this life. In his *Published Essays*, Eric Voegelin writes that 'from the experience of life in precarious existence within the limits of birth and death there rises the wondering question about the ultimate ground' (Voegelin, 1996, p. 268). The Ground is not to be found in the things of the external world; it lies beyond the world, which Plato designated by the symbol of the *epekeina*. Our existence here is in tension between life and death. As such, it has the character of an In-Between state – a Platonic *metaxy*. And happiness is metaxologically mediated too. We move between knowledge and ignorance, happiness and misery in our metaxological being-in-the-world while being beyond it too. Symbols of the sacred call upon man in our search for the divine Ground, as we experience the 'joy of luminous participation' (Voegelin, ibid., pp. 287-8), whenever we respond to the theophany, in faith, hope and love.

After this excursus into Thomas we now return, in the next chapter, to the twentieth-century to consider the theistic philosophies of Charles Taylor and Bernard Lonergan, S.J.

Chapter Fourteen
Taylor and Lonergan: Beyond Happiness

How rarely can happiness be really innocent and not triumphant, not an insult to the deprived. How offensive it can be, the natural instinctive showing off of decent happy people.

Iris Murdoch

My aim in this chapter is to unpack and describe the notion of 'fullness' as it prefigures in Charles Taylor's *A Secular Age* (2007). David Walsh's criticism of Taylor (1931-present) in a footnote in the former's *The Third Millennium: Reflections on Faith and Reason* (1999) makes the point that in *Sources of the Self* Taylor 'has drawn our attention to the centrality of ordinary life within the modern worldview, but he fails to exhibit the capacity for transcendence that renders it worthy of celebration', (Walsh 1999, p. 232). I believe that Taylor's *A Secular Age* answers this criticism. In the last chapter of this work he calls the experiences of fullness 'conversions', a notion extensively explored by another Canadian, the Jesuit philosopher and theologian, Bernard Lonergan (1904-1984), in *Method and Theology*, whose reflections on the subject will be adumbrated towards the end of this chapter to fill in the gaps, as I see it, of Taylor's account of the subject.

Taylor

For Taylor, 'fullness' takes us beyond mere human flourishing and relates us to the realm of the transcendent. Of course the notion of flourishing was given full voice by Aristotle in his *Nicomachean Ethics*, as we saw in chapter two; the word he employs is *eudaimonia* which is usually translated as 'happiness' but which can also be rendered as 'flourishing'; Taylor is thus critiquing this eudaimonistic ethic.

Taylor diagnoses this shift to secularity, where belief in God is no longer axiomatic despite the undoubted search for the spiritual that also abounds. Aristotelian 'flourishing' is understood as leading an ethical life, by cultivating the moral and intellectual virtues, in the *polis*. Flourishing in the city-state or society needn't have any reference, though, to ultimate reality. 'Flourishing' is a secular symbol. 'Secularism' may be defined as the space emptied of God or of any reference to transcendent reality. 'Fullness', by contrast, explicitly relates us to the transcendent, however that is conceived. Before we define what Taylor means by 'fullness' and in keeping with Eric Voegelin's injunction that we return to the engendering *experiences* to which subsequent symbols give rise, let me begin with an experiential epiphany enjoyed by Bede Griffiths, the British Benedictine monk, which he reports in his autobiography and which Taylor cites in his introduction to *A Secular Age*:

> One day during my last term at school I walked out alone in the evening and heard the birds singing in that full chorus of song, which can only be heard at that time of the year at dawn or at sunset. I remember now the shock of surprise with which the sound broke on my ears. It seemed to me that I had never heard the birds singing before and I wondered whether they sang like this all year round and I had never noticed it. As I walked I came upon some hawthorn trees in full bloom and again I thought I had never seen such a sight or experienced such sweetness before. If I had been brought suddenly among the trees of the Garden of Paradise and heard a choir of angels singing I could not have been more surprised. I came then to where the sun was setting over the playing fields. A lark rose suddenly from the ground beside the trees where I was standing and poured out its song above my head, and then sank still singing to rest. Everything then grew still as the sunset faded and the veil of dusk began to cover the earth. I remember now the feeling of awe which came over me. I felt inclined to kneel on the ground, as though I had been standing in the presence of an angel; and I hardly dared to look on the face of the sky, because it seemed as though it was but a veil before the face of God (see Griffiths, 1979, 9; cited by Taylor, 2007, p. 5).

Following Taylor, we can describe this conversion experience as one of 'fullness'; Bernard Lonergan and Viktor Frankl would call it 'self-transcendence'. The space in which we live has a certain moral and spiritual shape and somewhere, in some condition or activity, there lies a 'fullness' or 'richness', as Taylor calls it. There 'life is fuller, richer, deeper, and more worth while, more admirable, more what it should be', as he puts it (Taylor, ibid., p. 5). We often experience it as 'deeply moving, as inspiring. Perhaps this sense of fullness is something we just catch glimpses of from afar off; we have the powerful intuition of what fullness would be, were we to be in that condition, e.g., of peace or wholeness ... of integrity or generosity or abandonment or self-forgetfulness' (Taylor, ibid.). These experienced moments bring joy and fulfilment; they are referred to by some as 'transpersonal experiences'. In such experiences it seems that ordinary reality is abolished or obliterated; they are experiences that unsettle and break through our feelings of familiarity and our tried and tested ways of being in the world. Something other shines through our consciousness and leaves us with a sense of the uncanny, which Jacques Lacan labels the Real. However, it is important to note, as Taylor does, that the experience of fullness may not always be identified with such limit or 'peak experiences', as Maslow calls them, be they uplifting and edifying or frightening and traumatic. They may be moments when 'the deep divisions, [Pascalian] distractions, worries, sadnesses that seem to drag us down are somehow dissolved, or brought into alignment, so that we feel united, moving forward, suddenly capable and full of energy' (Taylor, ibid., p. 6). These experiences touch on our highest capabilities and aspirations. They transform us. These experiences situate us morally and spiritually:

> They can orient us because they offer some sense of what they are of: the presence of God, or the voice of nature, or the force which flows through everything, or the alignment in us of desire and the drive to form. But they are also often unsettling and enigmatic. Our sense of where they come from may also be unclear, confused …. We are deeply moved, but also puzzled and shaken. We struggle to articulate what we have been through (Taylor, ibid.).

We think of Aquinas' reverential silence before the Mystery. So often instead of fullness we experience *ennui* or melancholic *acedia*, when fullness fails. Between these two extremes of fullness and forlornness lies ordinary human happiness which fulfils us in various ways even permitting us to flourish and to contribute to what we conceive of as the good. It is essential, Taylor opines, that we have continuing contact with the place of fullness. For the theist, of course, this place of fullness will be faith, but it need not be so theistically construed. Such faith-filled fullness brings peace and joy, a sense of satisfaction and completeness. The unbeliever may experience satisfaction with his lot or a sense of achievement but so long as his life is not ordered to God as the divine flow of presence in it, 'he still has some way to go' (Taylor, ibid., p. 7); perhaps he hasn't conquered his nostalgia for something really transcendent, Taylor contends.

For the theist, 'the account of the place of fullness requires reference to God' (Taylor, ibid., p. 8). For the atheist, fullness may be interpreted naturalistically in terms of human potential and possibility. Experiences of fullness vary but believers often say that it comes to them as a gratuitous gift, as grace; that it is dependent on a relationship of love; that it involves practices of prayer, of charity; often such people feel very far from such conditions of *caritas* and experience themselves instead as preoccupied with lesser, mortal things, that what is needed or required is a (Christian) conversion (*metanoia*) or opening out, a Heideggerian 'clearing' (*Lichtung*), a Platonic *periagoge* or Rilkean 'turning', a Murdochian 'unselfing' or Weilian 'décreation', whereby the ego is transmogrified. Such experiences of fullness seem to come from a power beyond me. What does this mean? Taylor answers thus: 'the best sense I can make of my conflicting and moral experience is captured by a theological view of this kind. That is, in my own experience, in prayer, in moments of fullness, in experiences of exile overcome, in what I seem to observe around me in other peoples' lives – lives of exceptional spiritual fullness, or lives of maximum self-enclosedness, lives of demonic evil, etc. – this seems to be the picture that emerges' (Taylor, ibid., p. 10). Let us repeat, such experiences may be construed differently, non-theistically. It seems to me, though, that God is the best explanation of them. Like Lonergan's, Taylor's hermeneutic is avowedly a Christian construal.

Of course he is aware of the postmodern problems associated with a word such as 'fullness'. We have just to think of Derrida's critique of the metaphysics of *presence* (Taylor describes Derridean deconstruction as a 'non-religious antihumanism' [see Taylor, ibid., p. 19]) or of Levinas' stress on the 'trace'. Taylor observes:

> "Fullness" has come to be my shorthand term for the condition we aspire to, but I am acutely aware how inadequate all words are here. Every possible designation has something wrong with it. The glaring one in the case of 'fullness' is that according to one very plausible spiritual path, visible clearly in Buddhism, for instance, the highest aspiration is to a kind of emptiness (*sunyata*); or to put it more paradoxically, real fullness only comes through emptiness. But there is no perfect terminological solution here, and so with all these reservations I let the word stand (Taylor, ibid., n8, p. 780).

These considerations of what constitutes "fullness" contrast with conceptualisations about 'flourishing'. We all have some conceptions of what human flourishing is, of what constitutes a fulfilled life, of what makes life worth living. These may be codified in moral codes or philosophical or religious practices. The question Taylor poses is: does the highest or best life involve seeking or acknowledging a good that is beyond, in the sense of independent of, human flourishing? The highest human flourishing could include our aiming at something other than human flourishing. Taylor calls these 'final goals' (Taylor, ibid., p. 16). Of course, in the Judaeo-Christian tradition the answer to the question just posited is affirmative. 'Loving, worshipping God is the ultimate end. Of course, in this tradition God is seen as willing human flourishing, but devotion to God is not seen as contingent on this. The injunction "Thy will be done" isn't equivalent to "Let humans flourish", even though we know that God wills human flourishing' (Taylor, ibid., p. 17). Many people on different religious paths detach themselves, or try to do so, from their own flourishing to the point of the extinction of the self. Flourishing is good or a good but seeking it is not our ultimate goal, for Taylor. But secular humanism does not accept any final goals beyond human flourishing or ordinary human happiness. By contrast, Taylor defines 'religion' in terms of 'transcendence', of that something that is higher than or beyond mere human flourishing. Christianity calls this *agape*. Fullness, construed theistically, is 'a condition in which our highest spiritual and moral aspirations point us inescapably to God, one might say, make no sense without God' (Taylor, ibid., p. 26); fullness, so, as a gift from God – fullness as the felt presence of God even in our secular society, our disenchanted world. This is what Eric Voegelin, in an equivalent symbol, calls the 'flow of presence'

St. Augustine had held that all times are present to God. 'His now contains all time', as Taylor puts it (Taylor, ibid., p. 57) – a *nunc stans*. So God's presence is the intersection of timelessness with time, as T. S. Eliot describes it as. Rising to eternity is participating in God's instant. All times are present to Him. This is the beyond of (ordinary) human flourishing which is so crucial to Christianity. But in a world 'shorn of the sacred' (Taylor, ibid., p. 80) many people, Taylor contends, are happy living for purely immanent goals; 'they live in a way that takes no account of the transcendent' (Taylor, ibid., p. 143). The 'secular' age is not only that age that is not tied to religion but the original sense of the secular was that which pertained to profane rather than sacred time; it posited time as purely profane. Of course Taylor realises that our moral and spiritual resources can be experienced as purely immanent; fullness may be formulated with an exclusively human reference – to human time. The move to immanentisation is a rejection of the Christian aspiration to transcend flourishing. Non-theistic Romantics could interpret Bede Griffiths' experience and description of a moment of fullness pantheistically as a worship of nature. It will all depend on one's hermeneutic reading. So if flourishing pertains to our human or profane time, fullness belongs to God's 'time', or eternity. The secular, so, points or refers to the affairs of the world, to temporality, as distinct from the City of God. (Communism and Fascism, as modes of anti-religion, attempt to capture something of a higher purpose but in purely immanentistic terms. Modernity is marked by this anthropocentrism in a way the mediaeval period was characterised, in the main, by theocentrism. Our contemporary culture attests to 'the eclipse of the transcendent' (Taylor, ibid., p. 307) – Buber had called it the 'eclipse of God' in his book of the same title.

The question is: can we find meaning in the malaise of modernity, in the 'malaise of immanence' (Taylor, ibid., p. 308)? The sense of emptiness and meaninglessness, of absurdity and nausea, well documented by Sartre and Camus, is ubiquitous. We seem to have lost a sense of the sacred, of truth and goodness and beauty and depth and sense, in our quotidian, dry, flat and banal, mundane modern lives, of the 'one thing necessary/needful', in our crass, capitalistic and cardboard culture. Taylor distinguishes *three* modes of these malaises of immanence: 1) the fragility of meaning (a theme Frankl makes central to his thought), the loosening of a sense of or search for an over-arching significance; 2) the felt flatness of attempts to solemnise important moments of our lives; and 3) the emptiness of the ordinary (see Taylor, ibid., p. 309). Transcendence is the answer for some – a return to or deepening relationship with the transcendent; for others who don't share such faith, they will seek their solutions in their own ways, perhaps in working for greater prosperity or peace or justice in a world no longer full of gods/God. For the theist, God's existence is felt and flows through all creation. As Schiller writes in *The Gods of Greece*: 'Life's fullness flowed through creation/And there felt what never more will feel/.... Everything to the initiate's eye/ Showed the trace of a God' (cited by Taylor, ibid., p. 316).

Wordsworth, too, speaks of this presence we are identifying, with Taylor, Lonergan and Voegelin too, as God where, in *Tintern Abbey*, Wordsworth writes the following:

A presence that disturbs me with the joy
Of elevated thoughts; a sense sublime
Of something far more deeply interfused,
Whose dwelling is the light of setting suns,
And the round ocean and the living air,
And the blue sky, and the mind of man;
A motion and a spirit, that impels

All thinking things, all objects of all thought,
And rolls through all things (II. 94-102) (cited by Taylor, ibid., pp. 357-8).

This is an epiphanic experience of the flow, of 'the fullness of joy' (Taylor, ibid., p. 358); it is the fulfilment which goes beyond flourishing and even morality and which is the real 'point of our existence' (Taylor, ibid.). This entails, for the Christian, participating in agapeic love, which calls us to go beyond flourishing and to transform our purely immanentistic perspectives and frameworks, supported as they are by a materialist mentality. Ultimately, it will mean more that pursuing our own happiness. The 'pursuit of happiness' in our contemporary commercial culture means the pursuit of private pleasure and self-satisfaction; the modern turn to the self/subject, as in realising my so-called higher or 'true self', is a turn to hedonism where the stress is predominantly on personal development and individual self-expression. As the anthropologist, Marshall Sahlins, asserted: 'A people who conceive life to be the pursuit of happiness must be chronically unhappy'. Self-cultivation represents the higher selfishness involving not mindless accumulation but engaging in tasks that are seen to be socially constructive and emotionally enriching or edifying. Taylor calls this the 'horizontal' focus and form of the modern worldview; this libertarian *Zeitgeist* lacks the vertical dimension – the irruption of the Wholly/Holy Other. The question is: can a life encased in a purely immanentistic order provide ultimate purpose or 'is this all there is'? Many seekers searching for the self rather than salvation say they are interested in 'spirituality' rather than 'religion' or institutionalised forms of expression. But this so-called spirituality can be saccharine and subjectivistic focused, as it is, on the self and its concerns (see Costello, 2002). This kind of spiritual quest is often New Age in its immanentistic understandings and frames of reference (see Taylor, ibid., pp. 508-9), as 'wholeness' is emphasised and cultivated rather than 'holiness' and sickness replaces sin in the 'triumph of the therapeutic' (see Rieff, 1966). This Age of (alleged) Authenticity signifies the retreat of Christendom (see Taylor, ibid., p. 514). It is this hegemony that Taylor is challenging. He calls such a secularist spin a 'closed world structure' (Taylor, ibid., p. 551), reminiscent of Bergson's notion of the 'closed soul', wherein Capitalism has replaced Christianity and where the entertainment media and advertising encourage egomania, self-satisfaction, the pursuit of pleasure and personal fulfilment. 'We feel called to happiness', says Taylor (ibid., p. 583); we *demand* to be happy. But alongside this is a longing for clarity or ultimate meaning, for God, if you like, whose call echoes in the human heart. Can we make sense of life without invoking something transcendent? Does the 'immanent frame', as Taylor calls it, and which Voegelin calls 'the immanentisation of the eschaton', sufice with its relegation of the religious sense of life? Can materialism or Marxism answer our questions about meaning? How do we make sense of our ethical actions or artistic experiences without speaking in terms of a transcendent being which 'interpellates us' (Taylor, ibid., p. 597)? The absence of a life of fullness would leave us, according to Taylor, 'in abject, unbearable despair' (Taylor, ibid., p. 600). Nietzsche had poured scorn on ordinary happiness, as we saw, describing it as a "pitiable comfort". Camus' Dr. Rieux, in *La Peste*, insisted too on aiming for something higher and engaged in ethical acts despite Sisyphean senselessness and the feeling of futility. There are rival notions of fullness but for the theist they will probably be mirages, (Baudrillardian) simulacra, merely immanentistic or naturalistic ontologies. The theist will want, therefore, to include Bede Griffiths' experience or any epiphanic experience we enjoy in our encounter with great music or art within the religious register, what Taylor is calling the fullness beyond flourishing. Commenting on happiness, Taylor has this to say:

> The belief in untroubled happiness is not only a childish illusion, but also involves a truncation of human nature, turning our backs on much of what we are .... Hasn't Christian preaching always repeated that it is impossible to be fully happy as a sinful agent in a sinful world? Certainly this illusion can't be laid at the foot of the Christian faith, however much contemporary Christians may be sucked into this common view of the "pursuit of happiness" today (Taylor, ibid., pp. 635-6).

Humanistic happiness is not what it is ultimately about. Taylor opines: 'If the transcendental view is right, then human beings have an ineradicable bent to respond to something beyond life' (Taylor, ibid., p. 638). Conversion. Self-transcendence. Transformation. Attunement or orientation or alignment of the soul to God, to the flow of divine Presence. For the Christian consciousness, so, human flourishing, which is the aim of an exclusive humanism, is not the final goal. Christianity needn't and shouldn't crush human flourishing but point beyond it to the fullness of redemption, to the 'richness which transcends the ordinary' (Taylor, ibid., p. 677), to the eschatological banquet promised in Paradise. This eschatological emphasis lifts us beyond a teleological tending towards attaining 'my happiness' in this historical 'here and now'. Taylor notes: 'Human happiness can only inspire us when we have to fight against the forces which are destroying it; but once realized, it will inspire nothing but ennui, a cosmic yawn' (Taylor, ibid., p. 717).

Taylor speaks of a desire for eternity in human beings, of 'a desire to gather the scattered moments of meaning into some kind of whole' (Taylor, ibid., p. 720). Doesn't love call for eternity, as Nietzsche rightly recognised? Doesn't joy strive for it? By contrast, 'the collapse of a sense of the eternal brings on a void, a kind of crisis' (Taylor, ibid., 722). Mallarmé gives voice to this feeling of *le Rien, le Néant*: 'Sprawled in the happiness in which only his appetites/Feed' (*Mallarmé* 1994, 12; cited by Taylor, ibid., p. 724). Taylor observes:

> The individual pursuit of happiness as defined by consumer culture still absorbs much of our time and energy, or else the threat of being shut out of this pursuit through poverty, unemployment, incapacity galvanizes all our efforts. All this is true, and yet the sense that there is something more presses in. Great numbers of people feel it: in moments of reflection about their life; in moments of relaxation in nature; in moments of bereavement and loss; and quite wildly and unpredictably. Our age is very far from settling in to a comfortable unbelief. Although many individuals do so, and more still seem

to on the outside, the unrest continues to surface. Could it ever be otherwise? (Taylor, ibid., p. 727).

In the concluding chapter of *A Secular Age* entitled 'Conversions' Taylor relates another epiphanic experience, that of Vaclav Havel – like Griffiths' one, it is an experience of what Taylor calls *conversion*. Griffiths' and Havel's experiences/ conversions broke them out of the immanent frame of focus. In *Letters to Olga* Havel records:

> Again, I call to mind that distant moment in [the prison at] Hermanice when on a hot, cloudless summer day, I sat on a pile of rusty iron and gazed into the crown of an enormous tree that stretched, with dignified repose, up and over all the fences, wires, bars and watchtowers that separated me from it. As I watched the imperceptible trembling of its leaves against an endless sky, I was overcome by a sensation that is difficult to describe: all at once, I seemed to rise above all the coordinates of my momentary existence in the world into a kind of state outside time in which all beautiful things I have ever seen and experienced existed in a total "co-present"; I felt a sense of reconciliation, indeed of an almost gentle assent to the inevitable course of events as revealed to me now, and this combined with a carefree determination to face what had to be faced. A profound amazement at the sovereignty of Being became a dizzy sensation of tumbling endlessly into the abyss of its mystery; an unbounded joy at being alive, at having been given the chance to live through all I have lived through, and at the fact that everything has a deep and obvious meaning – this joy formed a strange alliance in me with a vague horror at the inapprehensibility and unattainability of everything I was so close to in that moment, standing at the very "edge of the infinite"; I was flooded with a sense of ultimate happiness and harmony with the world and myself, with that moment, with all the moments I could call up, and with everything invisible that lies behind it and has meaning. I would even say that I was somehow "struck by love", though I don't know precisely for whom or what (Havel 1984, 331-2; cited by Taylor, ibid., pp. 728-9).

Men like Griffiths and Havel and others like them as well as sages and saints such as Francis of Assisi and Teresa of Avila, the mystics and the prophets of all time, have all radiated a sense of direct contact with transcendent reality. They have articulated fullness. Taylor writes: 'We need to enlarge our palette of such points of contact with fullness, because we are too prone in our age to think of this contact in terms of "experience"; and to think of experience as something subjective distinct from the object experienced; and as something to do with our feelings, distinct from changes in our being: dispositions, orientations' (Taylor, ibid., pp. 729-30). But they are experiences as well as events – heart-transforming, life-changing. There are those like Griffiths and Havel and St. Ignatius who have contemplatively grasped this fullness; they have left us their records and reflections. They have wrought paradigm shifts that signalled a move from an immanent

therapeutic perspective and framework to a spiritual one. 'The internal economy of
the immanent theory, say a Freudian one, in which the various forces which count
are purely intra-psychic, and are rooted in the patient's desires and fears, is now
disrupted. The genesis of guilt, alienation, internal division is now found at least in
part in the aspiration to something transcendent' (Taylor, ibid., p. 731). In so doing,
they upset the parameters of our time and raise up human life to the divine (*theiosis*).
They take us beyond immanent realities and challenge mainstream materialism as
well as the nature/supernature distinction. But as St. Thomas reminds us, grace
builds on nature; it doesn't abolish it. They are responding to transcendent reality
which Taylor has called fullness. Others may respond to it too but may misrecognise
it such as in the exclusive humanisms. Griffiths initially interpreted his experience
in the light of a Wordsworthian Romanticism; only later did he come to see it in the
light of Christian Revelation. Rilke, commenting on his poem 'Turning', that he
penned between the 18th and 20th of June, 1914, to Lou Andreas-Salomé, wrote:
'May this gazing out of myself, which consumes me to emptiness, be rid of through
a loving preoccupation with interior fullness' (Rilke, 1976; cited by Hederman
2000, 92). For Taylor, our sense of this fullness 'is a reflection of transcendent
reality (which for me is the God of Abraham)' (Taylor, ibid., p. 769). To find fullness
is to find God, ultimately for Taylor. It is to be converted. He writes: 'The convert's
insights break beyond the limits of the regnant versions of immanent order .... to a
larger, more encompassing one, which includes it while disrupting it' (Taylor, ibid.,
p. 732). While Taylor calls these experiences 'conversions', it is Bernard Lonergan,
S.J., who details the dynamics of such conversions in his *Method and Theology*
(1971) and so it will prove instructive to consider his thoughts on the subject. Taylor
defines conversion as 'breaking out into the broader field' (Taylor, ibid., p. 769)
but it is Fr. Lonergan, whom Taylor interestingly doesn't cite, who distinguishes
between *three* types of conversion and who offers a more systematic and nuanced
account than Taylor, one that can fill in some of the caveats in Taylor's considerations
of the subject. We now turn to Lonergan.

Lonergan

For Lonergan, by a differentiation of consciousness, we are engaged in a
moral pursuit of goodness, a philosophic pursuit of truth, a scientific pursuit of
understanding and an artistic pursuit of beauty in our attempt to be attentive,
intelligent, reasonable and responsible, as we experience, understand, judge and
decide; this is the crux of his transcendental method, as set by him in *Insight* and
Method in Theology. It is to this latter work that we will now look for his insights
into the nature and dynamic of conversion. Like Taylor, Lonergan holds that being
in love with God is 'the basic fulfilment of our conscious intentionality' (Lonergan
2005 [1957], p. 105), one which brings a 'deep-set joy' (Lonergan, ibid.). In his
Spiritual Exercises St. Ignatius calls such spiritual happiness 'consolation' (without
a cause).

A conversion ushers in a change in the direction of development, a change for the better as one grows in authenticity. Values are apprehended, scales of preference shift, as Lonergan puts it (see Lonergan ibid., p. 52). Conversion may issue in a violent change that disrupts psychological continuity but it may be preceded by transient dispositions. More commonly, conversion is a slow process of maturation as one finds out what it is to be intelligent, reasonable, responsible and loving. Conversion doesn't rest on this once and far all dynamic of change; 'conversion is life-long' (Lonergan, ibid., p. 118). The objectification of conversion provides Christianity with its foundations. Lonergan defines conversion thus: 'By conversion is understood a transformation of the subject and his world' (Lonergan, ibid., p. 130). Normally it is a prolonged process that results in a change of the course of direction of one's life. 'It is as if one's eyes were opened and one's former world faded and fell away …. Conversion is existential, intensely personal, utterly intimate. But it is not so private as to be solitary' (Lonergan, ibid.). Conversion affects all of man's conscious and intentional operations. 'It directs his gaze, pervades his imagination, releases the symbols that penetrate to the depths of his psyche. It enriches his understanding, guides his judgments, reinforces his decisions' (Lonergan, ibid., p. 131). Conversion is the basic step, after it comes the labour of thinking out everything from the profounder perspective. Conversion heralds in the transition from inauthenticity to authenticity. It is the work of (a good) conscience. The dark decreases and the light increases. Conversion occurs when man discovers what is inauthentic in himself and turns away from it and embraces instead the fullness of authenticity. It is cognate with the Christic edict: 'Repent, the kingdom of God is at hand!' Conversion manifests itself in deeds and words; it is radical revision.

According to Lonergan, there are *three* types of conversion. They are three modalities or fundamental forms of self-transcendence. 'Conversion may be intellectual or moral or religious. While each of the three is connected with the other two, still each is a different type of event and has to be considered in itself before being related to the others' (Lonergan, ibid., p. 238). He elucidates these three types thus: 'Moral conversion changes the criterion of one's decisions and choices from satisfactions to values' (Lonergan, ibid., p. 240). Moral conversion, thus, consists in opting for or choosing the truly good. 'Religious conversion is being grasped by ultimate concern. It is other-worldly falling in love. It is total and permanent self-surrender without conditions' (Lonergan, ibid.). It is 'fated acceptance of a vocation to holiness' (Lonergan, ibid.). For Christians it is God's love flooding our hearts through the Holy Spirit given in the gift of (operative) grace. Operative grace is religious conversion whereas cooperative grace is the effectiveness of such a conversion; it is 'the gradual movement towards a full and complete transformation of the whole of one's living and feeling, one's thoughts, words, deeds, and omissions' (Lonergan, ibid., p. 241). Intellectual conversion 'is to truth attained by cognitional self-transcendence' (Lonergan, ibid.). When all three occur within a single consciousness their relations can be conceived in terms of sublation in Karl Rahner S.J.'s sense rather than Hegel's. When religious conversion occurs, desire turns to joy and the subject is held, grasped, arrested, possessed, owned by an other-worldly love; it involves loving with one's whole heart, soul, mind and strength. 'Holiness abounds in truth and moral goodness, but it has a distinct dimension of its own. It is other-worldly fulfilment, joy, peace, bliss' (Lonergan, ibid., p. 242). The absence of such fulfilment, in contradistinction, reveals itself as despairing unrest, the absence of joy, depressive disgust with oneself or life, what St. Ignatius calls 'desolation'.

In relation to the ordering of these three types of conversion, Lonergan delineates their interrelationships thus: 'Though religious conversion sublates moral, and moral conversion sublates intellectual, one is not to infer that intellectual comes first and then moral and finally religious' (Lonergan, ibid., p. 243). By contrast, in terms of the causal viewpoint, there is first God's love and the eye of this love reveals values in their luminosity and splendour, while the strength of this love brings about moral conversion. Finally, one discerns in the light of this love the truths taught by the religious tradition; the seeds are thus sown for intellectual conversion. The religious conversion grounds both the moral and intellectual conversion; 'it provides the real criterion by which all else is to be judged' (Lonergan, ibid., p. 283). Religious conversion is the experiential event that gives the name 'God' its fundamental meaning. The word penetrates to all four levels of intentional consciousness: experience, understanding, judging and deciding. The whole man is thus evoked. And aside from conversions one has breakdowns or derailments, distortions (see Lonergan, ibid., pp. 243-71). In any single consciousness all three types of conversion may be present or lacking; any one may be present or two or all three of them. Conversion manifests itself in deeds and words. Conversion consists in a radical revision of formerly held opinions, beliefs or positions and 'transforms the concrete individual' (Lonergan, ibid., p. 338) completely.

To finish, fullness takes us beyond flourishing (ordinary happiness) and conversion issues in joy. For Taylor, Lonergan and Voegelin, the fullness of joy is found in an encounter with the divine Ground of being, who reveals Himself as Ground and Goal, origin and end. In this alone is man's (final) fulfilment. Taylor uses this term 'fulfilment' in a broader sense than the ordinary word which is usually used to describe whatever fulfils my own personal needs or self-satisfactions. He explains: 'I want to extend it to whatever realizes (what we see as) the highest and fullest form of life, even if this demands the sacrifice of personal "fulfilment"' (Taylor, 2007, ibid., note 9, p. 838). Writing about such fulfilment, Viktor Frankl, who managed to find meaning in a concentration camp, in *Man's Search for Meaning*, wrote that a thought transfixed him and it was this: that for the first time in his life he saw the truth that had been expounded by the poets and philosophers of all times, that love is the ultimate goal to which the human spirit can aspire, that life is about meaning and not happiness, that man's salvation is in and through love. Let me conclude this chapter with Frankl's words – in the following, final chapter the focus is exclusively on Frankl:

> I understood how a man who has nothing left in this world still may know
> bliss, be it only for a brief moment, in the contemplation of his beloved. In a

position of utter desolation, when man cannot express himself in positive action, when his only achievement may consist in enduring his sufferings in the right way – an honourable way – in such a position man can, through loving contemplation of the image he carries of his beloved, achieve fulfilment. For the first time in my life I was able to understand the meaning of the words, "The angels are lost in perpetual contemplation of an infinite glory" (Frankl, 1959, p. 49).

Chapter Fifteen
Frankl: Pleasure, Happiness, Joy

Happiness is like a butterfly; the more you chase it, the more it will elude you, but if you turn your attention to other things, it will come and sit softly on your shoulder.

Thoreau.

Every follower of Viktor Frankl (1905-1997) knows that happiness must not be pursued, that it must ensue; happiness happens. For Frankl, happiness is a by-product, a side-effect of man's search for meaning as the primary motivating factor. This chapter addresses the dialectic between happiness and meaning by showing parallels between Frankl's approach to the subject and the work of some other contemporary philosophers. The hermeneutics of Ricoeur seeks meaning 'in spite of' meaninglessness, misery and failure; the equivalent in Frankl would be the hope that the 'triumphant triad' (of healing, forgiveness and meaning) would overcome the 'tragic triad' (of suffering/pain, guilt and death). Charles Taylor, as we have seen, argues that finding meaning in fulfilment, what he labels 'fullness' and which he relates to transcendence (Frankl's 'supra-meaning'), is superior to immanentistic flourishing. As such, the philosophical positions adopted by Frankl, Taylor and others represent implicit critiques of an Aristotelian eudaimonistic ethic which has been so prevalent in the Western philosophical tradition and with which we began this book. Aristotle explicitly argued in his *Nicomachean Ethics* that every pursuit aims at some good and the Good or happiness is that at which all things aim (see Aristotle, 1978, p. 63). It will be shown, by reference to some logotherapeutic techniques, that Frankl's phenomenological psychology, lacking in the purely philosophical perspectives, is the empirical linchpin that consolidates the thesis that, 1) happiness should not be aimed at directly contra Aristotle, and 2) rather, finding or locating meaning in life is paramount, both philosophically and psychologically.

Nietzsche had proclaimed that life itself is interpretation; if this is true then philosophy is the interpretation of interpretations. For Ricoeur, there is interpretation where there is multiple meaning. There are diverse hermeneutics; a Freud sees everything in terms of a semantics of desire; a Nietzsche and an Adler see everything in terms of will to power, a Marx sees everything in terms of capital and class consciousness. If we could put all the hermeneutic readings together we may catch a glimpse of the Promised Land of ultimate understanding; it would be, in Ricoeur's felicitous phrase, a 'hermeneutics of God's coming, of the approach of his Kingdom' (Ricoeur, 2004, p. 20). Due to equivocal expressions being endemic in language, hermeneutics remains unsurpassable. No one reading of anything can give us an exhaustive explanation; our viewpoints are restricted and limited, our perspectives partial. All contributions are modest and myopic. We see only small sections of reality. Philosophers, as well as everyone else, grasp things generally from one point of view. So, in this chapter, I would like to explore a hermeneutics of happiness in relation to meaning. My thesis is Franklian: rather than speaking of 'the meaning of happiness' we should speak instead of 'the happiness of meaning'. Similarly, the meaning of life is a life of meaning.

At the end of *The Future of an Illusion*, Freud exclaims that he can offer us no consolation, no happiness, only harshness and resignation to *Ananke*, to the blows of fate and fortune, to what in 'Beyond the Pleasure Principle', he calls 'sublime' Necessity (Freud, 1920, p. 317). For Freud, tragic knowledge is reconciliation to the inevitable and self-understanding comes slowly through suffering. Ricoeur sums up the Freudian position thus: 'In this terrible battle for meaning, nothing and no one comes out unscathed. The "timid" hope must cross the desert of the path of mourning' (Ricoeur, 2004, p. 172). We work towards meaning which for Freud merely represents our infantile consolation. Freud strips the ego of its omnipotence; he wounds us well and forces desire to accept its own death. However, the reductive hermeneutics of Marx, Nietzsche and Freud are welcomed by Ricoeur (which doesn't mean that they are accepted). Because it is from a moment of destruction that we can find inspiration and instruction and on surer foundations than before. All three offer their deconstructive critiques of religion; for Marx, to believe in God is form of alienation; God is a projection for Freud (and for Feuerbach) and based on an infantile illusion. Nietzsche had proclaimed God dead. But none of them really ever speak of God, only the gods of men and these we will always have with us. According to the hermeneutic hypothesis of these three 'masters of suspicion', as Ricoeur calls them, 'man is a being sick with the sublime' (Ricoeur, ibid., p. 335). However, for Ricoeur, the Protestant, the sacred calls upon man confronting him with the ethical task of moving from slavery and sin to sanctity and sense. We are urged toward hope and happiness while realising that 'happiness is not our accomplishment: it is achieved by superaddition, by surplus' (Ricoeur, ibid., p. 412). If it comes, it comes as a gift, as grace. For Kant, whom Frankl controversially calls 'the greatest philosopher of all times' (Frankl, 1988, p. 122), we have an indirect duty to seek our own happiness, in so far as this is compatible with the moral law but we need to make ourselves *worthy* of happiness. Furthermore, happiness is one thing, being good is something else. In the *Groundwork of the Metaphysic of Morals*, Kant writes: 'To assure one's own happiness is a duty (at least, indirectly); for discontent with one's state, in a press of cares and amidst unsatisfied wants, might easily become a great *temptation to the transgression of duty*' (Kant, 1985, p. 64). He goes on to say that we all have the strongest inclination towards happiness but the 'prescription for happiness is, however, often so constituted as greatly to interfere with some inclinations, and yet men cannot form under the name of "happiness" any determinate and assured conception of satisfaction of all inclinations as a sum' (Kant, ibid.). For Kant, happiness is ethical if seeking to further it is done, not from inclination, but from duty, then such conduct has 'real moral worth' (Kant, ibid., p. 65). There is one end that may be supposed as actual in all rational beings, to whom imperatives apply and there is one purpose, happiness. It is a hypothetical imperative (see Kant, ibid., p. 79). Moreover, happiness is a nebulous or 'indeterminate concept', that 'although every man wants to attain … he can never say definitely and in unison with himself what it really is that he wants and wills' (Kant, ibid., p. 81). What is required for the 'Idea' of happiness as a whole is maximum well-being in my present and future state. But this is difficult, contends Kant. He asks:

> Is it riches that he wants? How much anxiety, envy, and pestering might he not bring in this way on his own head! Is it knowledge and insight? This might perhaps merely give him an eye so sharp that it would make evils at present hidden from him and yet unavoidable seem all the more frightful, or would add a load of still further needs to the desires which already give him trouble enough. Is it long life? Who will guarantee that it would not be a long misery? Is it at least health? How often has infirmity of body kept a man from excesses into which perfect health would have let him fall! – and so on. In short, he has no principle by which he is able to decide with complete certainty what will make him truly happy, since for this he would require omniscience …. What action will promote the happiness of a rational being is completely insoluble; and consequently that in regard to this there is no imperative possible which in the strictest sense could command us to do what will make us happy, since happiness is an Ideal, not of reason, but of imagination (Kant, ibid., pp. 81-2).

What he is saying here is that the categorical imperative cannot be based on any interest. Our duty must not be influenced by our interests. We can but imagine happiness.

For Ricoeur, who was much influenced by Kant, and following the lead of St. Paul, in spite of death and misery and meaninglessness, we hope and wager in ultimate meaning. This 'in spite of' sin and death, is the inverse, the shadow side, of the joyous 'how much more than' which pertains to the logic of superabundance and surplus. Hope works towards the Kingdom of God despite evil and totalitarianism which constitute the pathology of hope. For Kant, virtue is the obedience to pure duty and happiness is the satisfaction of desire. But perhaps, to venture a Hegelian synthesis here, duty is not incompatible with desire, or hope and happiness and meaning with sin, death and despair? To put it in Franklian terms, to retain the pessimistic perspective of the tragic triad without permitting the triumphant triad into the frame of reference is lopsided. As such, to Freud's 'cheerful pessimism', we may oppose Frankl's 'tragic optimism'. The glass, to take the clichéd example, is always half full and half empty at the same time. To put it another way, when the glass is half full it is also half empty. By focusing on the part that is full alone or empty alone one is incorporating a limited understanding of reality. Isn't wisdom the cognitive ability to discern both realities simultaneously and not one at the expense of the other, to have, as James Joyce put it, two thinks at a time? Blake had summarised such dialectical thinking thus: 'There is no progress without contraries'. So to the question: 'would you like a cup of coffee or tea?' the only dialectical answer is 'yes please'!

We should, therefore, not be in too much of a rush to leave the tragic in favour of the triumphant but to retain both perspectives in a delicate dialectical and dynamic tension; in Hegel's memorable phrase, we need to spend some time 'looking the negative in the face, and tarrying with it. This tarrying with the negative...' (Hegel, 1977, para. 32, p. 19) is one side of the dialectic and an important one lest we become humanistic hopefuls who toe the Dalai Lama line: 'The purpose of life is to be happy' as he puts it (Dalai Lama, 1996, p. xiii). The other extreme is Schopenhauerian pessimism. Frankl's shorthand is 'D = S-M' (the DSM!): '*despair is suffering without meaning*' (Frankl, 2000, p. 132). In such a situation we are prone to experience with Shakespeare's Hamlet the feelings he describes thus: 'How weary, stale, flat and unprofitable seem to me all the uses of the world. Fie on it!' (Act I, Scene II). But suffering need not be an obstacle to happiness – often it is a means to it, less a pathology than a path.

The modern-day moral injunction is: '*happiness as the supreme duty*', as Slavoj Zizek puts it in his *In Defense of Lost Causes* (Zizek, 2008, p. 44). But, against this tradition that Zizek is also critiquing, Frankl contends that meaning rather than happiness is the objective – what Ricoeur calls 'a hermeneutics of meaning' (Ricoeur, 2004, p. 139). Meaning is embodied in human intersubjectivity, 'in art, in symbols, in language, and in the lives and deeds of persons' as Bernard Lonergan, S.J., puts it in his *Method in Theology* (Lonergan, 1971, p. 57). In his discussion on what constitutes meaning, Lonergan cites three works of Frankl: *The Doctor and the Soul, Man's Search for Meaning, The Will to Meaning* and, with others, *Psychotherapy and Existentialism* (see Lonergan, 1971, p. 70). For Lonergan, it is incarnate meaning that combines many of the carriers of meaning: *Cor ad cor loquitur*. It can be intersubjective, artistic, symbolic, linguistic; it is 'the meaning of a person, of his way of life, of his words, or of his deeds' (Lonergan, ibid., p. 73). He notes: 'Meaning enters into the very fabric of human living' (Lonergan, ibid., p. 81). (Meaning is communicative, constitutive, efficient and cognitive). We move from an infant's world of immediacy into a world mediated by meaning (see Lonergan, ibid., p. 89) and in this world man discovers mind; he discovers logos which, as Frankl says, is deeper than logic (see Frankl, 2004, p. 122). Lonergan observes: 'There is an intelligence, a *logos*, that steers through all things. It is found in god and man and beast, the same in all though in different degrees. To know it, is wisdom' (Lonergan, 1971, p. 91). As Heraclitus, the Pre-Socratic, said: 'When you have listened not to me but to the logos it is wise to agree that all is one'. Philosophically, it is hermeneutics which 'studies the varying relations of acts of meaning to terms of meaning' (Lonergan, ibid., p. 92) and which, in terms of a hermeneutics of religion, interprets this Logos that was in the beginning. The Logos as Word is 'the bearer of all grace and of all reality', in Karl Rahner, S.J.'s beautiful words (Rahner, 1941, p. 41).

The *three* basic foundations of Frankl's existential analysis are: 1) the freedom of the will – we are free to search for meaning, 2) the will to meaning – we have a will to find meaning, and 3) the meaning of life – that life is always worth living. Hence, his redeployment of the ancient symbol *logos* in his 'logotherapy', where *logos* is intended to signify 'the spiritual' and denote 'meaning'. By contrast, 'logophobia' is a term we may use, following Voegelin's lead, to describe a fear and hatred of philosophy, of a refusal to engage in the search for meaning and the truth of existence. Voegelin, Lonergan and Frankl would hold that our *nous* is capable of comprehending eternal being, that *Geist* is the core of the human person. Man is a 'psycho-physico-spiritual entity' in Frankl's words (Frankl, 2009, p. 28). And Voegelin acknowledges Frankl's work in existential psychology and expresses his gratitude to him for rediscovering what Schelling called '"pneumopathology", Frankl's "noological dimension" of man, as well as the treatment of its diseases by "logotherapy" ... It would not be surprising if sooner or later psychologists and social scientists were to find out about the classic analysis of noetic existence as the proper theoretical basis for the psychopathology of the "age"' (Voegelin, 1990, pp. 278-9; commenting on both Frankl and Voegelin, Prof. David Walsh, a Voegelin expert, writes thus, in a private communication with the author: 'Frankl is essentially a parallel figure to Voegelin who appreciated him as doing something similar. The core convergence seems to be on the need for spiritual order, an order of the soul, as the basis for the life of reason'. And Fr. Brendan Purcell, an expert on Voegelin and Lonergan, wrote to me that: 'Voegelin admired Frankl and felt he had rediscovered Platonic "therapy"'). Rahner similarly writes that the human person is spirit (see Rahner, 1941, p. 9). He notes: 'To be human is to be spirit [*Der Mensch ist Geist*], i.e., to live life while reaching ceaselessly for the absolute, in openness toward God .... We are forever the infinite openness of the finite for God' (Rahner, ibid., p. 53). Spirit is the intellectual soul in man. And, according to Frankl's psychiatric credo, the spirit can never be sick, though it may be blocked.

So we are enjoined to find (spiritual) meaning in life, to seize the 'meaning of the moment' and to fulfil ultimate meaning through noetic existence. Frankl believes that 'the greatness of a life can be measured by the greatness of a moment .... a single moment can retroactively flood an entire life with meaning' (Frankl, 2009, p. 58). We do not know what life has still in store for us, or what 'magnificent hour may still await' us (Frankl, ibid., p. 69).

Frankl sets out *three* ways as to how we can find meaning: 1) by being creative, 2) by experiencing something (especially experiencing the True, the Good and the Beautiful) or encountering someone, and 3) by changing one's attitude to unavoidable suffering or unchangeable situations. The last one – attitudinal values – entails facing one's fate without flinching; the ancient Stoics gave prominence to this the last of human freedoms in their philosophical *therapeia*. It testifies to the enduring and 'defiant power of the human spirit'. As Plutarch puts it: 'The measure of a man is the way he bears up under misfortune'.

Lack of meaning or the impossibility to fulfil meaning potential is the main reason for the 'existential vacuum' of *ennui* and apathy, of doubt, despair, hopelessness and spiritual *acedia*. Such is the *taedium vitae*. Yes, Frankl says, 'things are bad' (Frankl, 2000, p. 89) but unless we seek to ameliorate them, everything will become worse! To live is to suffer but to survive is to find some meaning in suffering. Frankl often asked his patients why they didn't commit suicide, thus recognising with Camus, that the only philosophical question is whether we should commit suicide out of disgust with life. *If* there is meaning, it is unconditional and neither suffering nor dying can detract from it (see Frankl, ibid., p. 156). To trust there is is transcendental in the Kantian sense. Indeed, it is tempting to read Frankl as a transcendental Thomist. Religion is the fulfilment of this will to ultimate meaning (see Frankl, ibid., p. 153) and to this end, Frankl cites Einstein (1950): 'To be religious is to have found an answer to the question, What is the meaning of life?' and Wittgenstein (1960): 'To believe in God is to see that life has a meaning' (see Frankl, ibid.).

Franklian psychology teaches that *life does not owe us happiness, it offers us meaning*. Happiness, like success and satisfaction, are by-products of our pursuit of meaning. And all meaning converges in the highest meaning, that is to say, in transcendent reality. As such, our search for meaning is implicitly, if construed theistically (and it doesn't have to be so construed) a search for God, for the intelligent Ground of being, for the divine Logos. Ultimate meaning may be approached, it is never appropriated; by contrast, the meaning of the moment can be found and fulfilled. This involves being mindful of the moment as we tend and attend to, as well as profit from, the present instant and the call of the hour.

Franklian psychology and philosophy deny *three* attitudes: nihilism, which is the denial of meaning; reductionism, which is the denial of the will to meaning; and pandeterminism, which is the denial of our freedom to find meaning. Isn't neurosis an illness of the soul that has not found meaning in life, as Jung hypothesised? The most fruitful arena wherein meaning can be found is self-transcendence, that is, the human ability or capacity to reach or stretch out beyond ourselves. For Lonergan, 'Man achieves authenticity in self-transcendence' (Lonergan, 1971, p. 104).

The pursuit of happiness, by contrast, is the pursuit of self-fulfilment; it ignores (the ethical dimension of) the Other. For Frankl, this is the paradox of happiness and of pleasure too. For example, the more we seek pleasure or happiness (and later we will distinguish between the two), the less we find it. Why? Because pleasure is a by-product of having done something meaningful. Like happiness. At the heart of the pursuit of pleasure and happiness is ultimate failure and paradox. Happiness must not be aimed at directly; this is Frankl's constant refrain. We have to let it happen by not caring about it, or giving it our energy. The surest way to be unhappy is to fixate on happiness, to demand or desire it, to hyper-reflect on it. Seeking happiness is like chasing a rainbow – the faster one runs, the further it recedes. We need to surrender to it happening, to let go and forget about it. Self-transcendence is the ultimate ethical and spiritual 'beyond' of self-actualisation.

Hyper-intention is the excessive striving for a goal such as happiness or pleasure. Frankl encourages us to de-reflect from this egotistical pursuit of happiness. As such, we need to *find meaning* and *forget about happiness*. It is the noetic dimension of the human spirit that contains the core of our vast spiritual resources, amongst which is our human capacity for self-transcendence. We are not self-enclosed Leibnitzian monads; we open out to the Other. Self-transcendence is, in Rahner's words, a 'reaching for more' (Rahner, 1994, p. 47). We 'continually transcend everything toward pure being' (Rahner, ibid., p. 53), which is the fullness of absolute, supramundane, infinite Being. For Rahner, being is luminous, being is light. Being is lucidity. And the human person is a spirit reaching out into the divine domain that 'only the fullness of God's absolute being can fill' (Rahner, ibid., p. 54). For the theist, 'God is the meaning of humanity' (Rahner, ibid., p. 19), not happiness.

In the Preface to the 1992 edition of *Man's Search for Meaning*, Frankl tells us that the following was the advice he gave to his students:

> Don't aim at success – the more you aim at it and make it a target, the more you are going to miss it. For success, like happiness, cannot be pursued; it must ensue, and it only does so as the unintended side-effect of one's dedication to a cause greater than oneself or as the by-product of one's surrender to a person other than oneself. Happiness must happen, and the same holds for success: you have to let it happen by not caring about it. I want you to listen to what your conscience commands you to do and go on to carry it out to the best of your knowledge. Then you will live to see that in the long run – in the long run, I say! – success will follow you precisely because you had *forgotten* to think of it (Frankl, 2004, pp. 12-3).

According to Frankl, man lives and moves in his everyday life in a dimension whose positive pole is success and whose negative pole is failure. However, the *homo patiens* (the suffering man) who, by virtue of his humanness is capable of rising above his suffering moves in a dimension whose positive pole is fulfilment and whose negative pole is despair. A human being strives for success but that doesn't depend on his fate. By the very attitude he chooses, man is capable of finding and fulfilling meaning even in hopeless situations. For Frankl, there can be as much meaning in suffering as in success. As he states: '*Lack of success does not signify lack of meaning*' (Frankl, ibid., p. 110). This philosophical position is only comprehensible through Frankl's dimensional ontology, his construal of man as being body, mind and spirit, which form a biopsychospiritual unity – there is, of course, also the social dimension. Frankl allots to the attitudinal values a higher dimension that to creative and experiential values. Attitudinal values are the highest ones possible just as the meaning of inescapable and unavoidable suffering is the deepest possible meaning. One can have a successful career and yet feel that one's life is meaningless and feel caught or trapped in the existential vacuum ('ev'), below 'success' and at the right side of 'despair', in the diagram below (see Frankl, 1988, p. 75), in which case, we may speak, as Frankl does, of *despair despite success*. On the other hand, there is a phenomenon which can be described as *fulfilment despite failure*, localised in the upper left angle, marked by 'SQ' (San Quentin prison).

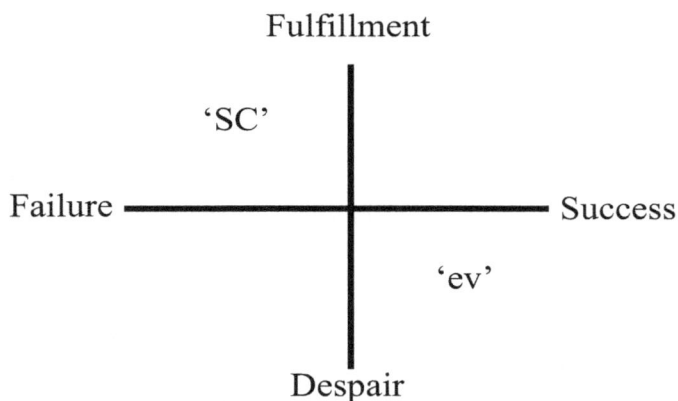

```
                    Fulfillment
                        |
        'SC'            |
                        |
Failure ————————————————+———————————————— Success
                        |
                        |     'ev'
                        |
                    Despair
```

In the prison of San Quentin Frankl met a man who bore witness to Frankl's contention that meaning may be found in life literally up to the last moment – in the face of death itself. The particular prisoner Frankl met was editor of the *San Quentin News* and he published a review of one of Frankl's books. He asked to interview Frankl and this was broadcast to the cells, to thousands of prisoners including those on death row. To one of them, who was due to be executed in the gas chambers in four days, Frankl was asked to address some special words. As somebody who had himself encountered Nazi gas chambers, he was in a unique position to expound on his philosophy of life. So he began: Either life is meaningful, in which case it doesn't depend on its duration or it is meaningless, in which case it would be pointless to prolong it. Frankl drew on Tolstoy's famous story, 'The Death of Ivan Ilyich' and made the point that prisoners, just like everybody else, can rise above their predicament and themselves and retroactively invest meaning in their lives. The message reached the inmates. Later, Frankl learned that the San Quentin news article which covered his visit took first place in a National Penal Press Journalism Contest and was selected for top honours from a representative group of entries from more than 150 American correctional institutions. It was penned by the prisoner in question who had fully agreed with Frankl that even in the depths of despair man can mould a meaningful life-experience and turn tragedy into triumph so that the existential vacuum can become transmuted into a value. People sentenced to death may 'triumph' where so-called successful people can feel caught up in despair. To this end, Frankl cites a study conducted in Harvard University where among 100 subjects who had graduated 20 years before, there was a huge percentage of whom who complained of a crisis and felt that their personal lives were pointless even though they had been very successful in their professional lives – they included lawyers, doctors and analysts. It is instructive to compare the experience of San Quentin with the Harvard one. In the light of Frankl's dimensional anthropology and ontology, despair is compatible with success, just as fulfilment of meaning is compatible with suffering and dying (see Frankl, 1988). As Goethe once remarked: 'There is no predicament that we cannot ennoble either by doing or enduring'.

Happiness and success and pleasure have one thing in common: they are substitutes for fulfilment, derivatives of the will to meaning, in this Franklian logo-philosophical, tri-dimensional perspective. Interestingly, it was John Stuart Mill who first counselled caution in relation to the direct aiming at happiness. In his *Autobiography* Mill muses: 'But I now thought that this end [one's happiness] was only to be attained by not making it the direct end. Those only are happy (I thought) who have their minds fixed on some object other than their own happiness .... Aiming thus at something else, they find happiness along the way .... Ask yourself whether you are happy, and you cease to be so' (Mill, 1929, p. 94). Henry Sidgwick, the English utilitarian philosopher and follower of Mill, made the same point in his *The Methods of Ethics*, that we should put happiness 'out of sight and not directly aim at it' (Sidgwick, 1963, p. 3). Pascal, for his part, tells us 'All men seek happiness. There are no exceptions' (Pascal, 1995, pp. 74-5). But this demand for happiness can wait; it must be postponed. The ancient Stoics taught us to withdraw into ourselves to find peace whereas others advise us to look outside ourselves. Pascal asserts: 'Happiness is neither outside nor inside us: it is in God, both outside and inside us' (Pascal, ibid., p. 407).

Let us repeat: the essence of existence is self-transcendence. Existence is both intentional and transcendent. Self-actualisation is possible only as a side-effect of self-transcendence (see Frankl, 2004, p. 115). For Frankl, our whole therapeutic culture stresses the idea that we ought to be happy, that we have a *right* to be happy, 'that unhappiness is a symptom of maladjustment' (Frankl, ibid., p. 118). But paradoxically, our burden is increased by unhappiness about being unhappy! Frankl continues:

> One must have a reason "to be happy". Once the reason is found, however, one becomes happy automatically. As we see, a human being is not one in pursuit of happiness but rather in search of a reason to become happy, last not least, through actualising the potential meaning inherent and dormant in a given situation .... Once an individual's search for a meaning is successful, it not only renders him happy but also gives him the capability to cope with suffering (Frankl, ibid., pp. 140-1).

Frankl is thus hugely critical of the Freudian pleasure principle and of Freud's emphasis on pleasure being the goal of life. Pleasure, far from being the goal of our endeavours and aspirations, is the consequence of attaining them, as Kant had pointed out. In *The Doctor and the Soul*, Frankl opines: 'Commenting on the hedonist ethics, eudemonism, Scheler has remarked that pleasure does not loom up before us as the goal of an ethical act; rather, an ethical act carries pleasure on its back' (Frankl, 2009, pp. 51-2). According to Frankl, life teaches most people that we are not here to enjoy ourselves (see Frankl, ibid., p. 53); we experience more unpleasurable sensations than pleasurable ones. People don't necessarily want pleasure; they want what they want. If we set up pleasure as the whole meaning of life, in the final analysis, life will seem meaningless. 'Pleasure cannot possibly lend meaning to life' (Frankl, ibid.). Now the man who first stated the supremacy of pleasure was Eudoxus (406-355 BC). For Eudoxus and Epicurus later, pleasure is the supreme Good (see Aristotle, 1978, p. 86). Aristotle, in his *Ethics*, summarises the main philosophical positions on pleasure thus: 1) some say that no pleasure is a good, 2) others say that some pleasures are good but that most are bad; and 3) even if all pleasures are good, pleasure itself cannot be the supreme good (see Aristotle, ibid., p. 250). For Aristotle, pleasure is necessary up to a point but excessive or insufficient enjoyment of pleasure is not. Pleasure is a constituent of happiness; it is not itself happiness however. According to Aristotle, (see Aristotle, ibid., p. 256) when people feel excessive pain in life they tend to pursue excessive pleasure, especially bodily pleasure as a cure for their suffering (Frankl makes a similar point when he says that when people are in the existential vacuum they usually fill it up with libidinal dynamics). But Aristotle advises us not to become slaves to self-indulgence, to avoid licentiousness and lead lives of temperateness and moderation instead. We ought 'to put on immortality' (Aristotle, ibid., p. 331) while realising that 'pleasure and pain permeate the whole of life' (Aristotle, ibid., p. 312). He observes: 'The best and most pleasant life is the life of the intellect, since the intellect is in the fullest sense the man. So this life will also be the happiest' (Aristotle, ibid., p. 331). Happiness, for Aristotle, is co-extensive with contemplation.

Frankl likewise critiques this 'will to pleasure' which he associates with Freud. As early as 1911 in 'Formulations on the Two Principles of Mental Functioning', Freud had written that the human organism strives 'towards gaining pleasure' (Freud, 1911, p. 36). The 'reality-principle' does not negate the dominance of the pleasure-principle; it merely postpones satisfactions, according to the Freudian formulation. The 'pleasure-ego' works for a yield of pleasure and attempts to avoid unpleasure. Of course, for Lacan, unpleasure can itself be a source of pleasure, an experience he labels *jouissance*. In 1920, in 'Beyond the Pleasure Principle', Freud announced, in his second theory of the instincts, that there was something 'beyond pleasure' and that is pain or the death drive (*Thanatos*). However, even the first sentence of this work suggests no abandonment of his previous perspective of nine years earlier: 'In the theory of psychoanalysis we have no hesitation in assuming that the course taken by mental events is automatically regulated by the pleasure principle' (Freud, 1920, p. 275). He says he is not concerned what philosophical system his hypothesis of the pleasure principle may be placed in; actually, it may be described as philosophical materialism. He still states his belief in 'the dominance of the pleasure principle in mental life' (Freud, ibid., p. 277). Of course, there are other principles, such as the reality-principle but for Freud this doesn't negate the pleasure-principle, as we have said. Freud wonders, 'If there is a "beyond the pleasure principle"' (Freud, ibid., p. 305). Even the death-drive, for Freud, is pleasurable in that '*the aim of all life is death*' (Freud, ibid., p. 311). Life is a circuitous path to death, death which the ego-instincts *desire*. The tendency of mental life is towards constancy, the removal of internal tension, what Freud calls (borrowing this phrase from Barbara Low) the *Nirvana principle* (see Freud, ibid., p. 329), a tendency, he writes, which 'finds expression in the pleasure principle' (Freud, ibid.). He concludes by opining that there are many processes in the mental life of man, 'matters over which the pleasure principle has as yet no control; but it does not follow that any of them are necessarily opposed to it' (Freud, ibid., p. 336). The search for pleasure is intense. In relation to the paradox of pleasure, Freud observes: 'Hence arises the paradoxical situation that the living organism struggles most energetically against events (dangers, in fact) which might help it to attain its life's aim rapidly – by a kind of short-circuit' (Freud, ibid., p. 312).

This 'pleasure paradox' is known in ethics too; pleasure and happiness, it is said, are strange phenomena; they do not obey normal principles. The paradox of hedonism points out that pleasure cannot be acquired directly only indirectly, which is the Franklian position too. Somewhere in *Either/Or* Kierkegaard says: 'most men pursue pleasure with such breathless haste that they hurry past it'. To secure it, we need to shun it. To give an example: suppose my best friend Darren enjoys martial arts. According to utilitarianism and most socio-psychological models of human behaviour, it is believed that Darren likes martial arts because he gets a pleasure from this activity. However, if you tell Darren this, he is likely to disagree. Yes, he does get pleasure from martial arts but this is not the process that explains *why* he practises martial arts. He is not saying to himself: 'I must do martial arts in order to obtain pleasure'. Martial arts are not just a means towards pleasure. Darren just likes martial arts. Pleasure and happiness cannot be reverse engineered. If you heard that philately, to take another example, was very pleasurable and started a stamp collection as a means towards happiness or pleasure, it would inevitably be in vain. To achieve happiness or pleasure, you must not seek it directly but motivate yourself towards things unrelated to pleasure or happiness, like the collection of stamps or martial arts. The pleasure-paradox means that if one sets oneself a goal to please oneself too highly (hyperintention) then the mechanism jams itself. To attain pleasure or happiness (and they are often mistakenly equated) we must put them out of sight. Aristotle had alerted us to the futility of purely pursuing pleasure because pleasure is not continuous. Furthermore, sooner or later finite beings will be unable to acquire and expend the resources necessary to maintain their sought-after goals of pleasure and ultimately we all find ourselves in the company of misery and miss out on the experience of joy.

At the bodily level we thirst for pleasure and sense experience – these come from the world; at the soul level we seek happiness and knowledge – these come from ourselves; but joy and wisdom pertain to the level of spirit, which is the deepest level; they come from God. One philosopher opines: 'Happiness is to pleasure what knowledge of truth is to awareness of sense data: a deeper level' (Kreeft, 1989, p. 126). Spirit is dynamic just as joy is infinite. Self-transcendence means that joy lies outside the self. Self-forgetfulness is the secret of joy. Pleasure is agitated aliveness, happiness 'has peace in place of agitation, but sleepy satisfaction in place of aliveness. Only joy has both peace and aliveness, aliveness without agitation and peace without sleepiness' (Kreeft, ibid., p. 142). Joy is not homeostasis; it does not obey the Freudian 'constancy principle'. Joy is pure affirmation. The same philosopher goes on:

> Pleasure is the restless mind moving along a line, never reaching the end. Happiness is the mind resting at the end. Joy is the mind eternally moving *at* the end, motion at a point .... Pleasure is moving; happiness is still; joy is moving while still. Pleasure is like work, happiness is like sleep, joy is like play. Pleasure is like action, happiness is like rest, joy is like contemplation (Kreeft, ibid., p. 143).

Desire is not an obstacle to joy as it is in Buddhism, where desire is seen as the cause of suffering. Christianity asks us instead to purify our desires, from selfish to unselfish and attach them to right objects (God rather than idols). 'For joy is always directed towards an object', Frankl writes (Frankl, 2009, p. 55). Joy is an intentional emotion. Frankl observes:

> How well Kierkegaard expressed this in his maxim that the door to happiness opens outward. Anyone who tries to push this door open thereby causes it to close still more. The man who is desperately anxious to be happy thereby cuts off his own path to happiness. Thus in the end all striving for happiness – for the supposed "ultimate" in human life – proves to be in itself impossible (Frankl, ibid., p. 55).

Further on in the same book Frankl repeats, in a Kantian vein:

> We see how misguided all striving for happiness is, how the desperate attempt to achieve happiness, to achieve pleasure as such, is condemned to miscarry. ... the striving for happiness is not one of man's basic drives; that, in general, life is not directed towards pleasure at all. Kant has remarked that man wants to be happy, but that what he ought to want is to be worthy of happiness. We hold, however, that man does not want to be happy. Rather, he wants to have a reason for being happy. Which is to say that all deflection of his desire from the object to the desire itself, from the aim (the reason for being happy) to the pleasure (the consequence of attaining the aim), represents a derivative mode of human striving (Frankl, ibid., p. 155).

In *Man's Search for Ultimate Meaning*, Frankl maintains that happiness is the side-effect of living out the self-transcendence of existence. 'Once one has served a cause or is involved in loving another human being, happiness occurs by itself. The will to pleasure, however, contradicts the self-transcendent quality of human reality. And it also defeats itself. For pleasure and happiness are by-products. Happiness must ensue. It cannot be pursued. It is the very pursuit of happiness that thwarts happiness. The more one makes happiness an aim, the more he misses the aim' (Frankl, 2000, pp. 89-90; see also, Frankl, 1988, p. 33).

To this end, Frankl quotes Albert Schweitzer: 'The only ones among you who will be really happy are those who have sought and found how to serve' (Frankl, 2000, p. 157). What is behind the emphasis on power or sexual pleasure, according to Frankl, is the frustrated 'will to meaning'. Self-transcendence, by contrast, involves living with intentionality, oriented towards values and meaning. If there is a *reason* for happiness, happiness ensues, automatically and spontaneously. Frankl observes:

> And that is why one need not pursue happiness, one need not care for it once there is a reason for it. But even more, one cannot pursue it. To the extent to which one makes happiness the objective of his motivation, he necessarily makes it the object of his attention. But precisely by so doing he loses sight of the reason for happiness, and happiness itself must fade away (Frankl, 1988, p. 34).

The very pursuit of pleasure and happiness is what thwarts it, and we end up experiencing our own grasping. The pursuit of happiness is a self-contradiction. Hyper-intention and hyper-reflection are likely to cause or create neurotic patterns of behaviour. Pleasure, no more than happiness, is not the goal of human strivings, rather, it is the side-effect of attaining a goal; it is this attaining of a goal that constitutes a reason for being happy. If there is a *reason* for being happy, happiness ensues. Frankl (Frankl, ibid.) depicts this philosophy in a diagram thus:

Pursuit of Happiness

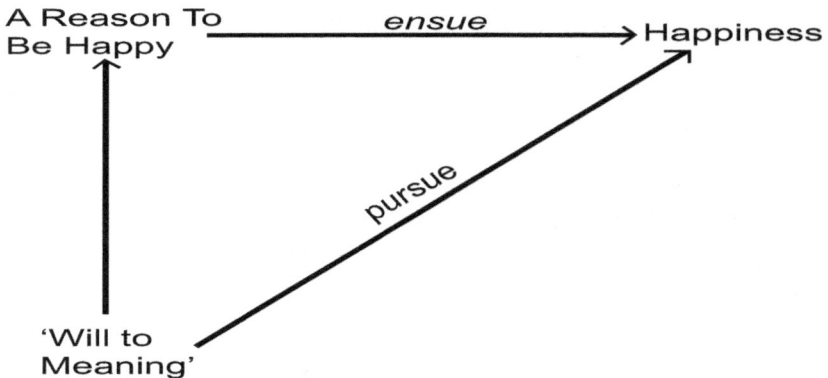

From Aristotle to Jefferson, happiness has been regarded as the principal goal of life but Frankl sides with Kant and Max Scheler who view it as a side-effect. Happiness is possible, like blushing, only in context – the context of a reason to be happiness. We cannot find a relationship with happiness itself, only with persons and actions. Happiness comes as a result of a task or experience or activity, of experiential, creative or attitudinal values. What about inducing happiness through drugs, through 'happiness pills'? Frankl responded to this once in Berkeley; it was raised by a student. Frankl answered that these can never be a *reason* for our happiness, though they may be a *cause* for it (happiness can be induced by a cause). Reason implies a psychological relationship just as cause implies physiological-biochemical one. Joseph Fabry, in his *The Pursuit of Meaning*, gives an example that delineates the differences between reasons and causes for happiness, thus: 'When someone is weeping because she lost a friend, she has a reason; but when someone is weeping while cutting an onion, the onion is not a reason for his tears – it is a cause' (Fabry, 1980, p., 82).

And what is true for happiness is also true for peak-experiences, in Maslow's sense: they too must ensue. Maslow himself said that 'hunting peaks is a little like hunting happiness' (cited by Frankl, ibid., p. 39). Thus, there is a self-defeating quality inherent in the pursuit of pleasure, peak-experiences, power, happiness, health and self-actualisation too. In *The Doctor and the Soul*, Frankl notes: 'This very "pursuit of happiness", however, again is foredoomed to fail' (Frankl, 2009, p., 237). It needs to be forgotten.The Franklian position on happiness is this one: abstain in order to obtain. *Abstinendo obtinere.*

In *On the Theory and Therapy of Mental Disorders*, Frankl observes: 'The path to pleasure and self-actualization leads over the path of self-giving and self-forgetting' (Frankl, 2004, p. 32). Later in the same work, he continues: 'the more he seeks his own pleasure, the more it escapes him, and finally the pleasure is completely lost' (Frankl, ibid., p. 123). We may liken it to insomnia. Sleep is a dove that flies away as soon as you make a grab for it. Or, to take another example, from the American conservative politician, William Bennett: 'Happiness is like a cat, if you try to coax or call it, it will avoid you; it will never come. But if you pay no attention to it and go about your business, you'll find it rubbing against your legs and jumping into your lap'. The striving and straining after happiness is, for Frankl, 'misguided' and 'neurotic' (Frankl, 2009, pp. 155 and 139, respectively). As Frankl puts it: 'Once one has served a cause or is involved in loving another human being, happiness occurs by itself' (Frankl, 2000, p. 89).

Elisabeth Lukas, a follower of Frankl, observes that at the level of psyche, we are pleasure-oriented but at the noetic level we are meaning-oriented (see Lukas, 2000, p. 14). Frankl explains a bit repetitively, it has to be said: 'Pleasure is also an effect that does not allow itself to be "grabbed at". Kierkegaard speaks analogously when he notes that the door to happiness opens outwards; it closes itself the more tightly as we try to push our way into happiness. We could say that the hunt for happiness scares it away – the fight for pleasure chases it away' (Frankl, 2000, p. 126; see also p. 192 where he writes: 'The hunt for happiness scares it away, the fight for pleasure drives it away'). Lukas elucidates the difference thus: she holds that logotherapy 'calls the popular "philosophy of happiness" of psychology into question. According to this philosophy, happiness is the fulfilment of needs. Taking the noetic dimension of human beings into consideration, happiness, however, means inner meaning fulfillment' (Lukas, 2000, p. 30) and later in the same book she opines: 'One is happy when one is good for something' (Lukas, ibid., p. 168). And lest we are inclined to think that only logotherapists hold these views, it is worth citing the well-known American cognitive psychologist, Steven Pinker. In *How the Mind Works*, drawing on the work of the evolutionary psychologist, Donald Campbell, who described humans as beings on a 'hedonistic treadmill' (cited by Pinker, 1997, p. 393), Pinker, commenting on the psychology of pleasure, notes that, 'the study of happiness often sounds like a sermon for traditional values. The numbers show that it is not the rich, privileged, robust, or good-looking who are happy, it is those who have spouses, friends, religion, and challenging, meaningful work' (Pinker, ibid.). Campbell sums up his research thus: 'The direct pursuit of happiness is a recipe for an unhappy life' (cited by Pinker, ibid.). For Frankl, this pursuit signifies a self-contradiction; the more we strive for it, the less we attain it. He notes that:

> ...the aim of both the hedonistic philosophy of the Epicureans and the quietistic philosophy of the Stoics, i.e., happiness and peace of mind (or, as the latter was called by the ancient Greeks, *ataraxia*), cannot possibly be the real aim of human behaviour, and they cannot for the a priori reason that they elude man exactly to the same degree that he strives for them (Frankl, 2010, p. 96).

Happiness cannot and should not be a matter of *intention*; it must remain a matter of *effect*. Happiness ensues as an unintended (side) effect of one's dedication and devotion to a cause (to serve) or person (to love). Frankl is explicit: the focus instead should be directed outward away from the pleasure-ego. 'In the final analysis, dereflection means ignoring one's self' (Frankl, 2004, p. 207). It is the logotherapeutic technique of dereflection that promotes such self-forgetfulness. Puttting it another way: self-transcendence is the basis of dereflection (just as paradoxical intention is the basis of self-detachment). Dereflection counters hyperintention and hyperreflection by directing attention outward away from the ego. As Dubois observes: 'Dereflection mobilizes the human capacity for self-transcendence' (Frankl, ibid., p. xxiii). A story is told about a man who was promised a hundred dollars if he would not think about a chameleon and although he had not, before that, thought about the lizard, now he couldn't stop thinking about it! But as soon as he was told to think about an elephant he stopped thinking about the chameleon! So dereflection puts the brakes on (pathological) hyperintention and acts a guidepost that turns the mind to other thoughts that are more meaning-centered rather than ego-encased. The Irish philosopher and novelist, Iris Murdoch, gives an example in her *The Sovereignty of Good*. Murdoch relates:

> I am looking out of my window in an anxious and resentful state of mind, oblivious of my surroundings, brooding perhaps on some damage done to my prestige. Then suddenly I observe a hovering kestrel. In a moment everything is altered. The brooding self with its hurt vanity has disappeared. There is nothing now but kestrel. And when I return to thinking of the other matter it seems less important. And of course this is something which we

may also do deliberately: give attention to nature in order to clear our minds of selfish care (Murdoch, 1970, p. 84).

In this example, dereflection ushered in self-transcendence and an alteration, therefore, in moral vision. Frankl likes the line from Bernano's *Diary of a Country Priest*: 'It is easier than one believes to hate oneself; grace consists in forgetting the self'. Frankl expounds: 'Persons do not exist for the sake of observing themselves and contemplating their own egos, rather, they exist in order to give themselves up, to give themselves away, to knowingly and lovingly devote themselves' (Frankl, 2004, p. 208). 'And only to the degree that persons transcend themselves in this manner do they also fulfil themselves, in the service of a thing, or in the love of another person! In other words, human persons are wholly human only when they are absorbed in some things or are completely devoted to another person. And only those who forget themselves are completely themselves' (Frankl, ibid., p. 233). We must 'let go' but this 'letting go' is a surrendering to 'more' rather than to 'less'. Frankl calls it 'dereflection', as we have said; Assagioli, the founder of psychosynthesis, (see Assagioli, 1965, pp. 58, 197, 302; he mentions Frankl as a parallel figure to his own work. He says that Frankl, whom he calls a 'spiritual existentialist' on p. 113, has emphasised the ethical element and religious tendencies in human nature on p. 36, and affirms the reality of spiritual experience, 'of the "noetic" or "noological" dimension (as Frankl aptly calls it)', p.195; see also p. 197), calls it 'disidentification'; Iris Murdoch calls it 'unselfing'; Simone Weil calls it 'décreation'; and Meister Eckhart calls it 'detachment'. A story illustrates the point nicely: it is the famous Zen story of the two monks, which is illustrative of our attachments and detachments and the problems we have in letting go:

Two monks were making a pilgrimage to venerate the relics of a great saint. During the course of their journey they came to a river where they met a beautiful young woman – an apparently worldly creature, dressed in expensive finery and with her hair done up in the latest fashion. She was afraid of the current and afraid of ruining her lovely clothing, so she asked the brothers if they would carry her across the river.

The younger and more exacting of the brothers was offended at the very idea and turned away with an attitude of disgust. The older brother didn't hesitate and quickly put the woman upon his shoulders, carried her across the river and set her down on the other side. She thanked him and went on her way, and the brother waded back through the waters.

The monks resumed their walk, the older one in perfect equanimity and enjoying the beautiful countryside while the younger one grew more and more brooding and distracted, so much so that he could keep silence no longer and suddenly burst out: "Brother, we are taught to avoid contact with women and there you were not just touching a woman but carrying her on your shoulders!" The older monk looked at the younger one with a loving, pitiful smile and said: "Brother, I set her down on the other side of the river; you are still carrying her."

The younger monk was unable to dereflect; he was tormented and preoccupied by his own ego-projections. Through dereflection the spiritual resources of self-transcendence are employed. For Frankl, love and conscience are two manifestations of self-transcendence. Conscience, according to the Franklian formulation, is creative and intuitive and irreducible to the Freudian superego. It is also fallible – because it is human it can err. It may pit us against the customs and conventions and moral mores of society. It has the power to 'discover unique meanings that contradict accepted values' (Frankl, 1988, p. 63); indeed, it is the organ of meaning and comes as a 'hint from Heaven'. Love, for its part, 'is that capacity which enables him [man] to grasp the other human being in his very uniqueness. Conscience is that capacity which empowers him to seize the meaning of a situation in its very uniqueness, and in the final analysis meaning is something unique' (Frankl, ibid., p. 19). Meaning is also objective whereas pleasure is subjective satisfaction.

Frankl distinguishes between sex, which remains at the level of bodily appearance; erotism, which pertains to psychic structure; and love, which represents a relationship with another person as a spiritual being; as such, real love belongs to the noetic sphere whereby one loves another not for what he *has* but for what he *is*. In *The Doctor and the Soul*, Frankl observes: 'The lover's gaze looks through the physical and the psychic "dress" of the spiritual core, looks to the core of the other's being' (Frankl, 2009, p. 134). Love is intentional and not just an emotional condition; it penetrates into the essence of another and *essentia* is not contingent upon *existentia*. Love is the eternal truth and can 'only be experienced *sub specie aeternitatis*' (Frankl, ibid., p. 142). It is a spiritual movement in which the salvation of the other is apprehended. Love performs a metaphysical act; in this spiritual act of love we apprehend the other's *haecceitas* and his *entelechy*. Frankl's dimensional ontology of the human subject is faithful to St. Thomas' view that man is a *unitas multiplex* – a unity in multiplicity/diversity. It is Rilke, the poet, who speaks about such a sacral love from the depths of an ardent spirituality that is rooted in the senses. In his letters on love, Rilke offers the famous prescription: 'I hold this to be the highest task of a bond between two people: that each should stand guard over the solitude of the other' (Rilke, 1975, p. 33). For Rilke, love and work (which for Freud is the aim of life) together constitute the supreme happiness, and love is work! (see Rilke, ibid., p. 37). Love is not merging or uniting; if this is our understanding then the Other becomes introjected into ourselves. Love is shared loneliness. Love consists in two solitudes saluting each other (see Rilke, ibid., p. 45). Rahner describes love as 'the luminous will willing the person in his or her uniqueness' (Rahner, 1994, p. 81) and knowledge is 'but the luminous radiance of love' (Rahner, ibid.). Love is grace and enchantment. Who knows, lovers may find shared meanings to survive and maybe even thrive.

Meaning is more than being (see Frankl, 1988, p. 128). Our Augustinian hearts are indeed restless until they have found and fulfilled meaning outside our egos. 'Human existence is not authentic unless it is lived in terms of self-transcendence' (Frankl, ibid., p. 52). Frankl is adamant: 'Self-transcendence is the essence of existence' (Frankl, ibid., p. 50). It is the model of the spiritual or noetic unconscious and discloses 'the essential transcendence of the spiritual unconscious', as Frankl puts it in *Man's Search for Ultimate Meaning* (Frankl, 2000, p. 61). Conscience is transcendent. Frankl exhorts us to the master of our will but servants of our conscience; in this respect, he speaks of 'the transcendent quality of conscience' (Frankl, ibid., p. 59), as it whispers ultimate meaning. The task of conscience is to disclose to man the *unum necesse* – the one thing necessary. Conscience reaches down into unconscious depths and stems from an unconscious ground; it is the premoral understanding of meaning (see Frankl, ibid., p. 39). We need to listen to the still, small, silent voice of conscience and of grace in existence itself.

Meaning, however, cannot be bestowed; it must be found (by oneself). Meaning is not universal; humanity is (Voegelin speaks of 'universal humanity' just as Frankl speaks of 'monoanthropism'). Meanings are unique to the individual. And we find such meanings creatively, experientially and attitudinally. And for Frankl, we have the capacity to wrest and win meaning from life even up to our last breath. In *Psychotherapy and Existentialism*, Frankl notes: 'To look for the general meaning of man's life would be comparable to asking a chess player: "What is the best move?" There is no such thing as "the best move" apart from the one that is best within the context of a particular situation of a particular game' (Frankl, 1985, p. 67).

For Frankl, either life has meaning and if so it retains it or life has no meaning (see Frankl, 2000, p. 129). He quotes Albert Einstein: 'The man who regards his life as meaningless is not merely unhappy but hardly fit for life' (Frankl, ibid., p. 134). For Frankl, we don't really care for happiness as such but rather for that which *causes* happiness (see Frankl, 1988, p. 42). This is most noticeable in the case of unhappiness. Let us suppose someone is mourning the death of his beloved friend and he is offered some pills to tranquilise him and bring him relief from his depression. He may not actually want to anesthetise his grief. The drugs won't change anything; they won't revive his friend. In other words, the reason for being depressed remains. For Frankl, he will be concerned not with the *removal of* his depression but with the *reason for* his depression (see Frankl, ibid.).

For Lonergan, too, life has meaning and the human subject is self-transcending (see Lonergan, 1971, p. 286). Such self-transcendence is achieved primarily in loving; love has the quality of self-surrender and brings a 'deep set joy' (Lonergan, ibid., p. 105). Further on, Lonergan notes: 'For a man is his true self inasmuch as he is self-transcending. Conversion is the way to self-transcendence' (Lonergan, ibid., p. 357). Conversion, be it moral, intellectual or religious, is a modality of self-transcendence. Man reaches fulfilment and joy by living a life of meaning and by moving outside himself (only after he has come to rest in himself, from a position of self-esteem) beyond the realms of finite goods and into the transcendental realm in which God is known and loved (see Lonergan, ibid., p. 84). As Lonergan writes: 'Holiness abounds in truth and moral goodness, but it has a distinct dimension of its own. It is other-worldly fulfilment, joy, peace, bliss' (Lonergan, ibid., p. 242).

The Greeks understood it as a state of spiritual health, of *eudaimonia*, which literally translates as 'good-spirit-ness' – it is not about feelings or subjective satisfaction; it is wholly objective. If it is objective, then perhaps it is not in us; rather, we are in it. We can, thus, distinguish between 'feeling good' (happiness as subjective satisfaction) and 'doing good' (happiness as virtue). Suffering, as the Greek tragedians taught, is an occasion of wisdom and wisdom is an important ingredient in happiness. We can talk, therefore, of the objective happiness of subjective unhappiness. Our humanity is divine discontent. The American Declaration of Independence has as one of its promises the right to pursue happiness. Commenting on this, C. S. Lewis states: 'We Have No "Right" to Happiness' (Lewis, 1963, pp. 10-12; see also Lewis, 1970, pp. 317-322). It was Freud who asked in *Civilization and Its Discontents*: why aren't we happy, despite the fact that we have fulfilled most of our desires in our technological age. He answers that he doesn't know. But to suggest that happiness is one of our inalienable rights is the surest way to unhappiness. Children aren't even happy, no-one is really. Malcolm Muggeridge, the British author and convert to Catholicism, in a section entitled 'Happiness' in his book *Jesus Rediscovered*, writes:

> The sister-in-law of a friend of Samuel Johnson was imprudent enough once to claim in his presence that she was happy. He pounced on her hard, remarking in a loud, emphatic voice that if she was indeed the contented being she professed herself to be then her life gave the lie to every research of humanity …. The pursuit of happiness, included along with life and liberty in the American Declaration of Independence as an inalienable right, is without any question the most fatuous that could possibly be undertaken. This lamentable phrase – the pursuit of happiness – is responsible for a good part of the ills and miseries of the modern world (Muggeridge, 1979, p. 179).

Earth is not heaven and the modern world certainly is not! Pascal points out the following: 'There are only three sorts of people: those who have found God and serve him; those who are busy seeking him and have not found him; those who live without either seeking or finding him. The first are reasonable and happy, the last are foolish and unhappy, those in the middle are unhappy and reasonable' (Pascal, 1995, no. 160, p. 82).

Throughout this chapter, indeed throughout the book, we have been touching on the difference between pleasure, happiness and joy, it is now time to make this more explicit with reference to Frankl's tri-dimensional ontology. In *Surprised by Joy*, C. S. Lewis states that there is a difference between these three (see Lewis, 1955, p. 181) but doesn't tell us in what the difference consists. That said, he does link joy to self-forgetfullness and in Franklian fashion observes: 'Only when your whole attention and desire are fixed on something else … does the "thrill" arise. It is a by-product' (Lewis, ibid., pp. 194-5). However, it is Frankl's tri-dimensional ontology that permits us to detail the dynamics of the distinction.

In terms of the relationship between pleasure, happiness and joy and relating them to Frankl's dimensional ontology, I would like to advance the notion that pleasure pertains to the somatic, happiness to the psychical and joy to the noetic. Somatic 'happiness' is pleasure, psychic 'happiness' is happiness, while noetic 'happiness' is joy. Hence, my schema (which gives the impression of being static and rigid, almost reified but there are, of course, interpenetrations and cross-currents present; as a heuristic/pedagogical and clarificatory tool, I believe it is useful):

Physical happiness (somatic):   Pleasure
Psychological happiness (psychical):   Happiness
Spiritual happiness (noetic):   Joy

We have been speaking a lot about pleasure and happiness, now let us say something about joy. Joy, in the Judaeo-Christian tradition, is the ultimate gift from God. It resides in the spirit, the noetic core or realm. And conscience is the voice of spirit. Joy has an air of eternity about it and opens us up to the Other. 'Enter into the joy of the Lord' (Matt. 25: 21), we are told. Joy is ek-stasis not homeostasis, which Frankl rightly critiques. Joy is ecstatic because it is a standing outside of oneself, as in self-transcendence. Joy is the ek-static experience of self-forgetfulness. Commenting on the final joy, in his *City of God*, St. Augustine shows that our own happiness cannot be properly located anywhere else but in contemplation and love of the inner life of God. Augustine relativises all the alternative descriptions of human happiness; for him all good points to the Good. But recalling Frankl's 'tragic optimism' let us say: we can be fairly happy, reasonably happy here! Josef Pieper, the great German Thomist philosopher, like Frankl, maintains that we cannot set out to obtain joy as if it were the direct object of our search. It is, he writes, in complete agreement with Frankl, a 'by-product' (Pieper, 1989, pp. 32-9), the result of knowing and 'doing' the truth. Joy follows on from truth and right.

Henri de Lubac, S.J., the French Catholic theologian, has some interesting and similar observations to Frankl and the other philosophers we have been considering in his small book of aphorisms entitled *Paradoxes of Faith* (see de Lubac, 1987). He, too, is of the opinion that suffering is part and parcel of the fabric of life and doesn't preclude joy. 'Suffering is the thread from which the stuff of joy is woven. Never will the optimist know joy' (de Lubac, ibid., p. 39). No, but the tragic optimist might! Suffering can be redemptive; it can bring blessings. Prayer, love and suffering are three ways which free us from sentimentality. 'Under the species of pain, the substance of joy is there, already …. There is only one way of being happy: not to be ignorant of suffering, and not to run away from it; but to accept the transfiguration it brings. *Tristitia vestra vertetut in gaudium*' (de Lubac, ibid., p. 173). ["But your distress shall be turned to joy" as in John xvi, 20). True happiness is the result of an alchemy, of an openness and orientation of the soul to the depths of the divine Ground of being. Real radiance is a centripetal force. 'I shall draw everything to me'. In relation to happiness, and on a Franklian note, de

Lubac observes: 'We only find it by not looking for it' (de Lubac, ibid., p. 113). Many promises of happiness, he contends, are 'swindles or childish dreams' (de Lubac, ibid., p. 182). The difference between joy and happiness is brought out in the following assertion: 'God has made us for Beatitude – and we meanly look for happiness. Happiness is what we conceive and desire spontaneously. It is a thing unworthy of us, and which the deepest part of our nature rejects. Beatitude is God' (de Lubac, ibid., pp. 210-2). So there it is: real joy is faith and found in the Father. Joy is the very life of Heaven. Joy is self-transcendence: joy points to its ultimate beyond, to God. Joy is not a feeling; it is one of the fruits of the Spirit. The road to joy: 'Thy will be done'. De Lubac summarises the relationship the Christian has to happiness, thus:

> The Christian does not ask for happiness. Jesus teaches him to ask for the Father's Name to be hallowed, for his kingdom to come, for his Will to be done. The Christian does not expect happiness. He expects the new heavens and the new earth, "which Justice inhabits". The Christian does not desire happiness. He hungers and thirsts after Justice. He is athirst for eternal life. The Christian does not hope for happiness. He hopes to see the glory of God. *Satiabor cum apparuerit gloria tua.* ... Happiness is all that and can be but that (de Lubac, ibid., p. 202).

Frankl's own experiences of spiritual self-transcendence are described in *Man's Search for Meaning*. He was in the concentration camp communing in his mind with his wife and struggling to find a reason for his sufferings, for his slow dying.

> In a last violent protest against the hopelessness of imminent death, I sensed my spirit piercing through the enveloping gloom. I felt it transcend that hopeless, meaningless world, and from somewhere I heard a victorious "Yes" in answer to my question of the existence of an ultimate purpose. At that moment a light was lit in a distant farmhouse, which stood on the horizon as if painted there, in the midst of the miserable grey of a dawning morning in Bavaria. "*Et lux in tenebris lucet*" – and the light shineth in the darkness (Frankl, 2004, pp. 51-2).

Love: this is the ultimate. Writing about such other-worldly fulfilment, Frankl tells us that love is the ultimate goal to which the human spirit can aspire and that life is about meaning, not happiness.

So any and every therapy worthy of the name ought to attempt to mobilise the vast spiritual resources of the noetic core of the human subject, which permit him to live a life of love. In this respect, it is worth citing the remarks of the great Catholic theologian, Hans Urs von Balthasar, who recognised this to be the central insight and aim of logotherapy:

> Therapy aims expressly at helping the individual to realize a life plan that is fulfilling, and to help in finding the courage to live according to this plan. A backwards oriented analysis of one's past, an analysis reaching back to

childhood and early infancy, is by no means sufficient for this aim. To merely unravel psychological knots and complexes is equally insufficient, because such unraveling can only come about when the individual is opened up to a new future, a meaningful engagement with a world and environment which is perceived as a meaningful whole. As a theologian, it appears to me that, in this regard, the term "logotherapy", with which Viktor Frankl names his method is a fortunate one, actually an indispensable term for every therapy which aims at real results, no matter how much individual healing methods diverge from each other (von Balthasar, 1986; untranslated. I thank Manfred Hillmann for translating this for me and for drawing this remark to my attention).

Similarly, that other great Jesuit genius, Karl Rahner, in his *Foundations of Christian Faith*, writes that a person may be made aware of experiences of transcendence in 'individual logotherapy' (Rahner, 2010, p. 59).

Plato insists that our souls be ordered to the *Agathon*; Aristotle advises us to think divine thoughts; and in terms of the Christian differentiation of consciousness, there is no more moving an account of dereflection than the advice given in *Philippians*: '...Whatsoever things are true, whatsoever things are honest, whatsoever things are just, whatsoever things are pure, whatsoever things are lovely, whatsoever things are of good report, if there be any virtue, and if there be any praise, think on these things' (Philippians 4: 8).

The transcendentals of the true, the good and the beautiful, beckon. They call, pointing to the transcendent Ground of all being, the Eternal Logos, source of all ultimate meaning, hope, purpose and joy – source and final solace.

Bibliography

Alain, *Propos sur le bonheur*. Éditions Gallimard, 1928.

Allendy, René. *L'amour*. Denoël, 1962.

Aquinas. *Treatise on Law*. (*Summa Theologica*, Questions 90-97). Introduction by Stanley Parry. Regnery Gateway, Illinois.

Aquinas. *Aquinas: Selected Philosophical Writings*. Selected and translated by Timothy McDermott. Oxford University Press, Oxford and New York, 1993.

The quotations from St. Thomas's *Summa Theologica* are indicated in the notes by numerals. (For example, 'II, II, 150, 1 ad 2' means Part II of Section II, question 150, article 1, reply to the second objection). The titles of the other works of St. Thomas cited in the text are abbreviated as follows:

C.G. = Summa contra Gentes.
Pot. = Quaestione disputatae potentia Dei.
Car. = Quaestio disputata de caritate.
In Met. = Commentary on Aristotle's Metaphysics.
In Eth. = Commentary on Aristotle's Nicomachean Ethics.

Aristotle. *Aristotle's Metapyhsics*. Trans. Hippocrates G. Apostle. The Peripatetic Press, Grinnell, Iowa, 1979.

Aristotle. *The Ethics of Aristotle*. Trans. J. A. K. Thomson. Penguin Books, 1986.

Aristotle. *The Art of Rhetoric*. Trans. H. C. Lawson-Tancred. Penguin Books, 1991.

Assagioli, Roberto. *Psychosynthesis: A Manual of Principles and Techniques*. Mandala, London, 1965.

Auden, W. H. *Another Time*. London, 1940.

Augustine. *Confessions*. Trans. Henry Chadwick. Oxford University Press, Oxford and New York, 1992.

Bacon, Francis. *Essays*. Wordsworth Editions Limited, Great Britain, 1997.

Balthasar, Hans Urs von. *Love Alone is Credible*. Trans. D. C. Schindler. Ignatius Press, San Francisco, 2004 (1936).

Bayley, John. *Iris*: *A Memoir of Iris Murdoch*. Abacus, London, 1999.

Ben-Shahar, Tal. *Happier*: *Finding Pleasure, Meaning and Life's Ultimate Currency*. McGraw Hill, London, 2007.

Boethius. *The Consolation of Philosophy*. Trans. V.E. Watts. Penguin, London, 1969.

Bok, Sissela. *Exploring Happiness*: *From Aristotle to Brain Science*. Yale University Press, 2010.

Brontë, Emily. *Wuthering Heights*. Penguin, London, 1965.

Buber, Martin. *Eclipse of God*. New York, Humanity Books, 1988 [1952].

Burke, Edmund. *A Philosophical Enquiry into the Origin of Our Ideas of the Sublime and the Beautiful*. Routledge and Kegan Paul, 1958.

Camus, Albert. *The Myth of Sisyphus*. Trans. Justin O'Brien. Penguin Books, 1975.

Chesterton, G. K. *Orthodoxy*. House of Stratus, North Yorkshire, 2001.

Clare, Anthony. *In the Psychiatrist's Chair*. Heinemann, London, 1992.

Comte-Sponville, André. *A Short Treatise on the Great Virtues*: *The Uses of Philosophy in Everyday Life*. Trans. Catherine Temerson. William Heinemann, London, 2002.

Conradi, Peter J. *Iris Murdoch*: *A Life*. Harper Collins, London, 2001.

Costello, Stephen J. *The Irish Soul*: *In Dialogue*. Liffey Press, Dublin 2001.

Costello, Stephen J. *The Pale Criminal*: *Psychoanalytic Perspectives*. Karnac, London and New York, 2002.

Costello, Stephen J. (ed.). *The Search for Spirituality*: *Seven Paths Within the Catholic Tradition*. Liffey Press, Dublin, 2002.

Costello, Stephen J. (ed.). *Credo*: *Faith and Philosophy in Contemporary Ireland*. Liffey Press, Dublin, 2003.

Costello, Stephen J. 'Lacan and the Lure of the Look', *The Letter*: *Lacanian Perspectives on Pyschoanalysis*, Autumn, 1996.

Costello, Stephen J. 'Freud's Moral Psychology and Its Implications for a Philosophical Ethics', *The Journal of the Irish Forum for Psychoanalytic Psychotherapy*, 1995.

Costello, Stephen J. 'What Type of Knowledge? The Fideist Position in Psychoanalytic Praxis', *The Letter*, Spring, 1997.

Costello, Stephen J. 'The Pale Criminal and the Need for Punishment: A Freudian Perspective', *The Letter*, Autumn, 1997.

Costello, Stephen J. 'The Real of Religion and Its Relation to Truth as Cause', *The Letter*, Summer, 1998.

Costello, Stephen J. 'Das Reale der Religion und seine Beziehung zur Wahrheit als Ursache', *RISS, Zeitschrift für Psychoanalyse, Freud-Lacan, Vatermetapher und Gesetz*, 47, 2000-1, Turia & Kant, Wien, pp. 25-39.

Costello, Stephen J. 'Klein's Little Criminals', *The Journal of the Irish Forum for Psychoanalytic Psychotherapy*, Summer, 1998.

Costello, Stephen J. 'Narrating Otherness: Between Hospitality and Hostility', *Philosophy and Social Criticism*, vol. 30, no. 7, 2004.

Costello, Stephen J. 'Philosophy, Death and the Unconscious', *The Review, Newsletter of the Association for Psychoanalysis and Psychotherapy in Ireland*, Issue 5, Spring/Summer, 2005.

Costello, Stephen J. 'Reflections on Ricoeur and Happiness', *The Review*, Issue 6, Autumn/Winter, 2005.

Costello, Stephen J. *18 Reasons Why Mothers Hate Their Babies: A Philosophy of Childhood*. Eloquent Books, New York, 2009.

Costello, Stephen J. *Hermeneutics and the Psychoanalysis of Religion*. Peter Lang, Oxford-Bern-Berlin-Bruxellles-Frankfurt am Main-New York-Wien, 2010.

Critchley, Simon. *On Humour*. Routledge, London and New York, 2002.

Dalai Lama and Cutler, Howard. *The Art of Happiness: A Handbook for Living*. Coronet, Philadelphia, PA, 1998.

De Bono, Edward. *The Happiness Purpose*. Penguin, London, 1977.

De Lubac, Henri. *Paradoxes of Faith*. Ignatius, San Francisco, 1987.

Derrida, Jacques. *Politics of Friendship*. Verso, London and New York, 1997.

Descartes, René. *Discourse on Method and the Meditations*. Penguin Books, 1968.

Desmond, William. *Philosophy and Its Others: Ways of Being and Mind*. State University of New York Press, 1990.

Dobson, Terry. *It's a Lot Like Dancing: An Aikido Journal*. Frog Ltd., 1994.

Dostoyevsky, Fyodor. *Crime and Punishment*. Trans. David McDuff. Penguin Books, 1991.

Epicurus. *Sentences Vaticanes* in *Epicurus: The Extant Remains*. Trans. Cyril Bailey. Clarendon Press, 1926, LXIX.

Epicurus. *Letters to Menoeceus*. In Diogenes Laertius, *Lives of Eminent Philosophers*. Trans. R. D. Hicks. Loeb Classical Library. Harvard University Press, 1991, vol. 2.

Epicurus. *Principal Doctrines*. In *The Essential Epicurus*. Trans. Eugene O'Connor. Prometheus Books, 1993.

Epstein, Mark. *Thoughts Without a Thinker*. Basic Books, New York, 1996.

Fabry, Joseph. *The Pursuit of Meaning: Viktor Frankl, Logotherapy, and Life*. Harper and Row, San Francisco, 1980.

Flanagan, Owen. *The Really Hard Problem: Meaning in a Material World*. MIT Press, Cambridge, Massachusetts, 2009.

Forrester, John. *Truth Games: Lies, Money and Psychoanalysis*, Harvard University Press, 1997.

Frankl, Viktor. *Man's Search for Meaning*. Rider, London-Sydney-Auckland-Johannesburg, 2004 (1946).

Frankl, Viktor. *The Doctor and the Soul*. Trans. Richard and Clara Winston. Souvenir Press, London, 2009.

Frankl, Viktor. *Man's Search for Ultimate Meaning*. Basic Books, New York, 2000.

Frankl, Viktor. *The Will to Meaning: Foundations and Applications of Logotherapy*. A Meridian Book, USA, 1988.

Frankl, Viktor. *On the Theory and Therapy of Mental Disorders*: *An Introduction to Logotherapy and Existential Analysis*. Trans. James Dubois. Brunner-Routledge, New York and Hove, 2004.

Frankl, Viktor. *Psychotherapy and Existentialism*: *Selected Papers in Logotherapy*. Washington Square Press, New York, 1985.

Frankl, Viktor. *The Feeling of Meaninglessness*: *A Challenge to Psychotherapy and Philosophy*. Ed., Alexander Batthyány. Marquette University Press, Wisconsin, 2010.

Freud, Sigmund. *The Standard Edition of the Complete Psychological Works of Sigmund Freud*. Trans. James Stratchey. The Hogarth Press, London, 1953-1974, vols. 1-24.

Freud, Sigmund. *The Complete Letters of Sigmund Freud to Wilhelm Fliess, 1887-1904*, ed. J. M. Masson, Cambridge, Mass:, Harvard University Press, 1984.

Freud, Sigmund. *Three Essays on the Theory of Sexuality* (1905), vol. 7.

Freud, Sigmund. *The Psychopathology of Everyday Life*, (1901), vol. 6.

Freud, Sigmund. *Civilization and Its Discontents*. Trans. Joan Riviere. The Hogarth Press and The Institute of Psycho-Analysis, London, 1982.

Freud, Sigmund. 'Psychopathic Characters on the Strage' (1905-6).

Freud, Sigmund. *Jokes and their Relation to the Unconscious* (1905), vol. 6.

Freud, Sigmund. 'Creative Writers and Day-Dreaming' (1908), vol. 9.

Freud, Sigmund. *Introductory Lectures on Psycho-Analysis* (1916-17), vol. 15.

Freud, Sigmund. *Five Lectures On Psycho-Analysis* (1910), vol. 11.

Freud, Sigmund. 'Why War?' (1933), vol. 22.

Freud, Sigmund. *The Ego and the Id* (1923), vol. 19.

Freud, Sigmund. 'On Psychotherapy' (1905), vol. 7.

Freud, Sigmund. 'On Transcience' (1916), vol. 14.

Freud, Sigmund. 'Humour' (1927), in *Art and Literature*. Penguin, London, vol. 21.

Freud, Sigmund. *The Future of an Illusion* (1927), vol. 21.

Freud, Sigmund. 'Beyond the Pleasure Principle' (1920), *On Metapsychology*: *The Theory of Psychoanalysis*. Penguin, London, vol. 11.

Freud, Sigmund. 'Formulations on the Two Principles of Mental Functionoing (1911), *On Metapsychology*: *The Theory of Psychoanalysis*. Penguin, London, vol. 11.

Gadamer, Hans-Georg. *The Relevance of the Beautiful and Other Essays*. Cambridge University Press, 1986.

Gadamer, Hans-Georg. *Truth and Method*. Continuum, London and New York, 2004.

Griffiths, Bede. *The Golden String*. Fount, London, 1979.

Hadot, Pierre. *Philosophy as a Way of Life*: *Spiritual Exercises from Socrates to Foucault*. Ed. Arnold Davidson. Trans. Michael Chase. Blackwell Publishing, USA, 1995.

Haidt, Jonathan. *The Happiness Hypothesis*: *Putting Ancient Wisdom and Philosophy to the Test of Modern Science*. Arrow, London, 2006.

Havel, Vacel. *Letters to Olga*. Knopf, New York, 1988 [1984].

Hederman, Mark Patrick. *The Haunted Inkwell*: *Art and Our Future*. The Columba Press, Dublin, 2001.

Hederman, Mark Patrick. *Manikon Eros*. Veritas, Dublin, 2000.

Hegel, G. W. *Phenomenology of Spirit*. Trans. A. V. Miller. Oxford University Press, Oxford-New York-Toronto-Melbourne, 1977.

Heidegger, Martin. *Being and Time*. Blackwell, 1962.

Heidegger, Martin. *The Fundamental Concepts of Metaphysics*: *World, Finitude, Solitude*. Indiana University Press, 1995.

Hopkins, Gerard Manley. *The Major Works*. Ed. Catherine Phillips. Oxford University Press, 2002.

Hume, David. *Dialogues Concerning Natural Religion*. Penguin Books, 1990.

Jamison, Kay Redfield. *An Unquiet Mind: A Memoir of Moods and Madness*. Picador, 1997.

Joyce, James. *A Portrait of the Artist as a Young Man*. Panther Books, London, 1985.

Kant, Immanuel. *Kant's Critique of Practical Reason and other Works on the Theory of Ethics*. Trans. Thomas Kingsnull Abbott, Longmans, Green, 1948.

Kant, Immanuel. *Critique of Practical Reason*, New York: Macmillan, 1993 [1956].

Kant, Immanuel. *Groundwork of the Metaphysic of Morals*, in H. J. Paton's *The Moral Law*. Hutchinson, London-Melbourne-Sydney-Aukland-Johannesburg, 1985.

Kearney, Richard. *The Wake of Imagination*. Hutchinson, London-Melbourne-Auckland-Johannesburg, 1988.

Kearney, Richard. *Poetics of Imagining*. Harper Collins Academic, London, 1991.

Kearney, Richard. *Strangers, Gods and Monsters: Interpreting Otherness*. Routledge, London and New York, 2004.

Kearney, Richard. *Modern Movements in European Philosophy*. Manchester University Press, 1986.

Kearney, Richard. *On Paul Ricoeur: Owl of Minerva*. Ashgate, 2004.

Kearney, Richard. *The God Who May Be: A Hermeneutics of Religion*. Indiana University Press, Bloomington and Indianapolis, 2001.

Klein, Melanie. *Envy and Gratitude, and Other Works 1946-1963*. Virago Press, London, 1988.

Kolakowski, Leszek. *Metaphysical Horror*. Penguin Books, 1988.

Kolakowski, Leszek. *Modernity on Endless Trial*. University of Chicago Press, 1990.

Kreeft, Peter. *Heaven: The Heart's Deepest Longing*. Ignatius Press, San Francisco, 1989.

Kristeva, Julia. *Black Sun: Depression and Melancholia*. Columbia University Press, New York, 1989.

Kundera, Milan. *The Art of the Novel*. Harper and Row, New York, 1988.

Lacan, Jacques. *L'angoisse. Le Séminaire. Livre X. 1962-63*. Unpublished.

Lacan, Jacques. *The Ethics of Psychoanalysis 1959-1960. The Seminar of Jacques Lacan. Book VII*. Tavistock/ Routledge, 1992.

Lacan, Jacques. *The Four Fundamental Concepts of Psycho-Analysis*. Ed. Jacques Alain-Miller. Trans. Alan Sheridan. Penguin Books, 1977.

Lacan, Jacques. *The Seminar of Jacques Lacan: Book II: The Ego in Freud's Theory and in the Technique of Psychoanalysis: 1954-1955*. Ed. Jacques-Alain Miller. Trans. Sylvana Tomaselli, Cambridge University Press, 1988.

La Rochefoucauld, François. *Maxims*. Trans. Arthur L. Humphreys. Wordsworth Editions, Hertfordshire, 1997.

Layard, Richard. *Happiness: Lessons for a New Science*. Penguin, Hammondsworth, 2007.

Lear, Gabriel Richardson. *Happy Lives and the Highest Good: An Essay of Aristotle's Nicomachean Ethics*. Princeton University Press, Princeton, New York, 2004.

Lear, Jonathan. *Happiness, Death and the Remainder of Life*. Harvard University Press, 2001.

Levinas, Emmanuel. *Totality and Infinity*. Trans. Alphonso Lingis. Duquesne University Press, Pittsburgh, Pennsylvania, 1969 [1961].

Levinas, Emmanuel. *On Escape*. Stanford University Press, 2003.

Lewis, C. S. *Surprised by Joy: The Shape of my Early Life*. Harper Collins, London, 1955.

Lewis, C. S. *Saturday Evening Post*. Vol. 236, Dec., 1963.

Lewis, C. S. *God in the Dock*. Eerdmans, Grand Rapids, Mich., 1970.

Lonergan, Bernard. *Method in Theology*. University of Toronto Press, 1971.

Lonergan, Bernard. *Insight: A Study of Human Understanding*. University of Toronto Press, 1992 (1957).

Lucretius, *De Natura Rerum (On the Nature of the Universe)*. Trans. R. E. Latham, revised by John Godwin, Penguin, 1994.

Lukas, Elisabeth. *Logotherapy Texbook*. Liberty Press, Toronto, 2000.

Marar, Ziyad. *The Happiness Paradox*. Reaktion, London, 2003.

McCabe, Herbert. *The Good Life: Ethics and the Pursuit of Happiness*. Continuum, London and New York, 2005.

McGahern, John. *That They May Face the Rising Sun*. London, Faber and Faber, 2002.

Marcus Aurelius. *The Meditations of the Emperor Marcus Aurelius*. Ed., and trans. A.S.L.F., vol. 1: Text and Translation; vol. 2: Greek Commentary, Oxford, 1944, repr. 1968.

Marías, Julián. *La felicidad humana*. Alianza, 1995.

Merleau-Ponty, Maurice. *The Visible and the Invisible*. Northwestern University Press, 1968.

Mallarmé, Stéphane. *Stéphane Mallarmé: Selected Poems*. Trans. Henry Weinfield, University of California Press, Berkeley, 1994.

Mill, John Stuart. *Utilitarianism, On Liberty, and Considerations on Representative Government*. Everyman's Library, London and Melbourne, 1972.

Mill, John Stuart. *Autobiography*. Harvard Classic, vol. 25, Charles Eliot Norton, ed. P. F. Collier and Son Company, New York, 1909.

Monk, Ray. *Ludwig Wittgenstein: The Duty of Genius*. Vintage, London, 1991.

Montaigne, de Michel. *The Essays of Montaigne*. Trans. George B. Ives. Harvard University Press, 1925.

Muggeridge, Malcolm. *Jesus Rediscovered*. Doubleday, New York, 1979.

Murdoch, Iris. *A Word Child*. Vintage, 2002.

Murdoch, Iris. *The Sovereignty of Good*. Routledge and Kegan Paul, London and Henley, 1970.

Murdoch, Iris. *Metaphysics as a Guide to Morals*. Chatto and Windus, London, 1992.

Murdoch, Iris. *Existentialists and Mystics*: *Writings on Philosophy and Literature*. Edited by Peter Conradi. Chatto and Windus, London, 1997.

Murray, Paul. *The New Wine of Dominican Spirituality*: *A Drink Called Happiness*. Burns and Oates, London and New York, 2006.

Nietzsche, Freidrich. *Beyond Good and Evil*. Trans. Helen Zimmern. In *The Complete Works of Friedrich Nietzsche*. Vol. 12, ed. Oscar Levy, Russell and Russell, 1964.

Nietzsche, Friedrich. *Ecce Homo*. Trans. R.J. Hollingdale. Penguin Books, 1979.

Nietzsche, Friedrich. *The Will to Power*. Trans. Walter Kaufmann and R. J. Hollingdale. Vintage, 1968.

Nietzsche, Friedrich. *The Gay Science*. Trans. Walter Kaufmann. Vintage, 1974.

Nietzsche, Friedrich. *Thus Spake Zarathustra*. Trans. Thomas Common. Wordworth Editions Limited, 1997.

Nietzsche, Friedrich. *Twilight of the Idols and the Anti-Christ*. Penguin, 1990.

Nietzsche, Friedrich. *The Complete Works of Friedrich Nietzsche*. Ed. Oscar Levy. Russell and Russell, 1964.

Norton, W. W. *The Norton Anthology of English Literature*. Vol. 2. New York, 1962.

Ortega y Gasset, José. *Man and People*. Trans. Willard Trask. W.W. Norton and Co., London and New York, 1957.

Ortega y Gasset, José. *History as a System*. W.W. Norton and Co., London and New York, 1961.

Ortega y Gasset, José. *The Origin of Philosophy*. W.W. Norton, London and New York, 1967.

Ortega y Gasset, José. *Obras Completas*. Revista de Occidente, Madrid, 1946-83.

Ortega y Gasset, José. *What is Philosophy?* Trans. Mildred Adams. W.W. Norton and Company, London and New York, 1960.

Pascal, Blaise. *Pensées.* Trans. A. J. Krailsheimer. Penguin Books, New York, 1995.

Paton, H. J. *The Moral Law.* Hutchinson, London-Melbourne-Sydney-Aukland-Johannesburg, 1985.

Pieper, Josef. *Lesiure, As the Basis of Culture.* Trans. Alexander Dru. Faber and Faber, London, no date given.

Pieper, Josef. *In Defense of Philosophy.* Trans. Lothar Krauth. Ignatius Press, San Francisco, 1002.

Pieper, Josef. *The Silence of St. Thomas.* Trans. John Murray. Henry Regnery Co., Chicago, Illinois, 1964.

Pieper, Josef. *Happiness and Contemplation.* Trans. Richard and Clara Winston. Faber and Faber, London, 1958.

Pieper, Josef. *Josef Pieper – An Anthology.* Ignatius Press, San Francisco, 1989.

Pinckaers, Servais. *The Pursuit of Happiness-God's Way: Living the Beatitudes.* Trans. Mary Thomas Noble. St. Pauls, New York, 1998.

Pinker, Steven. *How the Mind Works.* Penguin Books, London, 1997.

Plato. *The Symposium.* Trans. Walter Hamilton. Penguin Books, 1985.

Plato. *Phaedrus and Letters VII and VIII.* Trans. Walter Hamilton. Penguin Books, 1973.

Plato. *The Last Days of Socrates.* Trans. Hugh Tredennick. Penguin Books, 1969.

Plotinus. *The Enneads.* Trans. Stephen MacKenna. Faber and Faber, 1956.

Rahner, Karl. *Hearer of the Word.* Trans. Joseph Donceel. Continuum, New York, 1994 (1941).

Raher, Karl. *Foundations of Christian Faith: An Introduction to the Idea of Christianity.* Trans. William V. Dych. Crossroad, New York, 2010 (1976).

Ricard, Matthieu. *Happiness*: *A Guide to Developing Life's Most Important Skills.* Atlantic, London, 2003.

Ricoeur, Paul. *Freud and Philosophy*: *An Essay on Interpretation.* New Haven, Yale University Press, 1970.

Ricoeur, Paul. *The Conflict of Interpretations*: *Essays in Hermeneutics.* Continuum, London and New York, 2004.

Ricoeur, Paul. *Critique and Conviction.* Polity Press, 1998.

Ricoeur, Paul. *Figuring the Sacred.* Trans. David Pellauer, Fortress Press, Minneapolis, 1995.

Ricoeur, Paul. *Oneself as Another.* Trans. Kathleen Blamey, The University of Chicago Press, Chicago and London, 1990.

Ricoeur, Paul. *Fallible Man.* Trans. Charles A. Kelbley, Chicago, Regenery, 1965.

Ricoeur, Paul. *What Makes Us Think?*: *A Neuroscientist and a Philosopher Argue about Ethics, Human Nature, and the Brain.* Trans. M. B. DeBevoise. Princeton University Press, Princeton and Oxford, 2000.

Rieff, Philip. *The Triumph of the Therapeutic.* New York, Harper and Row, 1966.

Rilke, Rainer Maria. *Poems 1906 to 1926.* Trans. J. B. Leishman, London, 1976.

Rilke, Maria Rainer. *Sonnets to Orpheus with Letters to a Young Poet.* Trans. Stephen Cohn. Manchester, Carcanet, 2000.

Rilke, Maria Rainer. *Rilke on Love and Other Difficulties.* Trans. John Mood. W. W. New York and London, Norton, 1975.

Rodgers, Nigel and Thompson, Mel. *Philosophers Behaving Badly.* London and Chester Springs, Peter Own Publishers, 2005.

Rosset Clément. *Le principe de cruauté.* Editions de Minuit, 1988.

Rowe, Dorothy. *Wanting Everything*: *The Art of Happiness.* Harper Collins Publishers, London, 1991.

Russell, Bertrand. *The Conquest of Happiness.* Liveright Publishing Corporation, 1996.

Sartre, Jean-Paul. *Being and Nothingness*. Philosophical Library, 1956.

Sartre, Jean-Paul. *Existentialism and Humanism*. Trans. Philip Mairet. Methuen, 1987.

Schopenhauer, Arthur. *The World as Will and Representation*. Vols. 1 and 2. Trans. E. F. J. Payne. Dover Publications, 1966 (see also the 1969 version).

Schopenhauer, Arthur. *Parerga and Paralipomena: Short Philosophical Essays*. Vols. 1 and 2. Clarendon Press, Oxford, 1974.

Scruton, Roger. *On Hunting*. Yellow Jersey Press, London, 1998.

Seligman, Martin. *Authentic Happiness: Using the New Positive Psychology to Realize Your Potential for Lasting Fulfilment*. Nicholas Brealey, London, 2002.

Sidgwick, Henry. *The Methods of Ethics*. Book Savage Publishing, 1 Mar., 2001. MacMillan and Co., London, 1874, 1963.

Sophocles. *The Three Theban Plays*. Trans. Robert Fagles. Penguin Books, 1984.

Spinoza, de Benedict. *The Ethics* in *A Spinoza Reader: The Ethics and Other Works*. Ed. and trans. Edwin Curley. Princeton University Press, 1994.

Taylor, Charles. *Sources of the Self: The Making of the Modern Identity*. Cambridge University Press, 1989.

Taylor, Charles. *A Secular Age*. The Belknap Press of Harvard University Press, Cambridge, Massachusetts, and London, England, 2007.

Unamuno, Miguel de. *Tragic Sense of Life*. Trans. J. E. Crawford Flitch. Dover Publications, New York, 1954.

Vernon, Mark. *Wellbeing*. Acumen, London, 2008.

Voegelin, Eric. *What is History? And Other Late Unpublished Writings*. Edited with an introduction by Thomas Hollweck and Paul Carigella. *The Collected Works of Eric Voegelin*, volume 28. Louisiana State University Press, Baton Rouge and London, 1990.

Voegelin, Eric. *Published Essays 1966-1985*. Edited with an introduction by Ellis Sandoz. *The Collected Works of Eric Voegelin*, volume 12. Louisiana State University Press, Baton Rouge and London, 1990.

Wallwork, Ernest. *Psychoanalysis and Ethics*. Yale University Press, New Haven and London, 1991.

Walsh, David. *After Ideology: Recovering the Spiritual Foundations of Freedom*. The Catholic University of America Press, 1990.

Walsh, David. *The Third Millennium: Reflections on Faith and Reason*. Georgetown University Press, Washington, D.C., 1999.

Watts, Alan. *The Meaning of Happiness*. Rider, London, 1940.

Weil, Simone. *Gravity and Grace*. Routledge, London and New York, 1972.

Weil, Simone. *The Need for Roots*. Ark Paperbooks, London and New York, 1987.

Wilde, Oscar. *The Picture of Dorian Gray* in *The Complete Plays*, *Poems*, *Novels*, *and Stories of Oscar Wilde*. Paragon, London, 1993.

Winnicott, Donald. *Playing and Reality*. Routledge, London and New York, 2005.

Wittgenstein, Ludwig. *Tractatus Logico-Philosophicus*. Trans. D. F. Pears and B. F. McGuiness. Routledge and Kegan Paul, London, 1961.

Wittgenstein, Ludwig. *Philosophical Investigations*. Blackwell, Oxford, 1953.

Wittgenstein, Ludwig. *On Certainty*. Blackwell, Oxford, 1969.

Wittgenstein, Ludwig. *Culture and Value*. Blackwell, Oxford, 1980.

Wittgenstein, Ludwig. *Notebooks 1914-1916*. Second edition. Ed. G. H. Von Wright and G. E. M. Anscombe. Trans. G. E. M. Anscombe. Chicago University Press, Chicago, 1979.

Zizek, Slavoj. *On Belief*. Routledge, London and New York, 2001.

Zizek, Slavoj. *Welcome to the Desert of the Real*. Verso, London, 2002.

Zizek, Slavoj. *The Puppet and the Dwarf: The Perverse Core of Christianity*. The MIT Press, Massachusetts and London, 2003.

Zizek, Slavoj. *The Fragile Absolute or, Why is the Christian legacy worth fighting for*? Verso, London and New York, 2000.

Zizek, Slavoj. *Metastases of Enjoyment*. Verso, London and New York, 1995.

Zizek, Slavoj. *Violence*: *Six Sideways Reflections*. Profile Books, Great Britain, 2008.

Zizek, Slavoj. *In Defense of Lost Causes*. Verso, London and New York, 2008.

Zupancic, Alenka. *Ethics of the Real*: *Kant, Lacan*. Verso, London and New York, 2000.

About The Author

Dr. Stephen J. Costello is a philosopher, lecturer and logotherapist/existential analyst. He is Director of the Irish Viktor Frankl Institute of Logotherapy and Existential Analysis in Dublin and is a faculty member of the Viktor Frankl Institute of Logotherapy. He is the author of *The Irish Soul*: *In Dialogue*, *The Pale Criminal*: *Psychoanalytic Perspectives*, *18 Reasons Why Mothers Hate Their Babies*: *A Philosophy of Childhood*, and *Hermeneutics and the Psychoanalysis of Religion*. He holds a doctorate in philosophy and is a black belt in Aikido.

www.ingramcontent.com/pod-product-compliance
Lightning Source LLC
Chambersburg PA
CBHW021619270326
41931CB00008B/775